THE LIMITS OF CRITIQUE

the

LIMITS

OF

critique

RITA FELSKI

The University of Chicago Press
Chicago and London

RITA FELSKI is the William R. Kenan Jr. Professor of English at the University of Virginia and the editor of *New Literary History*. She is the author of several books, including, most recently, *Uses of Literature* and *Literature after Feminism*, the latter also published by the University of Chicago Press.

The University of Chicago Press, Chicago 60637
The University of Chicago Press, Ltd., London
© 2015 by The University of Chicago
All rights reserved. Published 2015.
Printed in the United States of America

24 23 22 21 20 19 18 17 16 15   1 2 3 4 5

ISBN-13: 978-0-226-29398-1 (cloth)
ISBN-13: 978-0-226-29403-2 (paper)
ISBN-13: 978-0-226-29417-9 (e-book)
DOI: 10.7208/chicago/9780226294179.001.0001

Library of Congress Cataloging-in-Publication Data

Felski, Rita, 1956– author.
    The limits of critique / Rita Felski.
      pages ;   cm
    Includes bibliographical references and index.
    ISBN 978-0-226-29398-1 (cloth : alk. paper)
    ISBN 978-0-226-29403-2 (pbk. : alk. paper)
    ISBN 978-0-226-29417-9 (ebook)
    1. Criticism. 2. Criticism—Methodology.
  3. Hermeneutics. 4. Suspicion. I. Title.
  PN81.F44 2015
  801'.95—dc23

                              2015010763

♾ This paper meets the requirements of ANSI/NISO Z39.48-1992
(Permanence of Paper).

CONTENTS

ACKNOWLEDGMENTS

Writing this book would have been much harder if friends and colleagues had not taken time out of their busy lives to offer comments, suggestions, and encouragement—in some cases, writing eloquent mini-essays that deserve publication in their own right. Thanks to Jeffrey Alexander, Elizabeth Anker, Timothy Aubry, Marshall Brown, Russ Castronovo, Claire Colebrook, Jim English, Winfried Fluck, David Glimp, Frank Kelleter, Bruno Latour, Victor Li, Heather Love, Ronan McDonald, John Michael, Tom O'Regan, Oana Panaite, Brad Pasanek, Andrew Piper, Robert Pippin, Ronald Schleifer, James Simpson, Simon Stern, Bill Warner, Chad Wellmon, and Jeffrey Williams. I owe a special debt to Toril Moi for her remarkable intellectual and personal generosity and her critical acumen, and to Allan Megill for detailed comments, exceptional patience, and much else besides.

I am grateful to everyone who invited me to test the ideas of this book in lecture form, especially to Amanda Anderson and Donald Pease. An early invitation to speak to the Department of Sociology at the University of Virginia was especially helpful in steering me away from several cliffs.

Other friends who have provided much-needed encouragement, advice, and good conversation include Cassandra Fraser, Susan Stanford Friedman, Michael Levenson, Ekaterina Makarova, John Portmann, and Sophie Rosenfeld, as well as my friends and fellow editors at *New Literary History*, Susan Fraiman, Kevin Hart, Krishan Kumar, Jahan Ramazani, Chip Tucker, and Mollie Washburne. Amy Elkins was a very able research assistant during the early stages of this project. My daughter, Maria, kept me sane.

I am deeply grateful to the Guggenheim Foundation for research support and also for research leave made possible by the William R. Kenan Jr. Charitable Trust and the University of Virginia. My thanks are also due to Alan Thomas for his very astute advice and his steady support of this project and to India Cooper for her careful and sensitive copy editing.

• • •

A few sections of the argument were first published, often in rather different form, as follows: "Critique and Hermeneutics of Suspicion," from *media/culture* 15, no. 1 (2012), contains material scattered across the introduction and chapters 1 and 4; parts of "Suspicious Minds," from *Poetics Today* 32, no. 2 (2011), appear in chapters 1 and 3; "Digging Down and Standing Back," from *English Language Notes* 51, no. 2 (2013) (http://english.colorado.edu/eln/), contains a chunk of chapter 2; "Fear of Being Ordinary," from *Journal of Gender Research* 3–4 (2014), references a few pages from my introduction and first chapter; and approximately half of chapter 5 first appeared under the same title in *New Literary History* 42, no. 4 (2011). I am grateful to the editors of these journals for allowing me to test out some of the ideas in this book in their pages.

Introduction

This book is about the role of suspicion in literary criticism: its pervasive presence as mood and method. It is an attempt to figure out what exactly we are doing when we engage in "critique" and what else we might do instead. And here I take my bearings from a phrase coined by the French philosopher Paul Ricoeur to capture the spirit of modern thought. What unites the writings of Freud, Marx, and Nietzsche, writes Ricoeur, is their conviction that radicalism is not just a matter of action or argument but also one of interpretation. The task of the social critic is now to expose hidden truths and draw out unflattering and counterintuitive meanings that others fail to see. The modern era ushers in a new mode of militant reading: what Ricoeur calls a *hermeneutics of suspicion*.

In the following pages, I pore doggedly over Ricoeur's phrase to clarify its resonance and relevance for the recent history of criticism. While coined to describe an earlier period of intellectual history, it seems all too prescient in capturing the mood of our own. Is it not evident to even the most guileless of graduate students that texts do not willingly yield up their meanings, that apparent content shrouds more elusive or ominous truths? Seizing the upper hand, critics read against the grain and between the lines; their self-appointed task is to draw out what a text fails—or willfully refuses—to see. Of course, not everyone subscribes equally to such a style of reading, but Ricoeur's phrase captures a widespread sensibility and an immediately recognizable shape of thought. As a result, it allows us to discern commonalities between methods that are often contrasted or counterposed: ideology critique versus Foucauldian historicism, forceful condemnation versus more suave and tempered modes of "troubling" or calling into question. The sway of such a sensibility, moreover, reaches well beyond the confines of English departments. When anthropologists unmask the imperialist convictions of their predecessors, when art historians choreograph the stealthy tug of power and domination, when legal scholars assail the neutrality of the law in order to lay bare its hidden agendas, they all subscribe to a style of interpretation driven by a spirit of disenchantment.

What follows, then, is neither a philosophical meditation nor a historical explanation but a close-up scrutiny of a *thought style* that slices across differences of field and discipline. I duly emphasize rhetoric and form, affect and argument. And while my focus is on literary and cultural studies—with occasional forays into other areas—many arguments in this book have a broader purchase.

My aim is not just to describe but to *redescribe* this style of thinking: to offer a fresh slant on a familiar practice in the hope of getting a clearer sense of how and why critics read. While the hermeneutics of suspicion has been amply discussed in religious studies, philosophy, intellectual history, and related fields, Ricoeur's phrase never took hold among literary critics, who preferred to think of themselves as engaged in something called "critique." (Now that scholars are casting a more jaundiced eye on their methods, it is gradually entering the critical conversation.) As we will see, the idea of critique contains varying hues and shades of meaning, but its key elements include the following: a spirit of skeptical questioning or outright condemnation, an emphasis on its precarious position vis-à-vis overbearing and oppressive social forces, the claim to be engaged in some kind of radical intellectual and/or political work, and the assumption that whatever is *not* critical must therefore be *un*critical. In what follows, I seek to reframe, reconsider, and in some cases refute these assumptions.

The act of renaming—of redescribing critique as a hermeneutics of suspicion—is crucial to this reappraisal. Ricoeur's phrase throws fresh light on a diverse range of practices that are often grouped under the rubric of critique: symptomatic reading, ideology critique, Foucauldian historicism, various techniques of scanning texts for signs of transgression or resistance. These practices combine, in differing ways, an attitude of vigilance, detachment, and wariness (*suspicion*) with identifiable conventions of commentary (*hermeneutics*)—allowing us to see that critique is as much a matter of affect and rhetoric as of philosophy or politics. We mistake our object if we think of critique as consisting simply of a series of propositions or intellectual arguments. Moreover, redescribing critique in this way downgrades its specialness by linking it to a larger history of suspicious interpretation. In what follows, for example, we will encounter the eagle-eyed detective tracking down his criminal quarry as well as the climate-change skeptic who pooh-poohs scientific data by pointing to hidden and questionable motives. In such cases, we can conclude, suspicion is not being harnessed to oppositional or transformative ends. In short, the aim is to de-essentialize the practice of suspicious reading by disinvesting it of presumptions of inherent rigor or intrinsic radicalism—thereby freeing up literary studies to embrace a wider range of affective styles and modes of argument.

At the same time, this book does not claim to offer a general history of suspicious interpretation (perhaps an impossible task!) but focuses on the rhetoric of literary and cultural studies over the last four decades, with an emphasis on developments in the United States. Nor, I should explain up front, is its method the close reading of a few canonical works. We already have many publications that meticulously assess the pros and cons of critique in Marx or Foucault or Butler, while remaining squarely within the horizon of "critical thinking." The questions that interest me are of a rather different order: Why is critique such a charismatic mode of thought? Why is it so hard to get outside its orbit? To what extent does it rely on an implicit story line? How does it orient the reader in spatial terms? In what ways does it constitute an overall intellectual mood or disposition? Such questions call for an approach that reads across texts as well as into texts, where phrases from an introductory textbook or primer can prove as revelatory as touchstone essays. Rather than summarize the works of individual thinkers, I trace the coils of collective modes of argument as they loop and wind across diverse fields. The emphasis is on critique as a genre and an ethos—as a transpersonal and widespread phenomenon rather than the brainchild of a few eminent thinkers.

What, then, are the salient differences between "critique" and "the hermeneutics of suspicion"? What intellectual worlds do these specific terms conjure up, and how do these worlds converge or diverge? "The hermeneutics of suspicion" is by no means a pejorative term— Ricoeur's stance toward the writings of Freud, Marx, and Nietzsche is respectful, even admiring. Yet "suspicion" is not a term around which scholars have been eager to rally, worrying, no doubt, that any reference to motive or mind-set will undercut their authority. There is an understandable wariness of being tarred with the brush of subjective or emotional response. To gauge the affective tone of scholarship, however, is not to spurn its substance but to face up to the obvious: modes of thought are also orientations toward the world that are infused with a certain attitude or disposition; arguments are a matter not only of content but also of style and tone. In sticking to the performance of such arguments, moreover, I intentionally refrain from peering into or diagnosing anyone's state of mind. My focus is on the ethos of argument rather than the hidden workings of consciousness, on rhetorical personae rather than historical persons.

Of course, one risk of focusing on suspicion is that of unduly exaggerating its presence. As I note in chapter 1, critique is a dominant approach, but it is far from being the only one. Helen Small observes that "the work of the humanities is frequently descriptive, or appreciative, or imaginative, or provocative, or speculative, more than it is critical."[1] This seems exactly right; everyday practices of teaching and writing and thinking span disparate activities and fluctuations of affect and tone. The point is obvious to anyone who has spent half an hour in the undergraduate classroom, where moods shift and slide as students and teacher commune around a chosen text: critical caveats are interspersed with flashes of affinity or sympathy; bursts of romantic hope coexist with the deciphering of ideological subtexts. And yet our language for describing and justifying these various activities remains remarkably underdeveloped. It somehow seems easier—for reasons we shall explore—to defend the value of literary study by asserting that it promotes critical reading or critical thinking. Think, in this context, of the ubiquitous theory course that often provides a conceptual toolkit for the English major, where "introduction to theory" effectively means "introduction to critical theory." In short, while critique is not the only language of literary studies, it remains the dominant metalanguage.

Let me specify at the start that this book is not conceived as a polemic against critique, a shouting from the rooftops about the obduracy or obtuseness of my fellow critics. My previous writing (in feminist theory and cultural studies, among other topics) owes an extended debt to traditions of critical thinking. I was weaned on the Frankfurt School and still get a kick out of teaching Foucault. I have no desire to reverse the clock and be teleported back to the good old days of New Critical chitchat about irony, paradox, and ambiguity. But it seems increasingly evident that literary scholars are confusing a part of thought with the whole of thought, and that in doing so we are scanting a range of intellectual and expressive possibilities. There is, after all, something perplexing about the ease with which a certain style of reading has settled into the default option. Why is it that critics are so quick off the mark to interrogate, unmask, expose, subvert, unravel, demystify, destabilize, take issue, and take umbrage? What sustains their assurance that a text is withholding something of vital importance, that their task is to ferret out what lies concealed in its recesses and margins? Why is critique so frequently feted as the most serious and scrupulous form of thought? What intellectual and imaginative alternatives does it overshadow, obscure, or overrule? And what are the costs of such ubiquitous criticality?

As I argue in chapter 1, such questions have implications that extend well beyond in-house disputes among literary scholars. Literary studies is currently facing a legitimation crisis, thanks to a sadly depleted language of value that leaves us struggling to find reasons why students should care about Beowulf or Baudelaire. Why is literature worth bothering with? In recent decades, such questions have often been waved away as idealistic or ideological, thanks to the sway of an endemically skeptical mind-set. In the best-case scenario, novels and plays and poems get some respect, but on purely tautological grounds: as critical thinkers, we value literature because it engages in critique! Looking closely at this line of thinking and situating it within a broader history of interpretation, my first chapter develops a line of argument against the assumption that suspicion is an intrinsic good or a guarantee of rigorous or radical thought.

One of the great merits of Ricoeur's phrase lies in drawing attention to fundaments of mood and method. Scholars like to think that their claims stand or fall on the merits of their reasoning and the irresistible weight of their evidence, yet they also adopt a low-key affective tone that can bolster or drastically diminish their allure. Critical detachment, in this light, is not an absence of mood but one manifestation of it—a certain orientation toward one's subject, a way of making one's argument matter. It is tied to the cultivation of an intellectual persona that is highly prized in literary studies and beyond: suspicious, knowing, self-conscious, hardheaded, tirelessly vigilant. I join Amanda Anderson in contending that "characterological" components—the attribution of character traits such as nonchalance, arrogance, or sentimentality to styles of thought—play a decisive part in intellectual debate, even though these components are rarely given their due.[2] Critique is not only a matter of method but of a certain sensibility—or what I will call "critical mood."

Ricoeur's second word, "hermeneutics," invites us to think about how we read and to what end. The following pages treat suspicious reading as a distinctive and describable habit of thought. While critique is often hailed for puncturing or deflating schemes, it is also an identifiable scheme in its own right. This attention to the rhetoric of critique has two consequences. First, it primes us to look closely *at* current ways of reading rather than through them, taking them seriously in their own terms rather than seeing them as symptoms of more fundamental realities (hidden anxieties, institutional forces). I strive to remain on the same plane as my object of study rather than casting around for a hidden puppeteer who is pulling the strings. At the same time, however, it also levels the playing field. Once we face up to the rhetorical and conventional dimension of critique, it becomes harder to sustain what I will call critique's exceptionalism—its sense of intrinsic advantage vis-à-vis other forms of thinking and writing.

Take, for example, statements such as the following: "Critique's task is to refuse easy answers, to withdraw the dependability and familiarity of the categories with which thought presents itself, so as to give thinking a chance to happen."[3] Variations on this theme, as we will see, saturate the recent history of criticism. Critique, it is claimed, just is the adventure of serious or proper "thinking," in contrast to the ossified categories of the already thought. It is at odds with the easy answer, the pat conclusion, the phrasing that lies ready to hand. In looking closely at the gambits of critique—its all too familiar rhetoric of defamiliarization—I question this picture of critique as outside codification. The point is not to deny that new forms of critique may emerge in the future—any form or genre is open to being remade in unexpected ways—but to question its claim to exceptional status, as opposed to or beyond convention.

Chapter 2, for example, details the spatial metaphors that undergird the practice of suspicious reading. It looks closely at the language of the critic-as-archaeologist who "digs deep" into a text in order to retrieve a concealed or camouflaged truth; it then turns to the rhetoric and posture of the critic-as-ironist who "stands back" from a text in order to defamiliarize it via the knowing equanimity of her gaze. These well-entrenched methods are associated with contrasting perspectives and philosophies, yet they partake with equal fervor of Ricoeur's hermeneutics of suspicion. Chapter 3 then proposes that suspicion and storytelling are closely aligned; critique weaves dramatic or melodramatic narratives in which everything is connected. The scholar-turned-sleuth broods over matters of fault and complicity; she pieces together a causal sequence that allows her to identify a crime, impute a motive, interpret clues, and track down a guilty party. (Even the deconstructive critic who clears the literary text of wrongdoing seeks, as we will see, to expose the shameful culpability of criticism.) Rather than being a weightless, disembodied, freewheeling dance of the intellect, critique turns out to be a quite stable repertoire of stories, similes, tropes, verbal gambits, and rhetorical ploys.

Paying close attention to these details of style and sensibility offers a fresh slant on the political and philosophical claims of critique—the subject of chapter 4. Critique is a remarkably contagious and charismatic idea, drawing everything into its field of force, patrolling the boundaries of what counts as serious thought. It is virtually synonymous with intellectual rigor, theoretical sophistication, and intransigent opposition to the status quo. Drawing a sense of philosophical weightiness from its proximity to the tradition of Kant and Marx, it also retains a cutting-edge sensibility, retooling itself to fit the needs and demands of new fields. For many scholars in the humanities, it is not one good thing but the only imaginable thing. Critique, as I've noted, just is the exercise of thoughtful intelligence and independence of mind. To refuse critique, by the same token, is to sink into the mire of complacency, credulity, and conservatism. Who would want to be associated with the bad smell of the uncritical? The negativity of critique is thus transmuted into a halo effect—an aura of rigor and probity that burnishes its dissident stance with a normative glow.

In querying the entrenchment of this ethos, I join a growing groundswell of voices, including scholars in feminist and queer studies as well as actor-network theory, object-oriented ontology, and influential strands of political theory.[4] It is becoming ever more risible to conclude that any questioning of critique can only be a reactionary gesture or a conservative conspiracy. Yet it may also be helpful to draw a preliminary distinction between those who harbor reservations about critique *tout court* and those who would condemn critique for not being critical or oppositional enough. The latter stance does not move away from critique but ramps and ratchets it up, lamenting its failure to live up to its radical promise. Its responses thus tend to run along the following lines: "To be sure, critique has its problems, but only because it has strayed from its true path as I define it," or "The hypercritical has turned hypocritical—let us interrogate its complicity with the status quo!" We are told that critique needs to become more negative (to avoid all risk of co-option) or more positive (so it can be truly dialectical). We are given the blueprint for a future critique that will transcend its current flaws and failings. In short, the disease also turns out to be the only conceivable cure; the insufficiencies of critique demand that it be magnified and multiplied, cranked up a hundredfold, applied with renewed vigor and unflagging zeal. Critique turns out to be, as scholars announce with a hint of satisfaction, an infinite task.

But what if critique were limited, not limitless; if it were finite and fallible; if we conceded that it does some things well and other things poorly or not at all? Rather than rushing to patch up every hole and frantically plug each sprouting leak, we might admit that critique is not always the best tool for the job. As such wording suggests, my own orientation is pragmatic—different methods are needed for the many aims of criticism, and there is no one-size-fits-all form of thinking that can fulfill all these aims simultaneously. And here the choice of terminology becomes crucial. In contrast to the powerfully normative concept of critique (for who, after all, wants to be thought of as uncritical?), the hermeneutics of suspicion does not exclude other possibilities (for Ricoeur, these include a hermeneutics of trust, of restoration, of recollection). Leaving room for differing approaches, it allows us to see critical reading as one possible path rather than the manifest destiny of literary studies.

My objection is not to the existence of norms as such—without which thinking could not take place—but to the relentless grip, in recent years, of what we could call an antinormative normativity: skepticism as dogma. There is a growing sense that our intellectual life is out of kilter, that scholars in the humanities are far more fluent in nay-saying than in yay-saying, and that eternal vigilance, unchecked by alternatives, can easily lapse into the complacent cadences of auto-pilot argument. It is a matter, in short, of diminishing returns, of ways of thinking that no longer surprise us, while closing off other paths as "insufficiently critical." At a certain point, critique does not get us any further. To ask what comes after the hermeneutics of suspicion is not to demolish but to decenter it, to decline to see it as the be-all and end-all of interpretation, to wonder, with Bruno Latour, whether critique has run out of steam.[5] That any attempt to rein in the ambitions of critique is often misheard as a murderous assault on critique, triggering dire predictions about the imminent demise of serious thought (the sky is falling! the sky is falling!), is a matter to which we will return.

I write this book, moreover, with at least one foot inside the intellectual formation of critique, as someone who has over the years deployed quite a few of its gambits. My hope is to steer clear of the hectoring tone of the convert, the sermonizing of the redeemed sinner with a zealous glint in her eye. The critique of critique only draws us further into a suspicious mind-set, as we find ourselves caught in an endless regress of skeptical questioning. Perhaps we can get the fly out of the fly bottle by choosing to redescribe rather than refute the hermeneutics of suspicion, to gaze at it from several different angles, to capture something of the seductive shimmer and feel of a certain sensibility. (Critique would not be so successful, after all, if it did not gratify and reward its practitioners.) Rather than an ascetic exercise in demystification, suspicious reading turns out to be a style of thought infused with a range of passions and pleasures, intense engagements and eager commitments. It is a strange and multifaceted creature: mistrust of others, but also merciless excoriation of self; critique of the text, but also fascination with the text as a source of critique, or at least of contradiction. It is negative, but not only or unambiguously negative. In what follows, I seek to be generous as well as censorious, phenomenological as well as historical, seeking to do justice to the allures of a critical style as well as pondering its limits.

This book had the working title "The Demon of Interpretation" — a phrase plucked from Steven Marcus's dazzling essay on Freud's method — but it eventually became clear that such a title was sending the wrong message.[6] Interpretation is not always demonic — only sometimes! We should avoid conflating suspicious interpretation with the whole of interpretation, with all the sins of the former being loaded onto the shoulders of the latter. This is to seriously shortchange a rich and many-sided history of engagement with texts of all kinds, sacred as well as secular. What afflicts literary studies is not interpretation as such but the kudzu-like proliferation of a hypercritical style of analysis that has crowded out alternative forms of intellectual life. Interpretation does not have to be a matter of riding roughshod over a text, doing symbolic violence to a text, chastising and castigating a text, stamping a single "metaphysical" truth upon a text. In short, it is a less muscular and macho affair than it is often made out to be. I will not be signing up for the campaign against what Deleuze and Guattari dub "interpretosis" — as if the desire to interpret were akin to an embarrassing disease or a mental pathology.[7] Interpreting just refers to the many possible ways of trying to figure out what something means and why it matters — an activity that is unlikely to come to an end any time soon. We do not need to throw out interpretation but to revitalize and reimagine it.

What form might such a reimagining take? As this book joins an animated conversation about the future of literary studies, it may be helpful to sketch out a few of its guiding premises at the start. Even at the high point of suspicious reading, there has always been a counter-trend of critics working within a more belletristic tradition, combining detailed, sometimes dazzling, literary commentary and appreciation with a declared animus toward sociological, theoretical, or philosophical argument. My own line of approach is rather different. This book, for example, does not take up arms against social meanings under the stirring banner of a "new formalism," a "new aestheticism," or a "new ethics," commonly heard phrases in the recent reappraisal of critique. I do not champion aesthetics over politics, talk up the wonders of literature's radical or intransigent otherness, or seek to tear it out of the sticky embrace of naïve or credulous readers. Rather, I propose, it is the false picture created by such dichotomies that is at issue: the belief that the "social" aspects of literature (for virtually everyone concedes it has *some* social aspects) can be peeled away from its "purely literary" ones. No more separate spheres! As the final chapter points out, works of art cannot help being social, sociable, connected, worldly, immanent—and yet they can also be felt, without contradiction, to be incandescent, extraordinary, sublime, utterly special. Their singularity and their sociability are interconnected, not opposed.[8]

It follows that there is no reason to lament the "intrusion" of the social world into art (when was this world ever absent?). Works of art, by default, are linked to other texts, objects, people, and institutions in relations of dependency, involvement, and interaction. They are enlisted, entangled, engaged, embattled, embroiled, and embedded. We will, however, look quizzically at the intellectual shortcuts and rabbit-out-of-a-hat analogies that can sustain the logic of critique—such as when a critic brandishes a close reading of a literary work as proof of its boldly subverting or cravenly sustaining the status quo. A text is deciphered as a symptom, mirror, index, or antithesis of some larger social structure—as if there were an essential system of correspondences knotting a text into an overarching canopy of domination, akin to those medieval cosmologies in which everything is connected to everything else. And yet political linkages and effects are not immanent, hidden in the convoluted folds of texts, but derive from connections and mediations that must be tracked down and described. Scratching our heads, we look around for detailed accounts of the actors, groupings, assemblies, and networks that would justify such claims. Where is the evidence for causal connections? Where is the patient piecing together of lines of translation, negotiation, and influence? Politics is a matter of many actors coming together, not just one.

What about the question of mood? Lamenting the disheartening effects of a pervasive cynicism and negativity, some scholars are urging that we make more room for hope, optimism, and positive affect in intellectual life. While I have a qualified sympathy for such arguments, what follows is not a pep talk for the power of positive thinking. There will be no stirring exhortations to put on a happy face and always look on the bright side of life. Academia has often been a haven for the disgruntled and disenchanted, for oddballs and misfits. Let us defend, without hesitation, the rights of the curmudgeonly and cantankerous! Reining in critique is not a matter of trying to impose a single mood upon the critic but of striving for a greater receptivity to the multifarious and many-shaded moods of texts. "Receptivity," in Nikolas Kompridis's words, refers to our willingness to become "unclosed" to a text, to allow ourselves to be marked, struck, impressed by what we read.[9] And here the barbed wire of suspicion holds us back and hems us in, as we guard against the risk of being contaminated and animated by the words we encounter. The critic advances holding a shield, scanning the horizon for possible assailants, fearful of being tricked or taken in. Locked into a cycle of punitive scrutiny and self-scrutiny, she cuts herself off from a swathe of intellectual and experiential possibility.

In the final chapter, I sketch out an alternative model of what I call "postcritical reading." (I too am a little weary of "post" words—but no fitter or more suitable phrase comes to mind for the orientation I propose.) Rather than looking behind the text—for its hidden causes, determining conditions, and noxious motives—we might place ourselves in front of the text, reflecting on what it unfurls, calls forth, makes possible. This is not idealism, aestheticism, or magical thinking but a recognition—long overdue—of the text's status as coactor: as something that makes a difference, that helps makes things happen. Along with the indispensable and invigorating work of Bruno Latour, the new criticism emerging from France (Marielle Macé, Yves Citton) offers a fruitful resource in thinking of reading as a coproduction between actors rather than an unraveling of manifest meaning, a form of making rather than unmaking. And once we take on board the distinctive agency of art works—rather than their imagined role as minions of opaque social forces or heroes of the resistance—we cannot help orienting ourselves differently to the task of criticism. Such a shift is desperately needed if we are to do better justice to what literature does and why such doing matters. The wager, ultimately, is that we can expand our repertoire of critical moods while embracing a richer array of critical methods. Why—even as we extol multiplicity, difference, hybridity—is the affective range of criticism so limited? Why are we so hyperarticulate about our adversaries and so excruciatingly tongue-tied about our loves?

The Stakes of Suspicion

Let us begin with the matter of "mattering." What lies behind the weird consonance of titles in criticism? What mind meld has spawned such synchrony and symmetry of wording? One volume after another buttonholes its readers in insistent, even indignant, fashion: *Why Does Literature Matter?*, *Why Literature Matters in the 21st Century*, *Why Poetry Matters*, *Why Victorian Literature Still Matters*, *Why the Humanities Matter*, *Why Milton Matters*, *Why Reading Literature in School Still Matters*, *Why Books Matter*, *Why Comparative Literature Matters*. That this verbal tic has gone viral—that mattering is exercising the minds of an expanding cohort of critics—points to a change of gears and an overhauling of priorities. The overall tone of such titles is one of exhortation combined with a whiff of exasperation. No more hair-splitting, nit-picking, angels-on-the-head-of-a-pin scholasticism! Leading questions can no longer be avoided: Why is literature worth bothering with? What is *at stake* in literary studies?

Pressures to tackle such questions are mounting from outside as well as inside the academy. Faced with an accelerating skepticism about the uses of the humanities in a market-driven age, literary studies find themselves in the throes of a legitimation crisis, casting about for ways to justify their existence. Why, after all, should anyone care about literature? Until recently, answers were thin on the ground, given the sway of a hypercritical sensibility along with a historicism fixated on past resonance rather than present relevance.

Among literary theorists, especially, talk about value was often met with a curled lip: spurned as antidemocratic, capricious, clubby, and in the thrall of a mystified notion of aesthetics. Critics continued to prefer some books over others and to explicate and elaborate on these books, sometimes with verve, acumen, and passion. Yet their reasons for doing so were often glossed over or else boiled down, as we will see, to the sole measure of their "criticality." To look back over the last few decades of literary debate is to encounter many of the same qualms, doubts, reservations, and misgivings that are now being voiced by outsiders, if for very different reasons. Literary theory, especially, cast its lot with a spirit of ceaseless skepticism and incessant interrogation; modeling itself on Mephistopheles in Goethe's *Faust*, it was "der Geist, der stets verneint"—the spirit that always negates. After decades of heady iconoclasm, after the bacchanalian joys of ripping up New Critical attitudes and scoffing at Leavisite platitudes, we are left nursing a Sunday morning hangover and wondering what fragments, if any, can be retrieved from the ruins.

To be sure, leeriness about values and norms is hardly unique to literary studies. Across the humanities, scholars are often trained not to articulate such values but to interrogate them, to recite the familiar Foucauldian mantra: Where does the discourse of values come from? What are its modes of existence? Which interests and power relations does it serve? Academics thrive in the rarefied air of metacommentary, honing their ability to complicate and problematize, to turn statements about the world into statements about the forms of discourse in which they are made. We conduct such interrogations endlessly, effortlessly, and in our sleep. When asked to justify our attachments and defend our commitments, however, we often flounder and flail about.

Michael Roth tackles this lopsidedness in his essay "Beyond Critical Thinking," noting that scholars are all too adept at documenting the insufficiencies of meanings, values, and norms; like tenacious bloodhounds, we sniff out coercion, collusion, or exclusion at every turn. We are often stymied, however, when asked to account for the importance of meanings, values, and norms in all forms of life, including our own. Rigorous thinking is equated with, and often reduced to, the mentality of critique. The result can be a regrettable arrogance of intellect, where the smartest thing you can do is to see through the deep-seated convictions and heartfelt attachments of others. "If we humanities professors saw ourselves more often as explorers of the normative than as critics of normativity," Roth writes, "we would have a better chance to reconnect our intellectual work to broader currents in public life."[1]

Literary studies, moreover, can avail itself of a distinctive and double-edged weapon: *the critique of literature versus literature as critique*. A toolkit of methods lies ready to hand to draw out what a text does not know and cannot comprehend. The scalpel of political or historical diagnosis slices into a literary work to expose its omissions and occlusions, its denials and disavowals. Reading becomes, as Judith Fetterley famously argued, an act of resistance rather than assent, a way of unbinding oneself from the power of the text.[2] For a significant cohort of critics, however, such an approach seemed jejune and lacking in finesse: a sign less of the text's failings than of an insufficiently subtle reading practice. Instead, things were flipped around: we no longer needed to aim critique at the text because it was already being enacted by the text. Literature could now be lauded for its power to defamiliarize and demystify, to lay bare the banality of the commonplace, to highlight the sheer contingency and constructedness of meaning. We did not need to be suspicious of the text, in short, because it was already doing the work of suspicion for us. Critic and work were bound together in an alliance of mutual mistrust vis-à-vis everyday forms of language and thought.[3]

Such a program has undeniable affinities with the agendas of those artists and writers estranged from, or at odds with, the mainstream of social life. Whether we are thinking of Flaubert's tirades against bourgeois bêtise or the caustic thrust of Brechtian alienation effects, Woolf's puncturing of male pomposity or Dadaist mockery of the museum as mausoleum, modern art has often sought to shake things up. It has been a thorn in the flesh, a fist in the eye, a forceful twisting and torquing and repurposing of ordinary language. What we might question, though, is the fervor with which "criticality" is hailed as the sole metric of literary value. We can only rationalize our love of works of art, it seems, by proving that they are engaged in critique—even if unwittingly and unknowingly. A particular novel or film thus serves as a meritorious exception to the ideologies that must be ritually condemned. All too often, we see critics tying themselves into knots in order to prove that a text harbors signs of dissonance and dissent—as if there were no other conceivable way of justifying its merits. In this respect, at least, we remain faithful descendants of Adorno and a modernist regime of aesthetic value. Both aesthetic and social worth, it seems, can only be cashed out in terms of a rhetoric of *againstness*.

And yet there are other salient desires, motives, agendas that drive acts of reading and that receive short shrift from critics scouring works of literature for every last crumb of real or imagined resistance. *We shortchange the significance of art by focusing on the "de" prefix (its power to demystify, destabilize, denaturalize) at the expense of the "re" prefix: its ability to recontextualize, reconfigure, or recharge perception.* Works of art do not only subvert but also convert; they do not only inform but also transform—a transformation that is not just a matter of intellectual readjustment but one of affective realignment as well (a shift of mood, a sharpened sensation, an unexpected surge of affinity or disorientation). Works of art, Chantal Mouffe notes, can trigger passionate attachments and sponsor new forms of identification, subjectivity, and perceptual possibility.[4] And here critique is stymied by its assumption that anything that does not "interrogate" the status quo is doomed to sustain it, that whatever is not critical languishes in the ignominious zone of the uncritical. Priding itself on the vigilance of its detachment, it proves a poor guide to the thickness and richness of our aesthetic attachments.

That the shake-up of the canon in recent decades and the influx of new voices and visions has altered our perceptions of what literature is and does is indisputable. Yet it hardly follows that such changes are best captured in the idiom of critique—rather than inspiration, invention, solace, recognition, reparation, or passion. Such an idiom narrows and constrains our view of what literature is and does; it highlights the sphere of agon (conflict and domination) at the expense of eros (love and connection), assuming—with little justification—that the former is more fundamental than the latter.[5] Anyone who attends academic talks has learned to expect the inevitable question: "But what about power?" Perhaps it is time to start asking different questions: "But what about love?" Or: "Where is your theory of attachment?" To ask such questions is not to abandon politics for aesthetics. It is, rather, to contend that both art and politics are also a matter of connecting, composing, creating, coproducing, inventing, imagining, making possible: that neither is reducible to the piercing but one-eyed gaze of critique.

In highlighting the salience of mood and method in criticism, I seek to kick-start a conversation about alternatives. What happens if we think of critique as an affective stance that *orients* us in certain ways? And as a particular cluster of conventions rather than a synonym for freewheeling dissidence or disembodied skepticism? Ideas and discourses, writes Peter Sloterdijk, "would dissolve like writing on water if they were not embedded in the ongoing processes of repetitive life that guarantee, among other things, epistemic characteristics and discursive routines."[6] Critique is not just a questioning of routine but a putting into places of new routines—a specific habit or regime of thought that schools us to approach texts in a certain manner. And here I turn to Ricoeur's two key words—suspicion and hermeneutics—in order to draw out their pertinence to literary and cultural studies. Why, after all, should we speak of suspicion—rather than, say, skepticism or paranoia—and in what sense does contemporary criticism remain a distinctively hermeneutic or interpretative exercise? Finally, the chapter gestures toward a wider history of suspicious interpretation that has yet to be written: a history that must surely qualify any view of the uniqueness or exceptionalism of critique.

SUSPICION AS MOOD AND METHOD

In surveying the recent history of theory, we must give credit to the extraordinary waves of energy and excitement it unleashed. For a generation of graduate students—including myself—who had been weaned on a bland diet of New Criticism and old historicism, the explosion of literary theories and critical methods was irresistible. The intellectual passions of the 1980s—the Macherey reading group, the late-night discussions of Cixous or Irigaray—were intense, feverish, and palpable. Suddenly, there was an overabundance of vocabularies at our disposal—a cornucopia of methods for connecting literary words to a larger world. Then, as now, I had misgivings about the vangardist tendencies that often tagged along with theory—as if only those schooled in the latest Parisian philosophies could escape a cloud of unknowing and the shame of ideological complicity. But, like many of my peers, I found the heady debates of the time indisputably interesting.

My first forays into theory occurred at the high point of Althusserian thought in the early 1980s—with its insistence that we were always already ensnared within ideology and interpellated by various state apparatuses. Its influential model of symptomatic reading—developed by Pierre Macherey, Fredric Jameson, and others—drew from psychoanalysis as well as Marxism: the language of literary and film studies grew weighty with references to symptoms and repressions, anxieties and the unconscious. Embarking on a feminist dissertation, I immersed myself in theories of the male gaze, femininity as masquerade, the features of a feminist aesthetic. Vocabularies proliferated and changed with an often bewildering speed: performativity and the panopticon, the mirror stage and the *mise en abyme*, interpellation and *l'écriture féminine*. The text was ruthlessly restrictive and repressive, closed, coercive, claustrophobic, exclusionary—or else the text was polyphonic, chaotic, carnivalesque, intrinsically unstable, convulsed by its internal contradictions and teetering on the edge of incoherence. Each new framework promised, with the roguish gleam of a salesman's wink, to overcome the limits of previous ones: to deliver the definitive theory of the subject or concept of power that would nail things down once and for all.

These frameworks would eventually yield ground to postcolonial studies and queer theory, to New Historicism and cultural materialism. Theory was contested, revised, and rewritten throughout the 1980s and '90s, in response to internal debates and disputes as well as the visibility of new political actors. There were vociferous demands for greater attention to historical details as well as the specifics of social identities, for precise calibrations of political inequity as well as an expansion of theoretical argument beyond its Eurocentric premises and preoccupations. Meanwhile the subject of postmodernism triggered a veritable avalanche of books and articles before suddenly expiring—like an overadvertised brand—around the turn of the cen-

tury. To immerse oneself in the last few decades of literary and cultural theory is thus to be caught up in a dizzying whirlwind of ideas,
arguments, and world pictures.

What is called "theory," in short, consists of many language games,
not just one: as David Rodowick shows in his illuminating history,
there are countless breaks, ruptures, dead ends and detours, fresh starts
and false starts, unexpected reversals and repetitions.[7] And yet these
language games also share certain resemblances. Stephen Greenblatt
and Catherine Gallagher summarize the stance of New Historicism as
being "skeptical, wary, demystifying, critical, and even adversarial" —
a description that perfectly matches virtually every other critical approach![8] In spite of the theoretical and political disagreements between styles of criticism, there is a striking resemblance at the level
of ethos — one that is nicely captured by François Cusset in his phrase
"suspicion without limits."[9] In what follows, I adopt an angle of vision
that reveals unexpected continuities among much-canvassed discontinuities. It is not that the differences between theories do not matter — in many circumstances they are crucial — but that an exclusive
fixation on these differences prevents us from asking equally important questions: What do forms of critique have in common? To what
extent do they prime us to approach texts in a given state of mind, to
adopt a certain attitude toward our object?

Let us call this attitude a "critical mood." That essays published
in *PMLA* or the *Journal of Philosophy* are unlikely to voice explo-
sive emotions or visceral passions does not mean that scholarship is
stripped of affect. Here the idea of mood gives us a helpful handle
for the low-key tone of academic argument. Mood, as discussed by
Heidegger and others, refers to an overall atmosphere or climate that
causes the world to come into view in a certain way. Moods are often
ambient, diffuse, and hazy, part of the background rather than the
foreground of thought. In contrast to the suddenness and intensity of
the passions, they are characterized by a degree of stability: a mood
can be pervasive, lingering, slow to change. It "sets the tone" for our
engagement with the world, causing it to appear before us in a given
light. Mood, in this sense, is a prerequisite for any form of interaction
or engagement; there is, Heidegger insists, no moodless or mood-free
apprehension of phenomena. Mood, to reprise our introductory com-

ments, is what allows certain things to matter to us and to matter in specific ways.

The notion of mood thus bridges the gap between thought and feeling. Mood accompanies and modulates thought; it affects how we find ourselves in relation to a particular object. There is more going on in literary studies than theoretical debates, political disputes, and close readings. Whether our overall mood is ironic or irenic, generous or guarded, strenuous or langorous, will influence how we position ourselves in relation to the texts we encounter and what strikes us as most salient. Critical detachment is not an absence of mood, but one manifestation of it, casting a certain shadow over its object. It colors the texts we read, endows them with certain qualities, places them in a given light.[10] A certain disposition takes shape: guardedness rather than openness, aggression rather than submission, irony rather than reverence, exposure rather than tact. We are talking here of an orientation in the phenomenological sense, a constellation of attitudes and beliefs that expresses itself in a particular manner of approaching one's object, of leaning toward or turning away from a text, of engaging in close—yet also critical and therefore distanced—reading. Like any other repeated practice, it eases into the state of second nature, no longer an alien or obtrusive activity but a recognizable and reassuring rhythm of thought. Critique inhabits us, and we become habituated to critique.

Critical mood and critical rhetoric are thus closely intertwined. The combative idiom of scholarship ("interrogate" is surely the most frayed word in the current lexicon) soaks us in an overall tonal atmosphere that can be hard to change. We become stuck in place. This just is, we feel, what it means to "do criticism"—so that other ways of doing things become remarkably difficult to imagine. Moods, in this sense, muddy the distinction between inside and outside, self and world. They often seem larger than our individual selves; they envelop and surround us, as if coming from elsewhere. "We find ourselves in moods that have already been inhabited by others," Jonathan Flatley writes, "that have already been shaped or put into circulation, and that are already there around us."[11] This is an apt way of describing the hazy and ambient nature of critical moods, which suffuse our milieu via the routines of scholarly life—the tone of the graduate seminar, the rhetorical pitch of the journal article—attuning us to our object of study in a certain way. As Heidegger puts it, "A mood is in each case already there, like an atmosphere, in which we are steeped."[12] The prevailing mood of a discipline accents and inflects our endeavors: the questions we ask, the texts we puzzle over, the styles of argument we are drawn to. Education is not just about acquiring knowledge and skills but about being initiated into a certain sensibility. And here suspicion precedes us and awaits us; it is "already there."

My concern is with pinpointing these details of sensibility and style rather than, for example, surveying the social or institutional conditions of criticism. What follows, then, is not a work of sociology or an intellectual history. There is, first of all, an extensive array of publications that offer such contextual analysis. As well as François Cusset's admirable and spirited survey of the US reception of French theory, we can tip a hat to the important accounts by Gerald Graff, John Guillory, Bill Readings, Christopher Newfield, Jeffrey Williams, and others. In *The Laws of Cool*, Alan Liu delivers an especially insightful analysis of how contemporary criticism links up to what he calls the "juggernaut of postindustrial knowledge work" in government bureaucracies, corporations, and the media. And there are also ample histories of criticism that include blow-by-blow accounts of the key ideas of major schools or detailed exegeses of major thinkers.[13] In what follows, I attend to patterns of thought rather than the careers of individual critics—the two being far from synonymous. (Some critics who are noted here because of their exceptional influence as virtuosos of suspicious reading—such as D. A. Miller—have since moved in very different directions.)

There can also be something dispiriting about a certain kind of contextual account: launching into a symptomatic reading of symptomatic reading; excavating the "professional unconscious" of criticism; presuming—on what authority, exactly?—to diagnose the anxieties, disavowals, and displacements of one's fellow critics. This is to concede too much to the premises of a suspicious hermeneutics—as if the only way to make sense of something were to assume the role of an eagle-eyed detective tracking down the invisible forces and maleficent entities that have conjured it into being. To explain acts of criticism in this way is to explain them away. Perhaps suspicious reading has something to do with Cold War politics, late capitalism, or postmodern paranoia—as various critics have speculated—but such big-picture accounts also run the risk of deflecting attention from the object at hand. We find ourselves falling back into the register of explanation-as-accusation, where accounting for the social causes of something serves as a means of downgrading it. X turns out, at the deepest level, to be about the more fundamental and foundational Y. A stark asymmetry separates the object explained (whose existence is reduced to external parameters) and the explaining subject (whose categories of analysis transcend such contingencies).[14]

In short, to foreshadow the Latourian spirit of the final chapter, I strive to treat critique as a distinct and distinctive actor—albeit one closely connected to and mediated by other actors. Suspicious interpretation, we could say, "takes on a life of its own"; it brings something new into the world; it attracts disciples, followers, allies, enthusiasts, fellow travelers, and adversaries; it moves into different spaces and places; it helps makes things happen. To look behind the practice of academic critique for prime movers and ultimate causes is, in this sense, to overlook the more crucial and interesting question of what it is and what it does as a habit of thought. The argument that follows does not and cannot eschew explanation entirely, but it seeks to prioritize understanding, in the classical hermeneutic sense. I attend to a hermeneutic of suspicion in its own terms and in its own right: to its moods and metaphors, its style and sensibility, and the distinctive world it calls into being.

Such words may bring to mind those disciples of Foucault who insist on the primacy and irreducibility of discourse. All well and good—with the proviso that we think of discourses as interacting with persons rather than "creating" or "constructing" persons—unfortunate locutions that make it sound as if human beings were vaporous entities fashioned purely from words. Let us cock a skeptical eye not only at one-size-fits-all social explanations but also at the dead end of linguistic determinism. Texts are far from being the sole actors in the world, and language does not conjure people, animals, things, out of thin air. Critique does not produce persons but must seduce persons, convincing them to throw in their lot with critique. Textual actors are linked to other kinds of actors in networks of cooperation, conflict, control, and cocreation.

Why, then, has critique caught on? Why has it proved so irresistible? For some preliminary clues, we can look to Amanda Anderson's important work on ethos and argument. As Anderson points out, ethos- or character-based assumptions—our tendency to attribute qualities such as complacency, naïveté, breeziness, or tough-mindedness to particular styles of thought—are everywhere in current debates. That is to say, ways of thinking and knowing are tied up with styles of self-presentation and performance, as we fashion for ourselves, or impute to others, a certain sensibility. And yet this phenomenon is rarely remarked upon. Caught between stringently antihumanist theories of language on the one hand and sociopolitical models of identity on the other, literary critics pay scant heed to how the nuances of character, temperament, tone, and manner play out in their own prose.

Anderson goes on to lament what she calls the "underdeveloped and often incoherent evaluative stance" of contemporary theory—drawing attention to a widespread skittishness, in the wake of post-structuralism, about voicing norms or defending judgments.[15] The result is what she calls, following Jürgen Habermas, cryptonormativism—that is to say, a resort to silent rather than explicitly articulated values. And it is here that ethos swoops in to assume an indispensable role. On the one hand, critique often defines itself in the negative, vaunting its wariness of positive norms and its canny distrust of theoretical systems. On the other hand, it smuggles in values and judgments via the charismatic aura bestowed on the figure of the dissident critic. As we will see, the authority of critique is often conveyed implicitly—not through propositions and theses but via inflexions of manner and mood, timbre and tone. Precisely because a certain kind of normative argument no longer seems possible, it is now the posture of the critic that carries disproportionate weight: ironic, reflexive, fastidious, prescient, an implacable foe of false dualisms and foundational truths.

In a related if more Foucauldian spirit, Ian Hunter proposes that literary theories can be understood as ways of working on, cultivating, and disciplining the self. Much of what counts as theory in literary studies takes the form of an ascetic exercise that is grounded in the suspension of ordinary beliefs and commitments. Via a training in specialized arts of reading, scholar-critics learn to look down on empirical knowledge, to disparage the staleness of the everyday lifeworld, to call into question the natural and self-evident. "In what historical or institutional circumstances," Hunter asks, "do people learn to become disdainful of certain knowledges as common sense and to become anxious about themselves for taking things for granted?"[16] Hunter underscores the contingency of such a skeptical mind-set, tracing its origins in a particular philosophical tradition as well as its successful implantation in the habitat of the American graduate school. What lies behind the success of poststructuralism is the allure of its technique of "self-problematization"—announcing their scrupulous abstention from commonsense beliefs and commitments, student-acolytes are inducted into a regime of rarefied knowledge. While the era of Theory with a capital *T* is now more or less over, this same disposition remains widely in force, carried over into the scrutiny of particular historical or textual artifacts.

Anderson and Hunter spur us to think about the rhetorical stances and personae we adopt and the ways in which argument links up with attitude. This line of thought resonates with my own interest in the affective and aesthetic aspects of critique even when—or perhaps especially when—it presents itself as a relentlessly hardheaded and dispassionate practice. The scission of thought from affect fails to acknowledge that mood brings the world into view in a certain way: it is how things matter to us. Mood, in this sense, is neither subjective nor objective, but the way in which the world becomes intelligible. What this means, as Matthew Ratcliffe points out, is that a posture of critical detachment no longer brings with it any particular epistemological privilege; it is just one kind of mood rather than an absence of mood.[17]

Both Anderson and Hunter also tackle the question of theory via its methods—its distinctive techniques and arts of argument. While accounts of literary theories typically center on their big-picture claims (about power, desire, society, language), such theories translate into quite specific—and highly regulated—ways of speaking, writing, and thinking tied to genre and milieu (the unspoken rules of the seminar, the scholarly article, the conference talk). And here it is often a matter of practical rather than abstract knowledge; the student learns by imitating the teacher, adopting similar techniques of reading and reasoning, learning to emulate a style of thought. Academic fields are shaped by what Howard Becker calls "tricks of the trade"—a shared pool of tried-and-tested techniques that are deployed to make arguments, read texts, or solve problems.[18] The tricks of the trade that characterize critique will occupy much of our attention: a motley collection of images, narratives, lines of argument, rhetorical moves, and displayed dispositions. *Critique is not just a matter of content ("knowing that" something is the case) but also a matter of style, method, and orientation ("knowing how" to read a text or pursue a line of reasoning), involving emulation of both tone and technique.*[19] Ways of thinking are also ways of doing.

YES, BUT . . .

By now, we are overdue for qualifications, concessions, demurrals. Before delving into the specifics of a suspicious hermeneutic, we need to make room for exceptions and counterexamples and try to do justice to alternative trends. Critique is by no means the only method in literary studies, with its presence being more unavoidable in some fields rather than others. It tends to be a mainstay of graduate rather than undergraduate education—at least in the United States, where the remnants of a liberal arts culture still encourage quite a few English majors to avow their undying love of literature. And there are, naturally enough, many scholars who choose to cultivate quite different gardens: biographical criticism, textual editing, the recovery of lost or neglected works, New Critical–style close readings, narratological or rhetorical analyses, belle-lettrism, computer-generated quantitative scholarship, empirical cultural history, and so on. Such areas of inquiry are not free of the long shadow of suspicion, but they do not orient themselves toward critique as their primary rationale and vindication. In literary studies, remarks Antoine Compagnon, old paradigms never really die but persist and coexist alongside the latest trends. Literary and cultural studies operate like a pluralist bazaar, in which new frameworks set up their stalls alongside the more traditional wares of formalist or humanist criticism.[20]

Moreover, even those approaches closely associated with critique are rarely single-voiced or unleavened with ambivalence. Rather than giving a simple thumbs up or thumbs down, textual commentary is often shot through with conflicting attitudes and warring emotions: curiosity, censure, generosity, irritability, affection, disapproval, hope. Critical attachments to literary works—what Deidre Lynch calls the "stickier language of involvement and affection"—are not so easily eradicated.[21] The Marxist critic warms to the utopian yearnings and subversive stirrings in the depths of bourgeois novels; the deconstructive critic leavens an austere prose with sallies of punning and playfulness; the scholar of scopophilia owns up to a fascination with Rita Hayworth's face. Even the most severe of symptomatic critics is capable of offering generous gestures toward the work she is analyzing—portraying it as more complex or worthy of attention than others. The category of the "interesting," as Sianne Ngai points out, often does considerable work in such discussions. As a form of judgment that is approbative yet curiously noncommittal, it allows critics to suspend many of the usual moral distinctions and bridge the divide between like and dislike.[22]

In some cases, moreover, critics simply transferred rather than eradicated their affections. While in the 1970s and '80s the very idea of literature seemed dulled by overfamiliarity and institutional respectability, the upstart realm of theory seethed with iconoclastic energies and exorbitant promises, generating intense involvement and waves of identification among a generation of scholars. Its sheer difficulty accentuated its allure to a certain kind of critic, convinced, akin to Burke commenting on the sublime, that the obscure is inherently more affecting and awe-inspiring than the clear. Indeed, there was often a fannish dimension to theory—evidenced in a cult of exclusiveness and intense attachment to charismatic figures.[23] That critics fell in love with a new object was not in itself a bad thing; at its best, theory offered rich philosophical ideas, counterintuitive yet compelling truths, challenges to commonsense beliefs, an often bewildering and head-spinning array of claims to struggle and contend with. Its disadvantages, however, gradually came to light when theory was treated as the new version of scripture and mechanistically "applied" to literary works in order to bash them into the requisite shape.

And there is, finally, a steady and irrepressible counterbeat in literary studies that needs to be mentioned—those critics eager to protect the text from the depredations of critique by stressing its sheer otherness and its separation from the social fray. This line of thought extends back to the "art for art's sake" movements of the nineteenth century and drives the various kinds of aestheticism and formalism that stake their claim throughout the twentieth. While the larger world is pictured as a zone of dull compulsion and coercion, the literary work is hailed by the formalist critic as a zone of radical ambiguity that promises a momentary freedom from such constraint. A recurring refrain is the *literariness* of literature—its decisive and determining difference from other forms of language use. We are urged to respect the autonomy or the singularity of the work and warned—at all cost— against imposing our own passions, prejudices, schemas, or meaning-patterns upon it. Once associated with New Criticism, this stance has regained traction via what has been dubbed the New Ethics. Inspired by a deconstructive hypersensitivity to the aporias and contradictions of language, such an ethics underscores our obligation as critics to respect the irreducible otherness of texts, to pay tribute to the ways they resist comprehension and trouble judgment. As Dorothy J. Hale puts it, such critics are convinced that "the ethical value of literature lies in the felt account with alterity that it brings to its reader."[24] Like a sheer cliff face, the literary work offers no steady footholds for interpretation; in its sheer recalcitrance, it repels our futile and facile attempts at appropriation.

This line of thought harbors a crucial kernel of insight—that the sharpened blade of critique cuts us off from those very qualities that demand sustained attention—while elaborating on literature's power to trigger disorientation, disturbance, and other dysphoric emotions.[25] Yet the critic feels impelled to beat off the barbarians by raising the drawbridge—a too-drastic response that cuts off the text from the moral, affective, and cognitive bonds that infuse it with energy and life. Thus the literary work is treated as a fragile and exotic artifact of language, to be handled only by curators kitted out in kid gloves. Such a vision of reading remains notably silent on the question of how literature enters life.[26] If critique is too punitive, this alternative stance seems too pious—genuflecting before the radical alterity and undecidability of texts, while looking disapprovingly at the countless readers who persist in using these texts in unseemly or inappropriate fashion—identifying with characters, becoming absorbed in narratives, being struck by moments of recognition. Is it possible to have an ethics of reading, wonders C. Namwali Serpell, that is not oriented around the self-evident merits of otherness and indeterminacy?[27]

Literary studies sorely needs alternatives to what I've dubbed elsewhere "ideological" and "theological" styles of criticism: a reduction of texts to political tools or instruments, on the one hand, and a cult of reverence for their sheer ineffability, on the other. And here my thinking draws from pragmatism and phenomenology as well as feminism and cultural studies. The latter fields have often invested heavily in the language game of critique, but they also offer some fruitful resources for rethinking literary value in ways that do not cut it off from nonexpert readers and ordinary life. In a previous book, for example, I took issue with a seemingly indestructible cultural meme of feminist critics as humorless harridans and thin-lipped puritans scowling over the sexism of dead white males.[28] Critique, of course, takes forms that are considerably more subtle and searching than such hackneyed images would suggest. But what these images obscure is that feminism also cranked up the level of positive affect and literary enthusiasm. Reclaiming the work of women writers, attending to overlooked genres, forms, and themes, triggering waves of excitement, recognition, and curiosity, it inspired more students to take the study of literature to heart. Feminists were among the first critics to emphasize the affective dimensions of interpretation, to talk about reading as an embodied practice, to conceive of literature as a means of creative self-fashioning.[29] Much the same can be said of cultural studies, which was less a matter of replacing art with politics, as disgruntled critics often charged, than of broadening the compass of aesthetic experience by looking beyond the New Critical cult of irony, difficulty, and ambiguity. Cultural studies offered a vocabulary for talking about the affective and formal richness of popular and mass-mediated art and made a wider variety of objects aesthetically interesting. In *A Feeling for Books*, for example, Janice Radway combines feminism and cultural studies to explore, in rich phenomenological and sociological detail, what she calls the "tactile, sensuous, profoundly emotional experience of being captured by a book."[30]

Most recently, queer theory—long associated with the charisma of negativity and a deconstructive troubling of identity—has fielded a number of significant challenges to the sovereignty of suspicion. Taking their bearings from Eve Kosofsky Sedgwick's influential essay on paranoid and reparative styles of criticism, critics have queried the affective tone, intellectual merits, and political payoff of entrenched styles of critique. José Muñoz draws on the tradition of German idealism and the work of Ernst Bloch to call for an "affective reanimation" of queer theory—a blending of critique with hope, passion, aesthetic pleasure, and utopian longing. Heather Love, working in a rather different vein, makes the case for an affectively muted "thin description" that she opposes to the compromised humanism of deep interpretation in both its critical and affirmative strains. And in their much-discussed special issue of *Representations*, Sharon Marcus and Stephen Best offer a skeptical assessment of symptomatic reading and plead for a renewed attention to the surfaces of aesthetic objects. (I return to some of these ideas at later points in my discussion.) In short, my argument adds to an ongoing and animated conversation about the limits of critique—even though the disaffection with a suspicious hermeneutics takes quite different and sometimes conflicting forms.[31]

HERMENEUTICS? SUSPICION?

I turn now to the key term of my argument. Paul Ricoeur is an exceptionally prolific philosopher who has written at length on narrative, metaphor, selfhood, time, evil, and many other topics. In what follows, I do not apply Ricoeur to literary studies or closely engage his version of hermeneutic phenomenology (for which I retain some sympathy).[32] Rather, I appropriate his phrase as a stimulus to thought, pushing it in directions that are rather different from Ricoeur's own. It is somewhat ironic, in fact, that Ricoeur's name is so closely tied to a term that plays only a modest role in his thought. "The hermeneutics of suspicion" may well be his most inspired coinage, yet the phrase crops up only a few times in his own writing. Moreover, while widely credited to his 1952 book *Freud and Philosophy*, this attribution is a mistake; in reality, Ricoeur came up with the term at a later date while reflecting on the trajectory of his own work.[33] What, then, does Ricoeur mean by "hermeneutics of suspicion," and how might this phrase offer a fresh slant on recent thinking in the humanities?

As we have seen, Ricoeur hails Freud, Marx, and Nietzsche as the creators of a new art of interpreting. They are, of course, hardly the first thinkers to hurl themselves against the barriers of doxa and dogmatism. The crucial difference: radicalism of thought now calls for intensive acts of *deciphering*, thanks to a heightened sense of the duplicity of language and the uncertain links between signs and meaning. Their aim is not just to underscore the unreliability of knowledge—a theme amply mined by previous generations of philosophers. Rather, these thinkers instantiate a new suspicion of *motives*—of the ubiquity of deception and self-deception. Rather than being conveyed in words, truth lies beneath, behind, or to the side of these words, encrypted in what cannot be said, in revelatory stutterings and recalcitrant silences. The task of the social critic is to reverse the falsifications of everyday thought, to "unconceal" what has been concealed, to bring into daylight what has languished in deep shadow. Meaning can be retrieved only after arduous effort; it must be wrested from the text, rather than gleaned from the text.

In this sense Ricoeur's triad of thinkers is engaged in a distinctively hermeneutic project: radical thought is now tied to painstaking acts of interpretation. "Henceforth," writes Ricoeur, "to seek meaning is no longer to spell out the consciousness of meaning, but *to decipher its expressions*."[34] That meaning must be actively deciphered via the scrutiny of signs testifies to its newly fraught and equivocal status. Apparent meaning and actual meaning fail to coincide; words disguise rather than disclose; we are entangled and held fast in sticky webs of language whose purposes we barely perceive and dimly comprehend. The complacency of consciousness—our belief that we can look into our own souls and discern who we really are—is rudely shattered; we remain, it turns out, strangers to ourselves. As Ricoeur puts it, the science of meaning is now at odds with the everyday consciousness of meaning.

Moreover, Marx, Freud, and Nietzsche are at war not only with the commonplaces of their own time but also the oppressive weight of the past. Ricoeur hails their work as a radical break—a leave-taking from traditional theories of interpretation anchored in the study of religious texts. What unites them, in spite of their differences, is a spirit of ferocious and blistering disenchantment—a desire to puncture illusions, topple idols, and destroy divinities. In *Freud and Philosophy* Ricoeur contrasts this iconoclastic verve to the yearning of the reader who approaches a text in the hope of revelation. Here meaning is disguised in a quite different sense. The reader luxuriates in the fullness of language rather than lamenting its poverty; the text's latent meaning "dwells" in its first meaning, rather than exposing, subverting, or canceling it out. To interpret in this way is to feel oneself addressed by the text as if by a message or a proclamation, to defer to a presence rather than diagnose an absence. The words on the page do not disguise truth but disclose it. Such a "hermeneutics of restoration" is infused with moments of wonder, reverence, exaltation, hope, epiphany, or joy. The difference between a hermeneutics of restoration and a hermeneutics of suspicion, we might say, lies in the difference between unveiling and unmasking.

Here Ricoeur reminds us of histories and theories of interpretation that receive scant attention in Anglo-American literary studies. (How often does even Gadamer or Ricoeur appear in a theory survey?) Thanks to a lingering aura of Teutonic fustiness, not to mention its long-standing links with biblical interpretation, hermeneutics was never able to muster the high-wattage excitement that radiated from poststructuralism. Even the work of the Italian philosopher Gianni Vattimo, one of the most sophisticated and prolific of present-day hermeneutical thinkers, has barely registered in the mainstream of literary and cultural studies. Things are little better in France, where, as Colin Davis puts it, "hermeneutics has often been understood reductively as the mystified quest for the single correct interpretation of a literary work."[35] In fact, critics in the United States and the United Kingdom often took their guidance from the leading lights of Paris and swallowed this view wholesale. Hermeneutics came to stand for a discredited form of "depth" interpretation—the hapless and hopeless pursuit of an ultimate meaning—that had been superseded by more subtle and sophisticated forms of thought.

Against such a background, my reliance on Ricoeur's phrase as a guiding thread through the labyrinth of criticism may strike some readers as misguided or downright perverse. Have I missed the memo and failed to notice that literary theory has ripped apart the axioms of hermeneutics and scattered them to the winds? In the heyday of structuralism, Jonathan Culler prophesied that its focus on structure would put an end to the tiresome business of interpreting literary texts. More recently, disciples of Foucault and Derrida have often insisted that their work is radically antihermeneutic in spirit, putting a massive dent in the project of interpretation.

There is no particular reason, I propose, to limit interpretation to a single-minded digging for buried truths. As I argue in the following chapter, depth is only one of the spatial metaphors on which literary critics rely. If we conceive of interpretation as a retrieval of non-obvious or counterintuitive meaning, its premises are clearly still very much in force. Indeed, rather than giving up interpretation, critics are practicing it ever more fervently and furiously, thanks to the spread of poststructuralist theories that school them in preternatural alertness and vigilance. *The unreliability of signs secures the permanence of suspicion*: no longer a temporary way station on the path to a newly discovered truth, it is a permanent domicile and dwelling place for criticism "after the linguistic turn." This entrenching of suspicion in turn intensifies the impulse to decipher and decode. The suspicious person is sharp-eyed and hyperalert; mistrustful of appearances, fearful of being duped, she is always on the lookout for concealed threats and discreditable motives. In short: more suspicion means ever more interpretation.

Given the surge of interest in questions of reading—close and distant, deep and surface—the neglect of the hermeneutic tradition in Anglo-American literary theory is little short of scandalous. Surely a correction of the record—and even some vigorous rebranding— is in order. Hermeneutics simply is the theory of interpretation and leaves room for many different ways of deciphering and decoding texts. While suspicion spurs interpretation, not all interpretation is

suspicious. While the retrieval of hidden truths is one kind of hermeneutics, not all hermeneutics require a belief in depth or foundations.
(Vattimo, for example, sees hermeneutics as nihilistic in its emphasis
on the inescapable and plural nature of interpretation.) Let us listen
to Richard Kearney—one of Ricoeur's most astute commentators—as
he explains that in hermeneutics "meaning emerges as oblique, mediated, enigmatic, layered, and multiform." Or to Ricoeur himself as
he declares that his hermeneutic philosophy addresses "the existence
of an opaque subjectivity that expresses itself through the detour of
countless mediations, signs, symbols, texts and human praxis itself."[36]
Interpretation, in this view, is a matter of conflict and disagreement, of
mediation and translation; it does not require a "transcendental subject" or a stance of heroic mastery. Interpreting, Ricoeur reminds us,
can be a matter of dispossession rather than possession, of exposing
ourselves to a text as well as imposing ourselves on a text. Hermeneutics will thus reappear in my final chapter, as a resource to be reimagined rather than an idol to be destroyed.

What of Ricoeur's second key word? What exactly do we mean
when we say that much of contemporary thought is endemically suspicious? What characterizes suspicion as an overall general orientation or mood? What are its tone and texture, feel and smell? Why
should we speak of suspicion rather than, say, paranoia or skepticism?
Where does suspicion spring from, and in what guises does it show
itself? And what exactly is at stake in the turn to—or away from—
suspicion?

The terminology of *paranoia* has established itself as a ready-to-
hand label for obsessive-fatalistic styles of interpretation. An early
salvo was fired by Eve Sedgwick in her influential essay on paranoid
and reparative reading. Taking stock of the state of queer theory and
literary studies more broadly, Sedgwick wonders at the ease with which
suspicious reading has settled into a mandatory method rather than
one approach among others. Increasingly prescriptive as well as excruciatingly predictable, its effects can be stultifying, pushing thought
down predetermined paths and closing our minds to the play of detail,
nuance, quirkiness, contradiction, happenstance. Knowing full well
that all-powerful forces are working behind the scenes, the critic conjures up ever more paralyzing scenarios of coercion and control. Like

the clinically paranoid individual, she feeds off the charge of her own negativity, taking comfort in her clear-eyed refusal of hope and her stoic awareness of connections and consequences invisible to others. Contemporary critique thus functions as a "strong theory" of explanation, interpretation, and prediction. In its exclusion of contingency and indifference to counterexample, it shades into tireless tautology, rediscovering the truth of its bleak prognoses over and over again.[37]

Sedgwick's essay—to whose subtle arguments such a precis cannot do justice—kick-started a process of soul-searching that is still going on. That a founding figure of queer theory was having second thoughts about a style of reading she had done much to promote was not easily dismissed. The essay's impact also hinged, in part, on its startling redescription of literary studies. By yoking a diagnostic category associated with irrationalism, obsession, and monomania to forms of reading that prided themselves on being hardheaded and dispassionate, it delivered a jolt to established frames of reference. In speaking of paranoia Sedgwick was not, of course, trying to analyze the maladjusted psyches of her friends, but to draw out salient parallels between a psychoanalytical concept and an influential style of interpretation.

This metaphorical or extended usage has proliferated in recent years; critics have seized on paranoia as a symptom of modernity and the anxieties of the professional class, to take just two examples.[38] Unlike some of her fellow critics, however, Sedgwick is highly conscious of, and attuned to, the paradoxes of imputing paranoia to others. In doing so, we find ourselves mimicking the very process we are trying to question—putting a negative spin on criticism with a negative spin, spurning obvious meanings for hidden truths that only we can discern, claiming to have privileged insight into the dubious or disingenuous motives of our fellow critics. It is in this sense that paranoia is reflexive and mimetic, as Sedgwick notes; accusing others of paranoia looks uncannily like a paranoid move. I prefer, then, to avoid terminology that conjures up the picture of a clinician peering suspiciously into the soul of a recalcitrant patient. Even if critics insist they are using the term in a metaphorical rather than strictly diagnostic sense, its effect is to cast a pathological shadow over styles of reading. We can disagree with aspects of critique without presuming to diagnose it.

If paranoia stains suspicious reading with overtones of pathology and manic obsession, the concept of *skepticism* endows it with a certain gravitas—an aura of loftiness and intellectual dignity. To describe a standpoint as skeptical is to situate it within a long history of reflection on the limits of knowledge that stretches back to the ancient Greeks. We are no longer in the world of psychological disorders but of philosophical propositions, epistemological arguments, and world views. And here we can draw countless connections—of direct influence as well as intellectual affinity—between present-day literary studies and a tradition of Western skepticism in which Hume, Kant, and Nietzsche feature as key players. Arguments in literary theory often assume not just the unknowability of the real world (external world skepticism) but also the rashness and risible naïveté of any claim to self-knowledge. Certain words—truth, reality, objectivity— have virtually vanished from scholarly writing, admissible only when garnished with an amplitude of scare quotes. And literature is often praised for its affinities with skepticism, for exposing the contingencies of meaning, the missteps of knowledge, the sheer duplicity and deviousness of language. It is not just that literary critics do not know certain things but that, as Michael Fischer puts, it, they actively work at unknowing them.[39]

My angle of approach, however, is somewhat aslant of these arguments about truth and falsity, knowledge and the limits of knowledge. The allure of suspicion extends beyond the philosophical premises on which it relies; the discreet murmur of sensibility and style proves just as salient as the cut-and-thrust of quarrels over epistemology. Moreover, while there are moments when suspicion spills over into a full-blown skepticism, other critics—especially those with strong political commitments—question what is currently in place in order to clear the horizon for a new order of meaning, as Ricoeur puts it. Skepticism, in other words, implies a world view, a metaphysics or anti-metaphysics. Suspicion, however, denotes an affective orientation— one that inspires differing lines of argument and that does not always terminate in the grand abyss of radical doubt.

As a broader and less prejudicial term, "suspicion" is thus ideally suited to an inquiry into the style and sensibility of critique. It points to an overall disposition that can coexist with very different political or philosophical beliefs—or with none. It also has the advantage of being a word in everyday use, connecting styles of academic reading to a broader cultural history of interpretation. While critics often contrast their own heightened vigilance to a mentality of unthinking trust and sheeplike assent, suspicion turns out to be more ordinary than such rhetoric would suggest. We can thus bypass the exceptionalist tendencies of critique, opening up an ampler and more expansive frame of reference.

So what exactly is suspicion? The British psychologist Alexander Shand offers some suggestive pointers. In an essay drafted during the First World War, he describes suspicion as an elusive and complex attitude, a secondary emotion composed out of basic affects such as fear, anger, curiosity, and repugnance. It is a sensibility that is oriented toward the bad rather than the good, encouraging us to presume the worst about the motives of others—with or without good cause. Shand surmises that suspicion originally served a biological function as an aid to survival, priming us to be alert and vigilant, to watch out for lurking predators and other dangers, its intensity rising as we feel ourselves or our loved ones to be under attack. It is also directed to the future, anticipating and second-guessing possible motives, preparing us for dangers that have not yet come into view. Suspicion thus involves "a general, deliberate and secret preparation for evil eventualities that is possessed by no other emotion."[40]

Shand underscores the visual and interpretive drive of suspicion— aspects that help explain why it meshes so seamlessly with scholarly thought. It calls for a heightened sense of watchfulness; we find ourselves constantly scanning our environment for possible dangers or keeping a close eye on an adversary. Citing some apropos lines from Shakespeare—"suspicions all our lives shall be stuck full of eyes"— Shand underscores the visual hyperalertness and sharpened attentiveness that typify suspicion. It is a stance incompatible with distraction, relaxation, ease, or indifference. Rather, we are always "on the lookout"—scrutinizing, scanning, searching, surveying, observing, gazing, examining. This looking is not a yielding gaze of pleasure, absorption, or entrancement but a sharp-eyed and diligent hunt for information, as we press beyond appearances to ferret out hidden dangers. In other words, we are both wary of something yet also exceptionally attentive to its presence.

In this sense, suspicion is driven by conflicting aims. On the one hand, we distrust someone or something—and are tempted to steer clear of a potential source of danger. On the other hand, we are also compelled to keep a close eye on what bothers us, so as to prepare for the eventuality of an attack. Know thine enemy! We remain physically close while psychically removed. Our attitude is guarded, tense, wary, defensive. And here suspicion is defined by qualities of sustained patience and reflectiveness that distinguish it from more elementary emotions such as fear or anger. Leery of the intentions of others, we must appraise, ponder, weigh things up. Because we are convinced that things are not as they seem, we are driven to decode and decipher, to push beyond the obvious, to draw out what is unseen or unsaid. Suspicion, as previously noted, is thus a fundamentally semiotic sensibility; it pivots on the treatment of phenomena as signs.

So far, so good—and yet Shand's essay also alerts us to a salient contrast between suspicion in its everyday sense and its intellectual doppelganger. Suspicion, he observes, is synonymous with doubt and uncertainty; it springs from a lack of knowledge. To suspect something, after all, is not to know it for a fact: it is to speculate and second-guess rather than to be sure. A mistrust of someone's motives is compounded by the nagging fear that our own mistrust may not be justified and that we could be jumping to unwarranted and unjust conclusions. Making false accusations, after all, can have consequences that are just as catastrophic as being overly trusting and naïve. For this very reason, we can be tormented by our own suspicions, adding yet another layer of anxiety to the mix.

This torment is memorably illustrated in Alfred Hitchcock's appropriately named *Suspicion* (1944). The viewer is invited to take the part of the wealthy, straitlaced heroine (Joan Fontaine) as she oscillates between conflicting views of her situation and her recent marriage. Is her husband, played by Cary Grant, a feckless but fundamentally good-hearted fellow? Or is he a sleek and sinister sociopath who is secretly plotting her murder? In a famously noir-ish scene, he carries a glowing glass of (poisoned?) milk up the stairs toward his wife, his body framed by a spiderweb of shadows; the following morning the glass of milk is still standing, untouched, on her bedside table. Hitchcock conjures up a world in which the most ordinary household objects are transformed into symbols of ambiguity and dread. The film layers doubt upon doubt, urging us toward constant vigilance while also inviting us to question our tendency to jump to premature conclusions. It is not just a depiction but a nail-biting re-creation of the phenomenology of suspicion.[41]

In Hitchcock's film, then, being suspicious means dwelling in a state of excruciating uncertainty, oscillating between mutually exclusive interpretations of the same events. It is in this sense that we talk of our suspicions being cleared up as we pass, in Shand's words, "from the doubt of suspicion to the certainty of knowledge."[42] Yet this description seems ill suited to the hermeneutics of suspicion as a critical method. Such a method, after all, does not exclude knowledge but is inspired by knowledge—namely the insight into clandestine or counterintuitive meanings that is claimed by the expert reader. This reader rarely doubts the merits of his own doubt; he is unlikely to retract or regret his own suspicions; he does not lie awake at night worrying that the text might turn out to be innocent of all wrongdoing. Indeed, it is precisely this assurance that is targeted by critics such as Tim Dean, who worry that suspicious reading promotes a sense of misplaced confidence and superiority—cutting the critic off from being touched by the genuine strangeness and otherness of the work of art.[43] Such an attitude is surely of a very different order to the paralyzing anxiety that grips Hitchcock's heroine as she is torn between opposing explanations of her husband's erratic actions. When we speak of someone being "under suspicion" in life or in the law, we admit the ambiguity and uncertainty of the person's status and the limits of our knowledge—he or she could, after all, turn out to be entirely innocent. As a style of academic reading, however, the hermeneutics of suspicion knows its vigilance to be justified. Something, somewhere—a text, an author, a reader, a genre, a discourse, a discipline—is always already guilty of some crime.

PREHISTORIES OF SUSPICION

What sustains this conviction that the text is up to no good? What lies behind the belief that something shady or sinister must be going on? Though my argument is not primarily cultural-historical, it is necessary to at least briefly acknowledge a broader horizon of suspicious interpretation. Critique often lays claim to an exceptional status, as a marginal, oppositional, or radical practice. To reframe critique as one form of suspicious reading among others is to break down such dichotomies, to locate it within a diffuse network of discourses and dispositions, to make room for multiple antecedents and acknowledge its entanglement with other words and other worlds. The picture of critique looks rather different once these mediations and translations are brought into view.

The history of critique, in short, is not a matter of drawing a single straight line from Marx, Freud, and Nietzsche to the doubting Thomases of contemporary American graduate programs. Forms of affiliation and influence are rarely so simple or straightforward. The traditional history of ideas often makes it sound as if styles of thought emerge fully formed from the heads of a few genius-philosophers, to be bequeathed to a forelock-tugging populace of groveling and grateful beneficiaries. Yet suspicious reading does not just spring fully formed from the minds of three eminent "masters of suspicion." Its lineage is more varied—arising out of multiple milieux, embracing collective forms as well as institutional norms, and involving a motley cast of actors and characters. Ideas, attitudes, sensibilities well up from below as well as above, wander across cultural and political boundaries, and insinuate themselves into different places and spaces. Let us look briefly at four salient strands in the prehistory of suspicious interpretation.

We have already noted the tradition of *philosophical suspicion.* This tradition is often the first thing that springs to mind when casting around for reasons why literary critics are so powerfully drawn to a spirit of skeptical questioning. Such a spirit, after all, is often hailed as the driving force and guiding spirit of modern intellectual history. Before Ricoeur's triad of Freud, Marx, and Nietzsche, there was Descartes, with his enshrining of doubt as a philosophical method, as well

as Kant, with his famous injunction "Sapere aude"—dare to know—
where a stance of critical questioning and self-questioning is hailed
as the means by which humanity will free itself from its self-incurred
tutelage. The intellectual culture of early modern Europe is gripped by
an exhilarating sense of philosophical awakening that binds reason
to the act of critique; the pursuit of truth requires a sweeping away of
the illusions and superstitions of the past. Critique and crisis are intertwined historically as well as etymologically.[44]

Thereare, to be sure, differences between those Enlightenment
thinkers who see their own skepticism or doubt as rationally justified
and a later tradition of post-Enlightenment philosophy that will subject the very idea of reason to excoriating judgment. In the latter instance, critique is steadily transmuted into a "perpetual agitation" and
unsettling of the given whose work can never be completed.[45] Nietzschean thought, especially, ratchets up a sense of the illusions and falsifications of language, even as twentieth-century critical theory engages in a blistering scrutiny of the deep-etched alienation of social
life. In its most influential variants, including the Frankfurt School
and a tradition of post-'68 Parisian thought, critique takes on an asser-
tively political as well as philosophical cast, while embracing a quasi-
tragic sensibility that strips away hypocrisy and skewers the sentimentality of false hope. Modern critics are, in Michael Walzer's words,
specialists in complaint.[46] Even if their argument presses forward to a
final remedy, the key refrain is a blistering excoriation of society. Dissatisfaction serves as evidence of clear-sightedness; a melancholic estrangement from ordinary life, embodied most poignantly in a figure
such as Adorno, is the price to be paid for this sharpened perception.
Meanwhile, those unwilling to come on board with critique can be reproached for their hidebound attachments to traditional forms of life.
Such attachments become newly shameful in the time-consciousness
of modern thought, which looks to the future as a hoped-for deliv-
erance from the failings of the past. Modernity, as Robert Pippin remarks, sees itself as a rapidly unfurling wave of critiques, genealogies,
unmaskings, dismantlings, and intellectual and aesthetic revolutions.[47]

From the late nineteenth century onward, moreover, a *literary
suspicion* presses increasingly to the fore—one that is shaped by, yet
also quite distinct from, philosophical reflection. It is not just that lit-

erature engages in acts of critique—voicing caustic commentary on
social mores or brooding over the painful and inescapable limits of
self-knowledge. In the experimental ferment known as modernism,
writers are drawn to formal devices that systematically block readers
from taking words at face value. Suspicion is not merely a matter of
content or theme, manifest in the jaundiced perspectives of solipsis-
tic narrators or misanthropic characters. Rather, it is also triggered in
readers via the properties of the literary medium. Opening a book,
they are confronted with an array of perplexing or contradictory signals that require intensive acts of deciphering. Readers are forced to
read against the grain of the text, to question motives and cast around
for concealed clues. Suspicion and interpretative unease, as Margot
Norris notes apropos of James Joyce, are actively provoked by literary
texts rather than being imposed on literary texts.[48]

Traditional-minded critics rallying to the defense of the canon lay
the blame for suspicious reading at the door of political correctness
and the corrosive influence of theory. The irony here is that it is often
literature itself, rather than an overattachment to Althusser or Derrida, that teaches readers to tread warily and read skeptically. Rather
than being innocent victims of suspicion, literary works are active in-
stigators and perpetrators of it. That we have learned to read between
the lines has everything to do with the devices deployed in modern
works of art: unreliable narrators, conflicting viewpoints, fragmented
narratives, and metafictional devices that alert readers to the ways in
which words conceal rather than reveal. Reading Kafka is more than
enough to make one paranoid; the texts of Beckett anticipate many
of the tenets of poststructuralism. Suspicious readers are preceded
and often schooled by suspicious writers. Indeed, much of what has
counted as theory in recent decades riffs off, revises, and extends the
classic themes of literary and artistic modernism.[49]

And here Ricoeur's own remarks on literary form are rarely
brought into conversation with his philosophical hermeneutics. In
his opus *Time and Narrative*, he writes, "It may be the function of the
most corrosive literature to contribute to *making a new kind of reader
appear, a reader who is himself suspicious*, because reading ceases to
be a trusting voyage made in the company of a reliable narrator, becoming instead a struggle with the implied author, a struggle lead-

ing the reader back to himself."⁵⁰ That the perspectives of modern narrators are clouded and self-deceiving forces the reader to assume a newly vigilant stance. The unreliable narrator is not just a formal device but a cultural catalyst, training readers to take on an inquisitorial role and to query the trustworthiness of another's words and, ultimately, perhaps, their own. Titles such as *Notes from Underground* and *The Turn of the Screw*, *Pale Fire*, and *The Remains of the Day* serve as signposts for a virtual armada of deceptive or self-deceiving narrators who school readers to discount or delve behind obvious meanings. Narrative ellipses, ironic juxtapositions, and stylistic or tonal incongruities serve as red flags that we are not to take words on trust. Suspicion is invited—indeed demanded—by a text, as the only feasible way of dealing with implausible statements, shaky rationalizations, or clashing perspectives. Literary works thus train their readers in a hermeneutic of suspicion—a hermeneutic that can subsequently be put into play in order to query the sacrosanct authority of these same works.

In tracing the tracks of a suspicious sensibility, however, we must also cast our net beyond the obvious suspects of philosophy and literature and account for other key actors. Reflecting on the chaotic upheavals and tumultuous violence that mark the dawn of the twentieth century, Shand worries that the spread of suspicion is destroying "harmonious co-operation between classes." Excessive suspicion, he declares, has catastrophic consequences for communal and collective life: inspiring revolutionary tendencies across Europe, it fractures the body politic and serves as a catalyst for political dissent. What Shand laments is what later critics will celebrate—the association of suspicion with a history of popular resistance. Those who have been "deceived and plundered," he admits, are more likely to harbor mistrust of the motives of others. And here we can point to histories of *vernacular suspicion* that often fly below the radar of a conventional history of ideas.

Individuals do not need to consult Freud or pore over Nietzsche, in other words, to know that words cannot be trusted and that language can serve as a conduit of power. Such knowledge is also derived from the harsh blows of experience as they rain down with disproportionate force on the downtrodden and the disenfranchised. Servants have often been skeptical of the promises of their masters; factory workers learned to treat the words of their bosses with a pinch of salt; African American slaves developed an oblique practice of signifying to convey their disdain for those who enslaved them. Here we find ourselves in the territory so brilliantly described by Michel de Certeau. Such tactics epitomize what he calls the "art of the weak": the array of skirmishes, evasions, and dodges by means of which individuals strive to gain a momentary advantage on a terrain they do not command.[51] Suspicion, in such situations, is knotted into the fabric of everyday life.

Fearful of retaliation or retribution, subordinates are unlikely to voice their dissent in public; its expression remained oblique, fugitive, discreet. Distrust of one's betters is signaled via oblique looks and knowing grimaces, passed down in oral traditions of myths, songs, and jokes, conveyed via acts of foot-dragging or feigned ignorance. It makes up what James C. Scott calls a hidden transcript, a form of critique that is voiced offstage, muttered behind the backs of a more dominant group.[52] This gritty skepticism about manifest meanings echoes the suspicious hermeneutics outlined by Ricoeur—even if not expressed in the form of a coherent philosophical system. A culture of mistrust serves as a tactic of self-protection on an uneven playing field, inspiring a wariness of glib promises, an attitude of rancor or weary resentment, an oblique mockery of the self-importance of the important. Apparent consent to the state of things coexists with a tacit attitude of ingrained wariness and cynical disbelief.

At pivotal moments, these subterranean currents of resentment rise to the surface, swelling into open rebellion and public dissent. In the late nineteenth and the twentieth centuries, new social actors—workers, women, racial, ethnic, and sexual minorities—elbow their way into the public sphere. Traditions of folk suspicion are now overlain with a newly assertive and confrontational language of political critique. In the language of Ernesto Laclau and Chantal Mouffe, we can say that a state of subordination is transformed into a state of antagonism. That is to say, while the disenfranchised cock a skeptical eye at those who claim to be their betters, it is only at certain times that this mistrust is translated into an explicitly political idiom—one that invokes an oppositional identity and voices demands for autonomy and equality. Resistance is no longer furtive but confident, collective, and public.[53]

When scholars in the humanities assume that there is something intrinsically seditious about suspicion, this history is usually what they have in mind. As we will see in chapter 4, an overriding justification of critique is the political claim to come "from below," to be a conduit for the interests of the downtrodden and oppressed. And yet vernacular suspicion is promiscuous rather than partisan, attaching itself to a broad spectrum of views. At present, for example, it can often take forms that are much less likely to garner sympathy from professors at Berkeley or Birkbeck: right-wing populism, hostility toward big government, grassroots opposition to multiculturalism and a scapegoating of migrants, disdain for out-of-touch intellectuals and an energetic debunking of their scholarly credentials. What has become of critique, Bruno Latour wonders, when French villagers know that 9/11 was really an inside job and an entire industry is devoted to showing that the Apollo Program never landed on the moon? When arguments about the social construction of truth are used to dismiss evidence of global warming and to discredit the motives of the scientific community? When it comes to dealing with urgent social and ecological problems, we are witnessing what looks like an excess of distrust rather than a surplus of belief. "Maybe I am taking conspiracy theories too seriously," writes Latour, "but it worries me to detect, in those mad mixtures of knee-jerk disbelief, punctilious demands for proofs, and free use of powerful explanation from the social neverland many of the weapons of social critique. Of course conspiracy theories are an absurd deformation of our own arguments, but, like weapons smuggled through a fuzzy border to the wrong party, these are our weapons nonetheless."[54] In such circumstances, is the piling up of yet more skepticism really what we need?

There is, in short, nothing automatically progressive about a stance of suspicion—nor is such a stance inherently marginal, oppositional, or even unusual. Several decades ago, Peter Sloterdijk flagged an increasing tone of cynicism and alienation in popular culture. Thanks to this climate of "chic bitterness," he argues, the intellectual's tactics of triumphant exposure have come to seem ever more superfluous.[55]

The contrast on which this exposure relies—between mass credulity and the brave lone voice of intellectual skepticism—no longer carries much force. Irony and irreverence saturate TV dramas and talk shows; conspiracy theories spawn on the Internet; a nonchalant coolness and world-weariness sets the tone in fashion and music. What is the use of demystifying ideology when many people no longer subscribe to coherent ideologies, when there is widespread disillusionment about the motives of politicians and public figures, when "everyone knows" that hidden forces are at work making us think and behave in certain ways? An entrenched disbelief—indeed, a legitimizing of the status quo *through* disbelief—pervades contemporary culture, writes Jeffrey Goldfarb; cynicism is a shared sensibility among the haves and the have-nots.[56] In such circumstances, familiar divisions between the savvy and the sappy, the critically enlightened and the sheeplike naïveté of the mass, lose their last shreds of purchasing power.

There is, moreover, a final piece to the puzzle that is often overlooked, perhaps because of its very closeness. Academic cultures are governed by distinctive protocols and behaviors, including a stance that we might call *professional suspicion*. That is to say, a detached, dispassionate, and skeptical demeanor has become a defining stance of modern purveyors of knowledge. Such a demeanor allows for real gains and cannot be waved away as merely a self-interested bid for status and prestige on the part of a professionalized New Class.[57] Nevertheless, these close ties to expert thought and practice make it very hard to sustain a view of critique as synonymous with marginality, resistance, or a politics from below. Critique is a form of contemporary "knowledge work" that is grounded in the values of analytical distance, professional autonomy, and expertise—qualities that critics reproduce in their own modes of discourse even as they question them.[58]

The figure of the detective, for example, serves as a prototype of a "science of suspicion" that takes shape in the nineteenth century. As we will see in chapter 3, he stands for a new kind of expert—able to decode hidden signs of criminal activity and to translate these clues into a language of causes and motives. A nascent science of criminology calls for the deciphering of forensic detail, even as the interrogation of suspects assumes a greater role in police work, requiring skills in reading involuntary gestures or fleeting changes in expression that will draw hidden truths to the surface. The invention of the lie detector is one striking example of such institutionalized suspicion, as new technologies are harnessed to extract the buried secrets of the criminal mind. Modern legal systems are grounded in a generalized distrust, presuming that there are hidden forms of malfeasance to be uncovered: faked documents, deceptive testimony, concealed crimes. Suspicion permeates the practice of the law, molding its protocols, forms of reasoning, and bureaucratic processes, inspiring acts of surveillance, investigation, interrogation, and prosecution. It causes new kinds of objects to proliferate and replicate: dossiers, documents, files, lists, statistics, photographs, rules, memoranda, files, specimens. It is here that Ricoeur's philosophical account of the sources of a suspicious hermeneutics comes up short. Such a hermeneutics is not just the brainchild of three "heroic naysayers" and mavericks scribbling through the night in their solitary studies. It is also a broader cultural sensibility composed out of the steady drip-drip of bureaucratic acts, a loose constellation of practices and postures that is diffused throughout society via the legal and executive branches of the modern state. In short, suspicion is less heroic and more humdrum and routinized than we might think.

In such situations, to be sure, the affective force of suspicion is muffled; it is now an institutionally mandated attitude rather than a sign of personal neurosis, philosophical skepticism, or political dissent. The suspicion of the detective or the criminal prosecutor is a low-key affair: a curiously nonemotional emotion that overlaps, in key respects, with the general attitude of detachment that serves as the mark of the modern expert. The rise of the professions in the late nineteenth century gives rise to a distinctive demeanor: the dispassionate individual able to address himself to a given task without being distracted by matters irrelevant to the task at hand. Imperturbability confirms an ability to rise above the tug of personal or political allegiances, to devote oneself to perfecting the skills and procedures that define particular types of specialized knowledge. The criteria that count most are those of proficiency and professional competence, defined in the light of a prevailing ethos of scientific objectivity. This ethos is neither an illusion nor a universal ideal, Lorraine Daston and

Peter Galison observe, but a distinctive orientation that crystallized over time: a composite of "gestures, techniques, habits, and temperament ingrained by training and daily repetition."[59]

Foucauldian critics have often sought to puncture this ideal of disinterestedness—which continues to stamp, nonetheless, the tone and tenor of their own writing. On the one hand, the ideal of objectivity—along with allied notions such as truth or rationality—is traced back to modern regimes of power and thus implicitly or explicitly discredited. On the other hand, these same critics adopt a stance of what we can call "procedural objectivity" that screens out any flicker of emotion, tamps down idiosyncratic impulses, and steers clear of the first-person voice. Even as it is relentlessly queried at the level of content, in other words, objectivity crops up again in the form of ethos, in the writer's own self-effacement and willed impersonality. As we will see in chapter 4, critique is often drawn to a tone of cool and dispassionate reflection rather than distraught condemnation. There is a powerful rhetorical effect that springs from the appearance of neutrality; political analyses seem more persuasive when the scholar has no obvious axe to grind. In this regard, the Victorian critic tracing out concealed genealogies of power in *David Copperfield* or *Little Dorrit* is not unlike the detective scanning a crime scene for buried clues or the clinician scrutinizing the patient's body for signs of pathology. In each case, specialized skills in interpretation and a dispassionate demeanor serve as the imprimatur of expert authority.

Let us note, finally, an *aesthetic* version of this professional detachment that plays into current critical arguments. Like scientific objectivity, the idea of artistic autonomy has a complicated history as a mode of relation that manifests itself in both things and minds: the making of institutions and objects (museums, fields of study, literary prizes) as well as the shaping of attitudes toward art works (what Bourdieu calls a "pure gaze" that considers a poem or painting "as art" in relation to prior works rather than in terms of direct moral, social, or practical gains.)[60] This mode of relation is not equally or evenly distributed; art's claim to autonomy seems more compelling to professional circles of artists, authors, and critics than to lay audiences less mindful of the distance between art and everyday life.[61] Its qualities are crystallized in a series of exemplary personae: the disinterested judgment of the Kantian subject, the nineteenth-century aesthete as dandy and aristocrat of style, the modernist writer brooding over his estrangement from the fray of ordinary life, the sangfroid of the New Critic carving out a distance from the impressionistic judgments of ordinary readers. These figures all speak to a view of art as something that sets its own agenda via specialized criteria, modes of response, and forms of judgment.

Present-day attitudes to this history are notably conflicted. The constellations of thought associated with Kantian philosophy or New Criticism currently find few takers in literary and cultural studies. The stance of the dandy, by contrast, is widely emulated, thanks not only to queer theory but also to a surge of interest in theatricality, parody, and performance. The dandy's debonair stoicism combines knowing distance with aesthetic flair and the verbal flash of wit and aphorism, rendering it appealing to a certain intellectual temperament. As we will see, critique increasingly takes the form of a battle of art against nature, in which the act of "denaturalizing" is held up as the scholar's most urgent task. And here the dandy's immaculate self-consciousness and disdain for sentimental effusions is perfectly attuned to the scholarly zeitgeist, allowing the critic to carve out a skeptical distance from the mainstream without lapsing back into an earnest language of reason and truth or an old-school worship of art.[62]

Disentangling these strands of suspicion thus affords a more comprehensive picture of the influences that bear on present-day criticism. It also helps explain the confidence of critique—its assurance that its own stance of vigilance and mistrust is justified. The shake-up of literary studies over the last few decades is often hailed as a break with a benighted past, and yet critique draws much of its conviction from past models. Its practitioners can rest assured that there is nothing whimsical, arbitrary, or capricious about their own thinking, thanks to a substantial prehistory of suspicious reading. However much it vaunts the solitude or estrangement of the critic, critique is also a collective act—one that draws strength from a communal "we" extending across time as well as space. Critique does not simply cut off, estrange, or isolate but also collects, composes, and gathers together; it creates imagined or real communities around a sensibility, ethos, and practice of reading.

This point is worth emphasizing, given that the anomic and anti-social aspects of critique are afforded so much weight by both supporters and detractors. In inveighing against what he calls the "lonely politics" of Michel Foucault, for example, Michael Walzer surely mischaracterizes the impact of a major intellectual figure.[63] Foucault's politics can hardly be called "lonely" once we take on board the multitudes of his followers, disciples, devotees, fans, and enthusiasts. The point holds more generally: a critical stance serves as a means of forging connections with like-minded others; an ethos of detachment can inspire copious and heartfelt attachments. As we will see in chapter 5, any form of thought—critique included—must gather supporters, forge pathways, generate alliances, and create networks in order to sustain its existence. Even if its affect is wary, skeptical, or negative, it is also engaged in the positive work of assembling allies and creating coalitions around a certain set of ideas. While it may rail against domestication, critique itself becomes a canopy, a dwelling, a resting place, a home.

· · ·

We have wandered some distance from the disciplinary heartland of literary studies, in the hope of offering a fresh slant on current critical method. Expanding the spatial and temporal coordinates of suspicious reading requires a redrawing of mental maps and orientations toward familiar landmarks. Most especially, it invites us to reassess an often selective and self-flattering genealogy of critique. The idea of critique, we could say, contains the answer to its own question: as a highly normative concept, it knows itself to be exceptional, embattled, oppositional, and radical. Whatever is not critique, by contrast, must fall into the camp of the credulous, compliant, and co-opted. In short, critique requires its antithesis in order to shore up its own virtues: the foil of a crushing system of domination or subjugation that turns out, nonetheless, to be strangely vulnerable to the threat of verbal exposure.

Such dichotomies seem less credible once we place critique within a broader spectrum of reading practices, engaging in comparative rather than oppositional thinking. A suspicious sensibility, it turns out, assumes various guises and crops up in many different milieus. It is cultivated by prosecutors and professionals as well as anarchists and avant-gardists; it thrives among cops as well as robbers, climate change skeptics as well as queer theorists. In short, suspicion is thoroughly enmeshed in the world rather than opposed to the world and offers no special guarantee of intellectual insight, political virtue, or ideological purity. My point here correlates with an argument recently made by Christian Thorne: forms of skepticism or antifoundationalism have no inherent or necessary political effects.[64] The result of this reframing is not simply "negative"—that critique is not outside power relations, institutional structures, or the unreflecting routines of everyday life. Rather, it is also "positive"—forms of thought long excoriated as insufficiently critical can be brought back in from the cold and may turn out to have important claims on our attention.

The ultimate hope is that we can wiggle our way out of the cleft stick in which we have been held fast. When it comes to its own self-justification, critique is drawn to an either/or schema: if we are not suspicious, we must be subservient; if we are not critical, we are doomed to be uncritical. And yet the alternatives to critique are not limited to gullibility, blind faith, and slavish compliance. We will have cause to query the equation of critique with "real" politics—a sleight of hand that exiles all other forms of thought to the Siberian wasteland of quietism, complicity, conservatism, or worse. And we will also dispute what Susie Linfield calls "the mistaken idea that chronic negativity equals fearless intelligence": the belief that the constitutionally suspicious are smarter and more sophisticated than the rest of us.[65] In order to engage in such counterfeints, however, we must first look more closely at the style and sensibility of critique: the subject of the next two chapters.

Digging Down and
Standing Back

Should we be close readers or distant readers? Dive in or draw back? Burrow into a text or slide and skitter along its surface? Thanks to a recent surge of interest in method, spatial metaphors are now front and center in literary debates. Critics stew over the implications of proximity versus distance and brood over the merits of surface and depth. Such metaphors are not just images but images-as-ideas that convey concepts and convictions via easily visualized word pictures. Critique revolves around figures of speech; argument relies on certain metaphorical entailments. In this chapter I examine how suspicious-minded critics deploy figures of textual depth *and* textual surface in staking out their claims. What do these figures tell us about practices of critique?

The fortunes of metaphor have soared in recent years; no longer just a decorative device or a baroque frill, it is acknowledged as an indispensable tool of thought. Metaphor, after all, is a matter of thinking of something in terms of something else—the basis for any kind of comparative or analogical thinking. Binding together the disparate and disconnected, it opens up fresh ways of thinking and seeing. Metaphors are orientation devices that yoke abstract ideas to more tangible or graspable phenomena, intertwining the less familiar with the already known. Putting things in an alternate light, they allow us to say things that could not otherwise be expressed. They are deeply entrenched and effortlessly deployed.[1] Some critics study metaphor, but all criticism hinges on metaphors or, more precisely, on metaphor clusters: constellations of images, families of figures or tropes.

While uses of metaphor are unavoidable, it matters which metaphors we use. Particular figures of speech prove more or less fruitful for a task at hand; analogies can smooth or derail the path of thought. Metaphors highlight and yet they also hide, allowing us to see certain things vividly while casting others into the shadows. Metaphor, in this sense, speaks to both creative and conventional aspects of language. Fresh metaphors spin connections that startle us into new ways of seeing; worn-out metaphors slow down our mental software, rendering it sluggish and stale. Figures of speech can become stubbornly entrenched and hard to budge, taking on a life of their own, dictating what and how we see. As a result, we are held hostage by our own pictures, configured by the force of our own figures.

Within literary and cultural studies, these pictures often cast readers and texts in spatial patterns or configurations, choreographing their placement and interaction. We think of the act of reading as involving a chasm of distance or a huddled proximity: we gaze up at the literary work in reverence or look down on it in caustic condemnation; we think of our analytical tools as probing deep into a text's crevices or striking against its glassy, unyielding surface. Such images sum up how a critic conceives the task of interpretation, creating a certain view of the relations between reader, text, and world. These spatial metaphors, however, convey not only ideas but also subliminal surges of attachment or disengagement, intimacy or estrangement. They prime us to adopt certain attitudes, so that we open the pages of a book already caught up in an anticipatory state of irritation or hope, empathy or skepticism.

My concern here is with two highly influential and widely disseminated schemas of suspicious reading. The first pivots on a division between manifest and latent, overt and covert, what is revealed and what is concealed. Reading is imagined as an act of digging down to arrive at a repressed or otherwise obscured reality. Like a valiant archaeologist, the critic excavates a rocky and resistant terrain in order to retrieve, after arduous effort, a highly valued object. The text is envisaged as possessing qualities of interiority, concealment, penetrability, and depth; it is an object to be plundered, a puzzle to be solved, a hieroglyph to be deciphered. By contrast, a second metaphor cluster emphasizes the act of defamiliarizing rather than discovery. The text is no longer composed of strata; the critic does not burrow down but stands back. Instead of brushing past surface meanings in pursuit of hidden truth, she stares intently at these surfaces, seeking to render them improbable through the imperturbability of her gaze. Insight, we might say, is achieved by distancing rather than by digging, by the corrosive force of ironic detachment rather than intensive interpretation. The goal is now to "denaturalize" the text, to expose its social construction by expounding on the conditions in which it is embedded.

The first of these methods is associated with a tradition of Freudian and Marxist thought, the second with the more recent sway of poststructuralism. Comparisons of these styles of reading often emphasize their intellectual and political differences. There is much scuffling and sparring between the fearless critic of ideology scouting for buried truths and the surface-dwelling ironist who distrusts all certainty and renounces critical authority. And yet their similarities at the level of critical mood or sensibility are less frequently noted. Both approaches, after all, seek to identify and taxonomize misperceptions by subjecting texts to analyses that place them in an unexpected and unflattering light. And both guard against any risk of deep involvement, absorption, or immersion in their object, priding themselves on their stoicism and lack of susceptibility to a text's address.

A recent issue of *Representations* called "How We Read Now" has triggered an avalanche of argument around the relative merits of depth versus surface reading. The special issue is framed as a stocktaking and leave-taking of the practice of symptomatic interpretation. Its contributors look skeptically at the methodological premises of such a practice—the belief that texts have hidden depths, possess an unconscious, or display symptoms—as well as its political rationale, that deciphering these concealed meanings is an act of insurgency or a strike against oppression. For the issue's editors, Stephen Best and Sharon Marcus, a turn to surfaces—with all their material, formal, affective, and ethical implications—offers an alternative to such a practice of excavation. "We take surface to mean what is evident, perceptible, apprehensible in texts; what is neither hidden nor hiding; what, in the geometrical sense, has length and breadth but no thickness, and therefore covers no depth. A surface is what insists on being looked at rather than what we must train ourselves to see through." Attending to surfaces, they suggest, promotes a practice of patient description rather than heroic interpretation, a greater critical humility, and a willingness to engage texts as they are. It is no longer a matter of treating the work of art in a reductive or instrumental fashion by slotting it into an imagined political agenda. Rather than signaling quietism or complacency, this renewed attentiveness to the work of art may itself constitute "a kind of freedom."[2]

In serving as a catalyst for a conversation about literary methodology, the *Representations* issue carried out a much-needed public service. I share Best and Marcus's reservations about the practice of symptomatic reading and especially their commitment to "looking at" rather than "seeing through." And I agree that critics, in their eagerness to demonstrate their skills in deciphering hidden meaning, have often failed to take texts at their word—missing things that seem obvious yet are worthy of sustained attention. It is less clear to me, however, that the metaphor of the surface is the best way of capturing the merits of the new directions they canvass. After all, the oscillation between surface and depth is a very familiar theme within aesthetics, a matter of complementary rather than mutually exclusive approaches.[3] A distrust of depth also runs through several decades of critical theory, where, as we will see, a turn to surfaces does not denote an end to interpretation. While poststructuralist critique rejects hidden truth and a dogged or naïve pursuit of ultimate meaning, it engages nonetheless in what I call a *second-level hermeneutics*—a method of reading that looks beyond the individual text to decipher larger structures of cultural production. Insofar as these structures are scrutinized in order to draw out counterintuitive and often unflattering insights, the critic is patently engaged in interpretation. Hermeneutics may be revised or refined, but it is not eradicated.

There is also, I argue, no necessary correlation between the attitude, ethos, or affective stance of critics and their attachment to metaphors of surface or depth. Depth interpretation does not have to be antagonistic; think, for example, of the religious believer who pores over the hidden mysteries of a sacred text in a state of reverence and joy. Conversely, an interest in surfaces does not automatically free us from the straitjacket of suspicion; indeed, as we are about to see, it is often been tied to a hypervigilant and deeply mistrustful stance. Surface reading can be just as suspicious as—indeed, more suspicious than—digging for hidden meaning.

DOWN UNDER

Why and to what end did critics start speaking the language of symptoms, repressions, anxieties, disavowals, rifts, cracks, and fissures? From the 1970s onward, this idiom steadily infiltrated and permeated literary, film, and cultural studies, along with the conviction that the primary task of criticism is to lay bare, make visible, and probe below the surface. The reasons for this terminological takeover included an overwhelming surge of interest in Freudian and Marxist thought, often blended with new linguistic and semiotic theories and applied to close readings of literary or film texts. In the United Kingdom, some of the most frequently cited figures in this style of thought included Antony Easthope, Catherine Belsey, Pierre Macherey, and John Ellis and Rosalind Coward, as well as *Screen* film theorists such as Steven Heath, Annette Kuhn, and Colin MacCabe. And in the United States, Fredric Jameson's *The Political Unconscious* set the tone for a subsequent generation of critics by gearing up an exceptionally powerful interpretative machine.

In the style of reading I call "digging down," we see spatial metaphors of surface and depth being yoked to a critique of culture. Digging is necessary because a text is composed of strata and its meanings are hidden from sight. Matters of import are shrouded, obscured, and inaccessible to the casual observer; they can only be mined via an exacting technique of close reading. What a text seems to be saying is either distracting or deceptive; its subterfuges must be resisted, its superficiality proclaimed. The task of interpretation is to burrow beneath these layers of concealment to arrive at a more fundamental grasp of how things are. Real meaning is at odds with apparent meaning and must be painstakingly exhumed by the critic.

Throwing his hat in the ring, Jameson declares that interpretation "always presupposes, if not a conception of the unconscious itself, then at least some mechanism of mystification or repression in terms of which it would make sense to seek a latent meaning behind a manifest one."[4] In other words, the act of interpretation is inherently mistrustful, driven by the desire to translate the words on the page into a more comprehensive and clarifying idiom. For Jameson, it is Marxism that plays the role of this master code, allowing the critic to redefine cultural artifacts as socially symbolic acts in order to restore a buried reality of material conditions. Turning to the works of Balzac, Gissing, and Conrad, Jameson shows, via a deployment of genre theory and a sequence of dazzling readings, how literary techniques bear the indelible traces of an overriding story of social struggle and class conflict. The coining of the phrase "political unconscious" was a stroke of genius that launched a thousand research projects; it captures both the overwhelming force and the essential elusiveness of the cause to which works of art are ultimately tethered. Jameson's unabashed claim that Marxist thought serves as the ultimate horizon of interpretation found few takers in the United States, but his phrase was rapidly absorbed into the lingua franca of literary studies, to be poached by scholars of diverse theoretical and political stripes. That literary texts could not help bearing witness to the very social conditions they sought to efface was soon folded into the common sense of criticism.

And yet there are different kinds of absence and various forms of concealment; latency or obscurity does not always signal repression, and not every act of interpretation qualifies as suspicious. All texts teem with meanings that are covert or implied: the shadowy presence of other forms or genres, the traces and residues of their historical moment, the many-layered connotations of words and combinations of words. All texts mean more than they say, inspiring critics to elaborate on the elliptical, to expound on the implicit. Interpretation just is this act of drawing out the nonobvious. Yet, as we have seen, such interpretation can be respectful, even reverential, in tone, with the critic adopting the role of a disciple or follower, aspiring to go beyond the text in the service of the text, to aid in the revelation of hidden mysteries. Here interpretation is a good-faith effort to draw out a text's implicit meanings.

It is only under certain conditions that implicit meaning turns into repressed meaning. "Repressed meaning," remarks David Bordwell,

"is what no speaker will own up to."[5] To invoke the language of repression is to put the text in its place by claiming a more discerning
vantage point; it is to lay bare truths that are counterintuitive and unflattering. When deployed in the service of political critique, moreover, a double charge is levied, as we will see in chapter 3: not only is a
text guilty of concealment, but this deception is systemic rather than
anomalous. Repression indicates not just a failure of knowledge but a
foreseeable failure rooted in a text's complicity with power relations.
Under such conditions, digging is an ethical and political imperative;
the role of the critic is not to augment or amplify a text's apparent
meaning but to draw out whatever it refuses to own up to. Appearance
is no longer a gateway to a deeper reality but a tactic for screening that
reality from view.

The links between interpretation-as-excavation and Freudian
method are impossible to miss. The image of digging for lost treasure
was frequently invoked by Freud to capture the distinctiveness of his
own approach. Not long after the discovery of Troy had inflamed the
public imagination, he assigned to himself the role of an archaeologist engaged in the retrieval of rare and precious objects. Just as excavation brings to light artifacts from distant civilizations whose myths
still shape our own, so psychoanalysis exposes the lingering effects
of childhood traumas on adult life. In both cases, the past retains its
grip upon the present. Like scattered shards and broken fragments of
Greek pottery, the memory scraps of the patient must be painstakingly
pieced together to form a larger whole. The model of archaeology connects space and time in a supremely satisfying manner, indicating that
what lies beneath forms part of an earlier, more fundamental reality.
In Freud's topography of the mind, the primitive aspects of the psyche are akin to the cultures of past civilizations; buried deep in the
ground, they serve as the foundations for later forms of life, testifying
to the present's ongoing debt to the past. Archaeology thus captures
the essential spirit of psychoanalysis, serving as a "mighty metaphor"
that resonated within and beyond Freud's time.[6]

Viewed in such a light, the conversations taking place in Freud's
study—interchanges that might otherwise seem halting, awkward,
circuitous, or inconclusive—could be recast as dramatic enterprises
of discovery, burnished with the romantic excitement and exotic

glamour of the archaeological find. To be sure, psychic phenomena turn out to be more complicated than the relics dug up by archaeologists, their structure more enigmatic and resistant to interpretation. Yet they also differ, Freud ventures, in being retained in their entirety. In contrast to the precious shards buried under layers of rubble and sand, the statues robbed of heads or arms, the fabled monuments destroyed by plunder or by fire, when it comes to the human mind "all of the essentials are preserved." What lies in the psyche is ambiguous and elusive, yet also indestructible. The archaeologist is all too aware of how much has perished, yet the analyst knows the opposite to be true: "Even things that seem completely forgotten are present somehow and somewhere, and have merely been buried and made inaccessible to the subject."[7] Nothing is ever definitely lost; absence can be alchemized into presence; silence can be made to speak.

Many of these tenets were taken over virtually unchanged into literary studies. The text, like the psyche, is pictured as being made up of multiple layers or strata; it fails to say what it means and does not mean what it says; absence points back to a determining presence, a hidden force, or a persistent pressure behind the scenes. "The silences of the text," remarks Alan Sinfield in his commentary on the plays of Shakespeare, "manifest moments when its ideological project is under special strain."[8] Instead of assuming coherence, the critic homes in on incoherence, hunting for those moments where language fractures or fails. The idea of repression is indispensable in this scenario; it transforms what look like accidental associations into buried connections, turning apparent contingency into hidden necessity.[9] What is denied, excluded, or ignored turns out to be fundamental and foundational; whatever seems to be last turns out to be first. Repression, in short, gives critics a never-ending job to do; it ensures the immanence of meaning and guarantees there are salient secrets to be discovered. The text is akin to a parapraxis or a dream: spurning its ostensible content, the critic delves into its murky depths to show how discomfiting realities are censored, sanitized, and rendered palatable.

As it turns out, orthodox Freudianism never gained much of a foothold in literary studies, attracting only a modest scattering of acolytes. It was often held up as a model to be avoided rather than to be emulated, excoriated for its flat-footed exegeses and monomaniacal obsessions. "Psychoanalytical literary criticism," writes Peter Brooks, "has always been something of an embarrassment."[10] It was only in the 1970s and '80s, after being blended with semiotics and the politics of social movements, that psychoanalysis finally breached the gates of literary and cultural studies. In being taken up by Marxists and feminists and later by queer and postcolonial critics, it acquired a fresh urgency and political edge, offering a way of grappling with the intractability of human desires, attachments and identifications. "Psychoanalysis," claimed E. Ann Kaplan in a statement whose convictions resonated throughout the 1980s and beyond, "will unlock the secrets of our socialization."[11]

This new form of psychoanalytical criticism made no bones about its disdain for old-style Freudianism with its clunky apparatus of authorial neuroses and phallic symbols. What it offered was something rather different: a blending of Freudian frameworks with linguistic and semiotic vocabularies in the service of sociopolitical critique. The personal ceded ground to the transpersonal—and yet the realm of culture was viewed as akin to an internally divided self, its codes and conventions screening a turbulent, conflict-ridden, social reality. Marjorie Garber, for example, pondering the hidden meanings of Jell-O and Jewishness, fake orgasms and Great Books, proposed that we "read culture as if it were structured like a dream, a network of representations that encodes wishes and fears, projections and identifications."[12] The goal of this analysis of symptoms—unlike the traditional interpretation of symbols—is to lay bare social conflicts and expose unconscious anxieties. A symptom is a kind of code, writes Garber, a means by which a body or a culture inadvertently reveals what lies beneath the surface, hinting at shameful or suppressed realities. The task of the critic is no longer the elaboration of the said but the retrieval of the unsaid.

The spatial logic of deep reading survives the move to literary and film studies, yet its temporal aspect is transformed. Both the archaeologist and the analyst are in pursuit of the past, whether the relics of past cultures or the repressed traumas of early childhood. What appears to be dead must be retrieved, resurrected, brought to light. For the literary or cultural critic, however, this transtemporal tie holds minimal interest. What the work of art represses is not the distant past but its own moment: that is to say, the political conditions or forces bearing down at the moment of its making. Depth, in other words, loses its associations with pastness; what is disavowed or concealed by the text is a "social context" that comes earlier only in the sense of being a foundation, explanation, or ultimate cause. We can discern here the rough outlines of a base/superstructure distinction that was taken over by many critics who had little interest in the tenets of Marxism. What novels or films repress is not the traumas of earlier historical epochs but their own.

A potent mix of Freudian and Marxist tenets thus drives the machinery of interpretation-as-excavation. Both forms of thought, after all, distinguish between surface appearance and a concealed reality; both insist that a seemingly serene and unruffled surface screens elemental yet deeply disturbing truths. Psychic repression and political oppression can be seen as two sides of the same coin — in both cases, something is being forced down, restrained, and muffled by a controlling force. Within this scheme, what is pushed out of sight is held to be of incomparably greater value, shimmering with a revelatory power; it testifies to a necessity and urgency that cannot be gainsaid. One strand of feminist argument, for example, was strongly drawn to this schema; women's status as an oppressed group echoed everything that was repressed in language and culture: desire, delirium, ecstasy, madness, chaos, excess. In the words of a widely referenced feminist film anthology: "Femininity became the underside, the repressed, of a classical or rational/conceptual discourse. It was aligned with the heterogeneity which always threatens to disrupt systems of signification."[13] Feminist critics invoked the power of the incalculable and unknowable, of whatever exceeded or overflowed the categories of language and rational thought.

The terminology of the "symptom" gave a quasi-scientific gloss to the language of criticism, while serving as a handy device for translating the invisible into the visible. Freud's patients, as they mixed up their words and fumbled nervously with their reticules, generated a cornucopia of signs for him to interpret. So too, a generation of critics scrutinized literary and cultural texts for their accidental or involuntary betrayal of repressed meanings. The parallels between the therapeutic session and the act of criticism were often emphatically underscored. In an analysis of *Heart of Darkness*, for example, a critic discovers unmistakable signs of "defensive disavowal" and declares her intent to blur the "distinction between text and embodiment. . . . Conrad's text becomes a corpus, a corpus marked by symptoms that 'speak.'"[14] The literary work is akin to the patient who unwittingly displays signs of neurosis or psychosis for the analyst to decipher. The goal of such a symptomatic reading is to yoke a text to a larger determining whole; it offers a way of binding the work of art to the social world that steers clear of the pitfalls of reflection theory—the belief that a text mirrors or should mirror a larger social context. The symptom points back to a larger reality without mimicking or copying that reality: the connection between text and world is indexical (causal) rather than iconic (based on visual or direct resemblance). This feature proved especially alluring to political critics, such as feminists eager to disassociate themselves from an "images of women" style of criticism that gauged texts in terms of their faithfulness to reality and was increasingly seen as theoretically naïve.

The job of the critic, then, is to demonstrate that texts are less cohesive, coherent, and unified than they seem. Literary and film scholars sounded ever more like geologists manqué, sprinkling their prose with references to faults, cracks, rifts, fissures, and fractures, scanning texts for features that subverted their unity and coherence. Thanks to these cracks, the lava of repressed desires and subterranean forces would inevitably force its way to the surface. "Textual signs," writes one critic, "act as symptoms, sometimes leading to diagnoses where patriarchy shows its marks as an oppressive disease, sometimes focusing rather on the fissures and gaps that the text opens up in the seemingly closed body of patriarchal discourses."[15] Such symptomatic tensions could take many different forms. Marginal or eccentric characters, incongruous, awkward, or clumsy stylistic usage, unresolved or mystifying plot elements, weird camera angles and odd filming techniques: all could be hailed as evidence of failed repression. Such a technique of highlighting the contradictory features of a text proved enormously appealing, allowing critics to demonstrate their alertness to ambiguous, paradoxical, or conflicting meanings. By importing theoretical vocabularies premised on semiotic instability, it became possible to avoid the taint of vulgar or ham-fisted interpretation leveled at traditional Freudian criticism.

One major advantage of this "gaps and fissures" approach lies in allowing the critic to blend critique and love, combining antagonism toward the text with admiration of the text. As we have noted, suspicion is rarely pure or unalloyed. By devoting herself to a close analysis of a novel or a film, after all, the critic implies that it is worthy of such sustained attention, that it contains more than meets the eye. And symptomatic reading was often the very closest of reading, combining meticulous and fine-grained analysis with programmatic theoretical or social claims. Canonical works of art, especially, could be "saved" via this approach, justified as legitimate objects of in-depth analysis as well as personal attachment and emotional investment. That such works embraced a dominant ideology was not disputed. And yet, it turned out, the hidden turbulence of repressed meanings could also trouble or disrupt this apparent compliance. Rather than simply being condemned for its sexist or racist beliefs, for example, a film or novel was now hailed as a contradictory knot of ideological tensions, allowing its more ambiguous or even progressive elements to be highlighted.[16]

To look below the surface of *The Bostonians*, for example, is to be apprised of signs of male hysteria; the text manifests "in its symptomatic discourse an anxiety about the boundaries of desire and identification that it cannot speak directly."[17] Like the New Critic, the symptomatic reader is fascinated by ambiguity and equivocation; unlike the New Critic, she sees such qualities as accidental or involuntary, triggered by the roiling forces of subterranean desires or warring ideologies. Nonetheless, suspicion can now be leavened by a qualified approval for texts that bear witness, however unwittingly and unknowingly, to real social conflicts. It becomes possible to rescue texts from the shame of the sheerly ideological, in Terry Eagleton's phrase, by underscoring their contradictory dimensions.[18] Such scrutiny of formal complexity freed criticism from the need for crude moral or political dichotomies—texts were no longer simply "good" or "bad" for women, for example—while still retaining a clear division between individual texts (portrayed as fissured and ambiguous) and the coercive uniformity of a dominant ideology or a larger social field.

This question of critique's affirmative dimensions remains something of a sore point for Jameson. Taking issue with those who would portray Marxist criticism as a sour-faced exercise in demystifying and debunking, *The Political Unconscious* concludes with a stout defense of the "positive hermeneutic" at the heart of Marxism, as analogous to that invoked by Ricoeur. Jameson's own use of non-Marxist intellectual traditions is eclectic and generous, and he rightly notes a vibrant and long-lived tradition of Left utopian thinking. Yet we might ask whether utopian thought offers a genuine alternative to critique or whether it simply constitutes the other face of critique: that the affirmative aspects of art are labeled "utopian"—i.e., defined in relation to a future no-place—only reinforces an endemic suspicion of the present, such that, as Latour remarks, all hopes are pinned on a world beyond this world.[19] Moreover, the romantic-imaginative yearnings of the works scrutinized in *The Political Unconscious* turn out, in the last instance, to portend a future "classless society"; the art work, even at its most radiant and effulgent, turns out to be an anticipation and confirmation of the tenets of Marxist thought. This is surely a very different kind of positive hermeneutic to that proposed by Ricoeur. There is no moment of revelation, no startling of consciousness, no transformation of thought; the world view of the critic is neither shaken nor stirred. What a text ultimately portends is foretold by a prior theoretical-analytical scheme.

By way of contrast, we can look at George Steiner's account of the fourfold structure of interpretation. Reading begins, according to Steiner, with an initial moment of trust: we venture a leap, taking the risk of an encounter with the unknown in the hope that there is something to be understood and that our effort will not be in vain. Trust in turn gives way to a tacit aggression, what he calls the invasive and extractive element of interpretation. We break a code, dissect the words on the page, ingest and consume the words we encounter. Here we find ourselves making sense of a text by translating it into our own categories. Such a prejudging, from the standpoint of hermeneutics, is not a naïve blunder or an act of egregious violence but the only entry point for understanding: we must begin, by default, with what we know. And yet, as Steiner points out, this incorporation may in turn trigger a reorientation. "We may be mastered and made lame," he writes, "by what we have imported."[20] The words we absorb may disconcert or disorient us, rattle our beliefs or draw us into unimagined worlds. We are altered by what we have ingested and consumed. A final moment is one of reciprocity and rest, in an assessment of what has been gained and lost. Whatever the value of Steiner's riff on the hermeneutic circle—clearly an ideal type rather than an empirical description of every act of reading—it has the advantage of factoring not only the aggressive aspects of interpretation but also that readers can be touched, troubled, perhaps even transformed by the texts they read.

This double-sidedness disappears, however, once dialogue gives way to the diagnosis of symptoms. Absence is translated into a ghostly presence, a passing allusion into a willful evasion, as the critic scans page or screen for signs of failed repression and demonstrates that a text is not in command of its own rhetoric. It seems uncontroversial that texts possess latent or nonobvious meanings, but what lies behind the conviction that these meanings are being actively stifled or squelched by an ideological censor rather than just being implicit, subsidiary, or peripheral? In a key film text of the 1980s, Annette Kuhn writes: "Since in dominant cinema, cracks in the smooth operation of ideology are by definition not there intentionally or consciously, the disjunctures of the text may be regarded as analogous to the symptomatic manifestations of such unconscious repressions."[21] This phrasing identifies, with admirable clarity, the assumptions that are being made. Individual films are slotted into the category of "dominant cinema," and dominant cinema is taken to be in sync with the smooth operation of ideology. This seamlessly interlocking system explains and justifies the hermeneutic aggression of the critic: a film is never just a specific film (not, at least, if it originates in Hollywood), but is also another brick in the wall of a hegemonic order. As David Bordwell points out, this style of reading yields a bifurcated method; mainstream films are held to betray their contradictions unwittingly, while avant-garde works do so knowingly and subversively.[22]

Given this starting presumption of ideological uniformity and coercive sameness, any deviation from this path can only be due to some glitch or mishap in the system. By first imputing a repressive ideology to the work of art, the critic can subsequently style herself as an oppositional reader, refusing its blandishments by teasing out its covert countermeanings. But where exactly is this political unconscious to be found? Is it seething and bubbling beneath the deceptive surfaces of Hollywood films and nineteenth-century novels? Or—to riff off Latour—is it housed in the scribbled notes, computer files, and footnotes of the critic's own workspace?[23]

If we are not held captive by this picture of the politics of culture, then the puzzle of textual ambiguity disappears. We are no longer nonplussed or confounded to learn that a Hollywood film or a Victorian novel contains contradictory meanings—a quality they share with countless other phenomena, which rarely offer a single, simple, seamless, explanation of how things are. Any text is jammed thick with implications, connotations, conflicting meanings, and associative echoes that will inevitable exceed any reader's immediate grasp. No work of art can yield up all its resonances in a single moment. There is always, as Ricoeur would say, a surplus of meaning. Why not think of a text as gradually yielding up its interpretative riches rather than being probed for its unconscious contradictions? In both cases, our preliminary hunches about what a text means are modified after a more careful reading. The key difference is that the text is no longer deemed unknowing and unwitting, in need of the critic's intervention in order to be freed from a coercive regime of ideological containment. There is no need to resort to repression, in other words, to account for contradiction, nuance, or implicit meaning.[24]

Within the frame of symptomatic reading, it is not only the text that is deemed oblivious to its own latent contradictions. So too is the ordinary reader or viewer who takes the text at face value. Just as the therapeutic session requires the intervention of a trained analyst who can decipher the import of a patient's words or gestures, so the fissures and gaps in the text are visible to the critic, whose reading unveils not just what the text does not know but what its intended audience fails to understand. The meanings of symptoms are available only to those eyes trained to draw connections between, in Garber's words, "seemingly unconnected, often wildly disparate things."[25]

These hidden signs thwart the awareness of a text's creator as well as the perceptiveness of ordinary readers; symptoms are, by definition, knotted into chains of causality that bypass the consciousness of those who speak or write. The surface/depth distinction, as Arthur Danto points out, circumvents and subverts the usual division of inner and outer, according to which persons are assumed to have privileged access to their own mental states.[26] These individuals are now the last to know, cut off from awareness of how their thoughts and actions are overdetermined.

There are striking parallels here to hermetic and Gnostic traditions of reading, with their distrust of accessible or apparent meaning. Within such traditions, all valued knowledge is secret knowledge restricted to a circle of initiates, and truth is synonymous with what is not and cannot be said.[27] In a similar manner, the elusiveness of meaning uncovered by the contemporary critic testifies to its value, as a rare and precious object to be unearthed after an endless labor of reading. And yet the mystery that is unveiled, as Jacques Rancière dryly remarks, is usually some variant of the ever-same theme, "an instance of domination either imposed or endured—even if it means that the mode of domination in question is merely the domination of language itself."[28]

A notable tension marks the practice of symptomatic reading: on the one hand, a fascination with fracture and rupture, with the aberrant, excessive, or unmotivated detail; on the other hand, an effort to fold these unruly signs back into some kind of coherent historical or political explanation. Increasingly, we find the former impulse gaining ascendancy, with critics striving to divest the symptom of its traditional associations with depth and a hidden core of meaning. In Pierre Macherey's influential *Theory of Literary Production*, translated in 1975, there are already signs of equivocation. Insisting that "the work is not what it appears to be," drawing on the language of mystification and deception, invoking the latent knowledge encrypted in the unconscious of the work, much of Macherey's argument seems to endorse a familiar division between surface illusion and deeper truth. At other points, however, Macherey insists that the goal of his analysis is to short-circuit any kind of analytical apparatus that opposes appearance to reality. The work, he writes, cannot conceal anything:

"Meaning is not buried in its depths, masked or disguised. It is not a question of hunting it down with interpretation. It is not in the work, but by its side on its margins."[29] Here we see the critic eager to cast off the mantle of archaeologist and to discard the premises of depth interpretation.

Macherey's claim that a precedent for this new style of reading could be found in the work of Freud himself, that psychoanalysis, all appearances to the contrary, was not an attempt to impose a master code on the mysteries of the unconscious, was to gain an increasingly sympathetic hearing. The 1980s and '90s saw the rise of prominence of what was often dubbed French Freud: a vigorous rebuttal of the old image of Freud as a doctrinaire thinker convinced of the scientific objectivity of his theories. Indeed, those who bought into this account were themselves at fault, exposed as careless, lazy, or irresponsible readers. Seizing on moments of linguistic equivocation and ambiguity in Freud's own arguments, critics found confirmation of their view that the work of psychoanalysis was a matter of construction rather than reconstruction, of fiction-building rather than fact. In the wake of Steven Marcus's groundbreaking reading of *Dora*, Freud was read as not just a modern but also a modernist writer, his work riven with doubt and moments of self-questioning, crisscrossed with multiple threads that could not be tied into a single, coherent thesis. "Freud's power as a reader," writes Lis Moller in an especially forceful rendition of this line of thought, lies in his "will to press his inquiry to the point where he encounters the unreadable—that which he *cannot* explain."[30] Pointing to moments of rupture and crisis, critics saw Freud's work as dismantling those very oppositions between depth and surface, truth and falsehood, manifest and latent reality, on which it seemed to rely.

Freud, in other words, was refurbished and rendered newly relevant for a changing critical context by applying essentially the same techniques that had been used to "save" canonical works of art. Clarity was now recoded as contradiction, authority as ambiguity, the expression of meaning as the evasion of meaning. Freudian theory was no longer prized for its sharp insights into hidden causalities, its bold conjectures, its powerful and programmatic explanations. Rather, it was now praised for its skeptical suspension of positive knowledge and its agitated swerving between mutually contradictory perspectives. It was assimilated, in other words, into an influential style of thinking that views irresolution, contradiction, and doubleness as the quintessential intellectual virtues.[31] Along similar lines, the idea of the symptom was wrested away from its association with psychic or historical depth; it was now a surface phenomenon that did not point back to any hidden meaning or ultimate cause and that could not be "cured" by the act of diagnosis. While troubling or muddying a work's apparent meaning, it did not lend itself to clear-cut resolutions, historical explanations, or political programs. In Jennifer Fleissner's words: "The symptom persists across the surface of the text itself, and it marks that which, in the text, persists beyond the moment of its historical inauguration."[32]

This skittishness about the claims of depth interpretation was to gather increasing momentum in literary studies. To impute a hidden core of meaning, critics argued, was to subscribe to a metaphysics of presence, a retrograde desire for origins, a belief in an ultimate or foundational reality uncontaminated by the play of signifiers. For those who subscribed to the tenets of poststructuralism, language was a primary, even primordial, force conjuring up what counts as reality rather than conveying or concealing it. In such a light, depth interpretation could only seem like a foolhardy exercise, a last-ditch attempt to deny the instabilities of meaning by clinging to the notion of a hidden, God-given kernel of truth. What, then, was to become of critique, by now firmly established as a core method in literary studies? How could literary scholars remain skeptical and vigilant without seeking to impose a new regime of authoritarian knowledge? Could the hermeneutics of suspicion yield to a suspicion without hermeneutics?

AGAINST NATURE

An alternate idiom thus pushes to the fore. Vertical metaphors yield to horizontal ones; the text is described as flat, shallow, empty, depthless, one-dimensional; it is a chain of signifiers, a verbal façade, a discursive structure, a weave of words. And the critic no longer digs down but draws away. Instead of foraging, nose close to the ground, for tempting truffles of truth, she stands back from the text to scrutinize it from afar. This quizzical gaze is designed to "denaturalize"— to show that there is nothing self-evident about its form or content. Whatever is the case is radically contingent and could be otherwise. There are no more masks to be ripped away, no mysteries to be uncovered, no ultimate truths or final vocabularies. Demystification without depth! While this approach takes issue with the excavation schema, it does not entirely supplant it; the two methods overlap in uneasy coexistence rather than slotting into a sequence of historical stages. The rhetoric of standing back stretches over decades, as we will see, while there are still scholars drawn to a depth hermeneutic and its language of symptoms, cracks, and fissures.

The shift in metaphors brings a change of tone and fine-tuning of technique. The critic no longer dirties her hands by burrowing into the text, scrabbling through layers of soil in pursuit of buried treasure. In standing back from the text, she also stands over it, looking down with a puzzled or ironic gaze. While the deep reader may be imperious in her hunt for truth, she is also passionately curious about hidden mysteries. The stance of the surface-oriented critic, by contrast, is more circumspect and equanimous. Weaned on Foucault, she looks skeptically at a Freudian language of repression and symptoms. Instead of reading deep, she prefers to reads wide, swapping the close-up view of the microscope for a wide-angle lens that offers a panoramic view of systems of discourse and grids of power.

She also speaks, persistently and pejoratively, of "nature." Stripped of its feel-good associations, nature now stands for everything that critique condemns: namely the realm of the it-goes-without-saying and the taken-for-granted. And the most urgent task of critique is to "denaturalize"—to turn what appears to be nature back into culture, to insist that what looks like an essential part of the self or the world could always be otherwise. It would be hard to overstate the pervasiveness of this antinaturalist rhetoric in contemporary scholarship. In a founding text of disability studies, Rosemarie Garland-Thomson announces her intent to "denaturalize" the cultural coding of disability in order to interrogate the conventions of representation within social narratives of bodily differences.[33] Questioning the rhetoric of black authenticity and Afro-centrism, Kobena Mercer argues that "the 'nature' invoked in black counter-discourse" is an ideologically loaded idea created by binary logic within a European culture that sought in turn to "naturalize" its own power.[34] And in a critique of the myth of American national identity, Paul Giles seeks "not only to denaturalize it, but also to suggest how its own indigenous representations of the 'natural' tend to revolve tautologously, reinforcing themselves without reference to anything outside their own charmed circle."[35]

In citing these few examples among countless possible others, I have no bone to pick with the critic's general line of argument, but am curious about the repeated resort to nature and naturalizing as the means by which it is made. The right to rail against social injustice, reinterpret images, or take issue with badly made arguments is not in dispute, but it is less evident that such rebuttals need to be framed as excoriations of nature. Reflecting on the guiding tenets of poststructuralism, Rey Chow ponders its untiring mistrust vis-à-vis "illusions of nature, origin, primordialness, authenticity, and so forth."[36] Suspicion, in this line of thought, must be directed not only at "nature" as an object, ideal, or value but also at "naturalness," as that quality possessed by any style of thought that fails to draw attention to its own contingency, that yields to the lure of the accepted, the obvious, the familiar.

Why have nature, the natural, and naturalizing gotten such a bad rap? We have already touched on one source of inspiration: the figure of the dandy, whose embrace of artifice and detachment is accompanied by a deep-seated distaste for anything associated with nature. In the tradition of aestheticism pioneered by Baudelaire and sustained by Wilde, Huysmans, D'Annunzio, and others, the Romantic vision of nature as a spiritual haven and solace is subject to withering scorn. The natural, rather, is portrayed as the realm of the automatic and unthinking, the tyranny of coercion and compulsion, associated with whatever is mandated either by biology's laws or society's norms. In the bohemian circles of the metropolis, writers and artists will reclaim the epithet of "unnatural" as a badge of honor and source of pride. "I ask you to review and scrutinize whatever is natural—all the actions and desires of the purely natural man: you will find nothing but frightfulness," declares Baudelaire in a famous paean to the glories of the artificial.[37] "Against nature" will become the rallying cry of a generation of disaffected decadents and aesthetes, its echoes resonating through the works of twentieth-century artistic and intellectual avant-gardes.

Another obvious influence is the heritage of Russian formalism and its idea of *ostranenie*, usually translated as "defamiliarizing" or "making strange." The language of everyday life, according to Viktor Shklovsky and his Soviet compatriots, has been dulled, deadened, and rendered inert by the force of habit. We look without really seeing, hear without really listening; we mechanically utter the common-places of speech like vending machines spitting out chocolate bars. What defines literary language, by contrast, is its power to invigo-rate perception, to employ devices that estrange us from the habitual and alienate us from the self-evident. For the Russian formalists, then, literature is intrinsically opposed to the quotidian, the familiar, the taken for granted. It is what allows us to break away from the "sec-ond nature" of ordinary language, to get off the treadmill of mundane speech and thought.

Critics drawn to this line of thinking often use "defamiliarize" and "denaturalize" as synonyms. Nature, in this sense, flips its usual mean-ing. It no longer has much to do with birds and beasts, fauna and flora; it does not conjure up some sphere of stark necessity or pri-mordial desire beyond the reach of convention and culture. Rather, the natural *is* the conventional, the world of social norms, rote per-ception, and the dead weight of routine. This automatic aspect of be-havior, moreover, is felt to have intensified in modernity; we take on the qualities of the machines that serve us, are programmed to be un-thinking consumers, behave repetitively and robotically like workers on a production line. Modern "culture," in a paradoxical reversal of the usual distinction, thus enforces the metaphorical sway of "nature" as second nature.

Yet there is a key difference between Russian formalism and con-temporary critique; it is now not just literature but the distancing gaze of *theory* that transforms the ordinary into the strange and alienates us from the commonplace. While philosophical thought has always pitched its tent at some distance from everyday life, this heightened suspicion of nature and the natural is a modern phenomenon. And here we can also discern the influence of phenomenology and its ingrained suspicion of the "natural attitude." The philosopher, according to Husserl, must shuck off those beliefs and attitudes that constitute his ordinary or everyday self; he forbids himself to partake of "the whole natural performance of his world-life. . . . All natural interests are put out of play."[38] Commonsense thought is a constant irritant and thorn in the side of the serious thinker. The natural attitude simply is the naïve attitude, the epitome of *Selbstverständlichkeit*, or taken-for-grantedness. Such naïve knowledge must be bracketed via the transcendental reduction for rigorous thinking to begin. The persona of the contemporary critic—engaged in endless self-problematizing, practicing an abstention from positive categories and norms, while looking skeptically at the natural and commonsensical—is clearly indebted to this intellectual tradition.[39]

Antinaturalism, then, sanctions iconoclasm on several different fronts; it allows critics to assail the authority of both biology and culture, to voice a mistrust of any and every form of constraint. "Nature," in short, encompasses several distinct but equally toxic belief systems. The idea of *human nature* comes under withering scrutiny from critics implacably opposed to universals, assailed with special vigor by feminist, queer, and antiracist critics conscious of its many historical uses in sanctioning social inequality. The notion of an *inner nature*, of a fateful inner self and personal calling, is viewed as a naïve Romantic holdover or a nakedly ideological belief in the autonomy and supremacy of the individual. What we think is inside is really outside: our sense of an inner reality is manufactured by external forces, and any sense we may have of our individuality or uniqueness is misplaced. And finally, the idea of *second nature* as a sense of ingrained casualness and acceptance of the way things are will be subject to ever more scathing judgment. From a theoretical point of view, there are now few crimes more heinous than "naturalizing" the cultural forms that surround us, causing them to seem self-evident rather than fabricated and fungible. As Eve Sedgwick remarks, "Theory has become almost simply coextensive with the claim (you can't say it often enough), *it's not natural*."[40]

This antinaturalism, moreover, is not just a matter of argument but also, as we've noted, a matter of attitude and tone. Critique is translated into critical style, expressed not only in what is said but in the manner of its saying and a distinctive mode of scholarly self-fashioning. To flip through the annals of recent theory is to encounter an unmistakable rhetoric: the vigilant weeding out of any traces of emotion or expressive voice, a syntax that piles one rhetorical question on top of another in an interrogative spiral while steering clear of definite propositions or affirmative statements, a deadpan citation of commonplace phrases in such a way as to expose their hollowness and hypocrisy. In the act of distancing herself from received wisdom, the critic models an exemplary self-consciousness and a heightened aesthetic sensibility. Foucault's style, especially, has triggered numerous imitations: famously impassive, scrupulously nonjudgmental, even when portraying sensational facts and shocking acts, it serves as a model and template for much contemporary prose.[41] Purged of obvious signs of affect and attachment, the temperature of critique is cool rather than hot.

We might think this metaphorical constellation (embrace of surfaces/distaste for nature) is quite new, but it is already evident in a work such as *Mythologies*, written over half a century ago. Barthes's primer on the French everyday life of the 1950s, with its stylish exegeses of margarine and murder trials, Einstein's brain and Garbo's face, Hollywood Romans and steak and chips, was, for many English-speaking students, their gateway to French theory. At several points, Barthes telegraphs his indifference to a depth hermeneutic that hunts for hidden meanings; he explicitly rejects a language of secrecy and concealment and waves away the tenets of Freudianism. "*Myth*," he declares, "*hides nothing*: its function is to distort, not to make disappear. There is no latency of the concept in relation to the form; there is no need of an unconscious in order to explain myth." The intentions of myth are not concealed or buried below the surface; they are simply naturalized, drained of history and politics. Myth draws the logic of social relations into the sphere of the self-evident, endowing them with a "natural and eternal justification."[42]

Myth, in other words, is Barthes's word for culture masquerading as nature. It does not identify a specific idea or ideology but covers all those modes of expression that fail to draw attention to their own contingency. It embraces, in other words, virtually the entire spectrum of culture, from TV advertisements to academic essays, from women's magazines to photography exhibitions. The essays in *Mythologies*, writes Barthes, were triggered by his impatience at the "'naturalness' with which newspapers, art, and common sense constantly dress up a reality which . . . is undoubtedly determined by history." Here Barthes acknowledges his debt to modes of semiotic analysis that allow him, in his own words, to blend acts of denunciation with detailed analysis in order to better account "for the mystification that transforms petit-bourgeois culture into a universal nature."[43]

Mythologies' vignettes on wrestling and striptease, on French guide books and politicians' photographs, aims to reverse this process, to "denaturalize" the falsely obvious, to look afresh at everyday phenomena in such a way to capture their strangeness. Barthes ponders the euphoric connotations of ads for laundry detergents and cleaning fluids, detects the ghost of the commedia dell'arte in the spectacle of modern wrestling, elaborates on the mythological resonance of wine, scrutinizes the cooking pages of women's magazines. By treating everyday texts like works of art, bracketing their function as information or entertainment in order to expound on metaphor, narrative, and visual design, he engages in the Sisyphean task of turning nature back into culture, of highlighting the artifice and arbitrariness of what seems self-evident.

Even in the mid-1950s, however, Barthes worried that the act of demystifying was starting to show signs of wear. Fifteen years later, he is ready to lament its status as an intellectual cliché and a new form of academic doxa. "Any student," he observes, "can and does denounce the bourgeois or petit-bourgeois character of such and such a form (of life, of thought, of consumption). . . . Denunciation, demystification (or demythification) has itself become discourse, stock of phrases, catechistic declaration."[44] Barthes himself would subsequently move away from critique in order to experiment with very different styles and sensibilities: the languorous and the euphoric, the epigrammatic and the flamboyant, the sensual as well as the semiological. His prose melts into forms that are more seductive and more vulnerable, entwining themselves around the textures and tones of words, invoking a state of dependency and desire. Criticism, he remarked at a later point in his career, is often affectionate: reacting against dispassionate analysis, he now dwells on the affective intensities of criticism.[45] Transmitted across the Atlantic, however, the technique of dispassionately scrutinizing surfaces while denouncing nature would enjoy a long and successful afterlife. In this reworking of critique, the task of the critic is not to unmask falsehoods in order to replace them with truths but to squelch the desire for such substitutes by stressing the radically contingent and contestable nature of belief. In Richard Rorty's words, such critics are the quintessential ironists, "always aware of the contingency and fragility of their final vocabularies and thus of their selves."[46]

To be sure, this ironic consciousness was often blended with activist commitments quite unlike Rorty's own. Detachment was not just a matter of disinterestedness, the "suspended animation" of the philosopher engaging in self-questioning for its own sake, but was infused with political and sometimes polemical energies.[47] From the 1980s onward, an elective affinity arose between "French theory" and a vanguard of queer theorists, feminists, and postcolonial scholars. And here the act of standing back acquired a sharp political edge, albeit one cast in the mode of disassociation. Radicalism now required a stance of hypersuspicion and tireless vigilance; critics looked skeptically not only at conservative or mainstream thought but also at a language of identity, pride, and empowerment embraced by oppositional social movements. By distancing themselves from such affirmative claims, they hoped to evade the metaphysical traps and conformist values that they saw lurking within the categories of everyday speech. Wary of compromise and fearful of co-option, they held fast to the view, expressed succinctly by Lee Edelman, that "critical negativity, lacking a self-identity, can never become an orthodoxy."[48]

From the perspective of actor-network theory (ANT), we can briefly note, a treatise on critical negativity turns out, by contrast, to have numerous identities—as a material and physical object, a contribution to a tenure file, a reckoning with one's scholarly rivals, a means of working through a midlife crisis, a well- or poorly selling commodity, an argument in active search of supporters and allies, an object that triggers a wide range of affective response ranging from enthusiasm to irritation. The much-invoked idea of an "antisocial thesis," in short, collides with the fact that such a thesis can only sustain itself by enlisting allies, generating attachments and connecting to networks—engaging in precisely those activities that would seem to undercut and disprove its own theoretical tenets. Negation thus collides with the ubiquity of relation—even though ANT would insist that the nature and variety of these relations are not well understood by gesturing toward an abstract notion of oppressive orthodoxy.

The trend toward denaturalizing was not universally embraced but was the subject of disputes and disagreements. Within the field of postcolonial studies, for example, stand-offs were frequent between a "poststructuralist" and a "materialist" wing; that is to say, between scholars intent on teasing out ambivalences in colonial discourse in order to deconstruct or denaturalize its claims and others eager to push beyond such discourse to retrieve more accurate accounts of geopolitical realities or subaltern identities. In literature departments, however, the linguistic turn and its denaturalizing methodologies won the day, such that postcolonial studies was often described as a supplement or surrogate of poststructuralism. To consult a widely used textbook, for example, is to see "postcolonial reading" defined as a "form of deconstructive reading most usually applied to works emanating from the colonizers (but may be applied to works by the colonized) which demonstrates the extent to which the text contradicts its underlying assumptions . . . and reveals its (often unwitting) colonialist ideologies and processes." The word "unwitting," as we have seen, is key.[49]

This increasing wariness of positive definitions promoted a proliferating rhetoric of constructionism across the humanities. When critics declare that sexuality or serial killers are socially constructed, their point is not to contrast this condition to a more natural, edenic, or primordial state. Rather, it is to take a sledgehammer to the very idea of nature and the natural, to drive home that what we take to be ingrained or self-evident is stamped by culture all the way down. The set of socially constructed phenomena becomes an ever-expanding field that subsumes every conceivable object and practice. And yet the ubiquity of this idiom does little to mute its charge. To describe something as socially constructed is to deliver an accusation or mount a reproach. It is, as Latour remarks, to seek to reduce something to dust by showing that it is made up.[50]

In Judith Butler's often-cited essay "Imitation and Gender Insubordination," for example, the suspicion of nature and rhetoric of constructionism are yoked to an intensive scrutiny of everyday assumptions about gender and sexuality. What exactly does it mean, asks Butler, for a gay person to "come out"? Any attempt to disclose or define one's sexuality, she suggests, will only precipitate new forms of concealment and mystification, thanks to the opaque and often intractable workings of erotic desire. To declare an identity as a lesbian or gay man is to risk being boxed into the categories of a disciplinary regime; it is to submit to new forms of expectation, regulation, and normalization. Perhaps one is most oppressed most insidiously, Butler remarks, in the very act of claiming to be out.

A suspicious hermeneutic is here applied to the conditions of consciousness and to what often seem to be the most intimate and intrinsic aspects of self. Our apprehension of ourselves as gay or straight, men or women, relies on a sense of naturalness that conceals the linguistic and cultural structures mandating our sense of who we are. The intertwined categories of biological sex, cultural gender, and sexual orientation are radically contingent, even though, in being assimilated and reproduced over time, they acquire the status of second nature. In this context, any sense we may have of our autonomy or uniqueness as persons turns out to be misplaced. The self, writes Butler, is the effect of a discourse that claims to represent that self as a prior truth. That is to say, what appears to be primary turns out to be secondary and subordinate; the self is demoted from a source or origin to an epiphenomenon thrown up by the implacable structures of language.

We see here many of the characteristics of fin-de-siècle critical theory: an exposure of the grip of linguistic and semiotic systems, an emptying out of selfhood and interiority, a vigilant interrogation of the power-laden structures of everyday language and belief. By yoking such tactics to the study of gender and sexuality, Butler's writings shook up and transformed feminism while also invigorating an emerging field of queer theory. It was already apparent that categories like "woman" or "gay" were less unified and cohesive than they appeared, and that those who belonged to subordinate groups were quite capable, in their turn, of manipulating or marginalizing others—in short, that the world did not divide cleanly into camps of oppressors and victims, the powerful and the powerless. One especially salient background was the infamous sex wars of the 1980s, when lesbians engaging in sadomasochistic sex were often shamed, shunned, and accused of complicity with patriarchy. Butler's essay thus spoke to a growing unease, in some circles, with the very language of identity.

That such language could be used to police, control, or exclude was no longer in doubt, even as attempts to define or pin down sexual identity are undoubtedly fraught with complication. Yet it hardly follows that attempts to speak of self, sexuality, or identity are automatically or invariably coercive. After all, people seek to articulate and understand themselves in different milieus and to very diverse ends. They speak, they hesitate, and they speak again: in classrooms and in bars, in therapists' offices and on talk shows, in custody disputes and in intimate conversations with lovers. They irritate or enthrall their audiences; they move listeners to tears or sway them to anger; they inspire confidences and counterrevelations in response. Some of these speech acts, no doubt, are inspired by self-delusion or misperception; others may bully, browbeat, or exclude. Yet they can also forge new attachments and solidarities, renounce or reaffirm past histories, offer fresh angles of vision or reaffirm crucial but long-forgotten insights. They serve differing needs and have countless uses. It is not that questions of power are irrelevant to such speech acts but that the writer must clarify their relevance by attending to specific cases. As Toril Moi puts it, "It is impossible to theorize power in language in advance of any utterance. . . . You need to understand who says what to whom, for what purpose, under what circumstances."[51] To nail one's colors to the mast of a series of theses about language and power, however, is to know ahead of time what one is going to find. Overlooking the nuances, subtleties, quirks, variations, and tonal differences in conversations about personhood, the critical theorist sees the grinding machinery of normalization and regulation—with disruption serving as the only conceivable loophole and escape hatch. In short, the metaphorical act of standing back has its own risks and epistemological losses. From a distance, things blur together, everything looks remarkably similar, and distinctions and details are lost. Farsightedness can be a hindrance as well as an advantage.

Moreover, it is worth noting that the distinction between depth and surface does not entirely disappear in the rhetoric of antinaturalism. The natural, normal, or intrinsic is now demoted to a mere façade; what seems to be an "inner psychic or physical necessity" is merely a surface sign that produces the misleading "illusion of an inner depth."[52] And yet this fictional status of personhood is hidden from sight, notes Butler, thanks to a stubborn attachment to Romantic notions of interiority and an unwillingness to relinquish a sense of our own uniqueness. The truth of superficiality, in other words, is a truth that is hard to access and concealed from view, buried under the sediment of everyday beliefs. The paradoxical quality of this perception is well captured by Raphael Samuel when he writes that critical theory is eager to expose the "artifice which a camouflage of naturalness conceals."[53] That is to say, metaphors of surface and depth switch places: it is superficiality that is now the hidden truth, while interiority is demoted to a deceptive façade.

One consequence of this ubiquitous antinaturalism is the erection of a forbiddingly high wall between ordinary language and the ethos of critique. There are, to be sure, very good reasons why scholars might wish to take issue with the ideas that surround them, and especially with the conviction that certain forms of life are authorized by divine or biological fiat. The language of "nature" has often been invoked to justify racial inequality, condone homophobia, and defend the subordinate status of women. In the 1999 preface to *Gender Trouble*, for example, Butler explains her "dogged effort to 'denaturalize'" as being driven by a desire to challenge the normative violence inherent in prevailing discourses of sexuality. The point is well taken, though it is worth asking whether the only alternatives are either to fix and solidify identities or to deconstruct them.[54] And yet the intellectual antipathy toward nature and the natural has steadily been stretched to the point of incoherence. It is one thing to point out that certain ideas are bad and also taken for granted. It is another to conclude that they are bad *because* they are taken for granted—in other words, that anything taken for granted is an agent of domination. Such an antinature animus, with its unblinking suspicion of anything tainted by convention, has the effect of assigning an automatically backward status to everyday language. Such language languishes in the perpetual gloom of unknowingness, even as a theoretically honed consciousness exposes an ever-widening circle of culture to the laser beam of critique.

And yet critical theory is, of course, soaked through and through with its own taken-for-granted assumptions that look eccentric, ab-

surd, or counterintuitive to outsiders. All forms of acting and thinking depend on "black boxes": beliefs and hypotheses so well established that they do not even register as beliefs but are part of the air we
breathe and the water in which we swim. Without such boxes, thinking could not take place; if we were to pause to test every assumption and interrogate every hypothesis, bridges would never be built
and books would never get written.[55] In short, critique overestimates
the transcendent force of its own self-consciousness and the extent
to which it can liberate itself from convention. Opposing critique to
common sense fails to acknowledge the commonsensical aspects of
critique. As Stanley Fish never tires of pointing out, we cannot access
all the conditions that make our speech possible; we cannot turn all of
our background into foreground; we cannot turn all that is unthought
into thought. To believe that we can "denaturalize" the assumptions
that make our thinking possible, that we can distance ourselves from
the very patterns of belief that make us who we are, is to chase the
old dream of philosophical transcendence, of the view from nowhere.
None of this implies that we cannot object to whatever we dislike or
wish to change. But we do better to direct our criticisms at the specific
ideas or issues at stake and dispense with the reproachful charge that
something is at fault just because it has been *naturalized*.[56]

CONCLUSION

We have considered two variants of critique: hermeneutics versus
genealogy, depth versus surface, the pursuit of truth versus the interrogation of nature. In the first scheme, the critic strives to recover
or retrieve something precious: interpretation pivots on a division
between what is concealed and what is revealed. False gods are cast
down in order to usher in a new regime of truth; critical doubt is deployed in the service of a final revelation. For a second group of critics, this hermeneutic is not yet suspicious enough, thanks to its pesky
attachment to final vocabularies and ultimate truths. Their response
is to sweep away the topology of depth, with its distinction between
the true and the false, reality and its concealment. There are no longer
hidden layers to be peeled back, mysteries to be unveiled, or secrets

to be salvaged. Instead, the object of analysis exists on a flat plane, disencumbered of dualistic distinctions and hierarchical ranking. The critic abstains from positive judgments, no longer asking "What does this text really mean?" but "How did this text come about?" or "What functions does it serve?" The reference point is no longer Freud but Foucault.

Foucault, of course, had little time for either Marxist notions of oppression or Freudian notions of repression. Power, he insists, is not something wielded by a dominant group; nor is it a purely negative force that punishes and prohibits. It manifests itself, rather, in the circulation of discourses that create forms of knowledge and produce certain kinds of persons. These discourses are decentralized and dispersed; we are caught, as it were, in a spiderless web. Moreover, capillaries of power do not distort or obscure an underling reality but bring into existence historically contingent forms of acting and being. The division between latent and manifest meaning thus fades from view. As David Hiley puts it, "For genealogy, there is no appearance/reality distinction; and if one wants to speak of disguise and unmasking, then there are only an endless series of masks. . . . The operations of biopower are hidden in the transparency of surface practices themselves."[57]

Thanks to this stress on surface, Foucauldian method was often hailed as an antidote to hermeneutics. According to Hubert Dreyfus and Paul Rabinow, for example, such a method did not qualify as a "hermeneutics of suspicion" because it did not involve a "search for a deep truth which has been purposefully hidden."[58] Their argument could find some justification in Foucault's own strictures against certain methods of interpretation in *The Birth of the Clinic* and elsewhere. In the essay "Nietzsche, Freud, Marx," for example, he explicitly rejects a view of the interpreter as "the good excavator of the underworld."[59] Rather than getting to the bottom of things, Foucault writes, the three thinkers invoked in his title are embroiled in the endless task of interpreting interpretations, caught in a perpetual play of mirrors. Any claim to pin down ultimate meaning collapses under the weight of its own contradictions. Reading, we might say, is more like falling into a bottomless pit rather than striking solid ground.

And yet the rationale for limiting suspicious interpretation to a reliance on depth metaphors and buried meanings—evident in both Dreyfus and Rabinow and in contemporary debates—seems arbitrary. After all, as we have seen, surface-oriented critics can be just as suspicious and distrustful as their deep-digging comrades, and even more intent on distancing themselves from ordinary beliefs and commonsense assumptions. As Jim Merod writes in his discussion of Foucault, what makes this line of thought a hermeneutic one is "the repeated emphasis on power as an elusive interrelational phenomenon, something that escapes detection but is prevalent and formative." The Foucauldian critic is an expert in tracking down an almost invisible quarry.[60]

We can encapsulate this similarity-in-difference via a distinction between "strong" and a "second-order" hermeneutics. To engage in a strong hermeneutics, as we saw in the case of Freudian archaeology, is to forcefully extract a deep but disavowed truth, to push aside surface phenomena in order to demonstrate that the text is radically other than it appears. A second-order hermeneutics, by contrast, stands back from a text in order to denaturalize its assumptions and position them within larger structures of power. Attention shifts from the "what" to the "how" of meaning, to the discursive conditions that allow a text to signify. In both cases, however, there is a commitment to drawing out undetected yet defining forces, to exposing what remains invisible to or unnoticed by others. Critique remains, in this sense, a fundamentally interpretative task.

As we've noted, moreover, styles of reading call up an ambient mood or disposition, encouraging critics to take up attitudes of trust or mistrust, affection or aversion. And here, the continuities between deep reading and distant reading leap to the eye, overshadowing, though not overriding, their differences. Both of these approaches, after all, bring a text into view in a certain kind of way. Both prime the reader to approach a text gingerly, with her guard up. Both encourage her to pit her wits against an imagined opponent, to treat a text as an antagonist, to assume that words and images must be misleading. Depth readers and distant readers agree that the responses of ordinary readers require not just amplification but ongoing adjustment and correction. Ordinary readers lose their bearings because of their tendency to take things at face value, their obdurate attachment to what is. In pouring cold water on these inclinations, the critic seeks to shock untrained readers out of their complacency. The work of critical analysis simply is this work of estrangement, the labor of disrupting continuities and severing attachments.

Both methods, moreover, treat a text as an inert object to be scrutinized rather than a phenomenon to be engaged. And in this sense, neither metaphors of depth nor surface get us very far in clarifying the coimplication and coproduction of reader and text. "Interpretation," remarks Alexander Nehamas in an argument that queries the language of the superficial versus the deep, "is not a geological project."[61] A work of art is a potential source of knowledge rather than just an object of knowledge—one whose cognitive impact and implications are tied up with its affective reach. We are intertwined and entangled with texts, in ways that require further consideration. We look expectantly toward these texts, cultivate moods and attitudes, project our obsessions and ride our hobbyhorses. Yet these texts are more than the sum of our projections: they can surprise or startle us, nudge us into unexpected moods or states of mind, cause us to do things we had not anticipated. Reading, in this sense, is neither a matter of digging below resistant ground nor an equanimous tracing out of textual surfaces. Rather, it is a cocreation between actors that leaves neither party unchanged.

· 3 ·

An Inspector Calls

What is the connection between critique and crime? And how do stories of detection shed light on contemporary protocols of suspicious reading? The parallels between critics and detectives have often been noted. Both pride themselves on their sharp-eyed gaze and powers of intellection; both decode signs, decipher clues, and brood over intractable puzzles. Literary scholars have often shown a soft spot for fictional sleuths of various stripes. From Sherlock Holmes to Sam Spade, criminal investigators have served as figures of fascination and identification, hailed as comrades in arms, alter egos, and kindred spirits. Both critics and detectives, to pick up on a phrase from Ernst Bloch, like to fish in murky waters.[1]

This affinity between sleuths and scholars has a long history—and takes various forms. While Edmund Wilson excoriated detective fiction in his essay "Who Cares Who Killed Roger Ackroyd?" it turned out that many critics cared a great deal—less about Agatha Christie than about detective fiction generally and its striking affinities with their own methods. As Marjorie Nicholson declared back in 1929, "Scholars are, in the end, only the detectives of thought."[2] Both classic whodunits and hard-boiled crime fiction have triggered copious analyses from philosophical, ideological, and formalist perspectives. And in the heyday of deconstruction, Edgar Allan Poe's "The Purloined Letter" spawned a virtual industry of commentary and metacommentary. Detective fiction has often been a playground for the latest theories of interpretation.

Sociological explanations for such affinities are not hard to come by. Literary scholars often feel sidelined by market-driven values; they chafe at bureaucratic structures that relegate them to the role of glorified grade givers and paper pushers; they are prone to bouts of alienation and anomie. So it's hardly surprising if they find themselves drawn to representations of charismatic loners whose quick-witted reasoning runs rings around the plodding procedures of the official police force. Fictional detectives, remarks Richard Alewyn, are often eccentrics and outsiders; they live alone in messy rooms, smoking opium or cultivating orchids, devoting themselves to artistic as well as intellectual pursuits.[3] Their brilliance is underestimated and their motives misunderstood by the commonplace minds that surround them. The parallels seem irresistible. Academics are obsessive problem-solvers, writes Dennis Porter, who find in the figure of the avenging investigator a style of intellectual heroism with which they can identify.[4]

The following pages, however, take a tack that is more rhetorical than sociological. I am less interested in the shared identities of scholar and sleuth — which, as we'll see, have taken a serious knock in recent years — than in overlapping methods of interpretation. Specifically, I pursue the analogies between detection and critique as styles of suspicious reading that blend interpretation with moral judgment. And here the similarities proliferate at a dizzying rate: a penchant for interrogating and indicting, a conviction that deceit and deception are ubiquitous and that everyone has something to hide, a commitment to hunting down criminal agents and a reliance on the language of guilt and complicity. I've already noted that the practitioner of critique shares with the detective a professionally mandated mood: an ambient attitude of mistrust that expresses itself in a refusal to let down one's guard. Let us now link mood to morality in order to throw out a hypothesis: *like the detective, the critical reader is intent on tracking down a guilty party.* Suspicion sets in motion a search for agents who can be held to account for acts of wrongdoing.

Accountability brings us to matters of cause and effect; we can only be held responsible for events if we play some part in making these events happen. To put it another way, guilt is inseparable from narrative. The critic, like the detective, must tell a persuasive story: both slot events into a chronological sequence, track down agents engaged in wrongdoing, and parcel out blame. In both cases, pinning down wrongdoing is a matter of establishing means, motive, and opportunity. Suspicious readings, in short, are forms of plotting that seek to identify causes and assign guilt. They partake of a larger cultural history of causality, in which varying forces—from language to society, from sexuality to power, from ancestry to the emotions—have been hailed as the ultimate explanation for why things happen.[5] At the same time, they are exercises not just in meaning-making but in moral-making, not just arguments but allegories, peopled with a cast of right-minded investigators and cunning adversaries. And here critique borrows heavily from the Manichean structures of the classical detective novel. Only by acting like detectives—interrogating and cross-examining the texts of culture—can we avoid being mistaken for criminals (those accused of political quietism, active complicity, or worse). Our *explanations* of literature and art are also tacit *accusations*, driven by a desire to identify fault, apportion blame, and track down wrongdoing.[6]

That storytelling is an integral part of reasoning and thinking is now a familiar idea. Several decades ago, Hayden White elaborated on the links between explanation and emplotment, showing that the writing of history relies on archetypal patterns of romance, comedy, tragedy, and irony. More recently, Roger Schrank has driven home the function of storytelling in the everyday exercise of intelligence. Knowledge, he argues, requires a putting into play of various schemas or scripts, without which higher-level thinking would be impossible. We would be paralyzed without an existing repertoire of plot patterns that allow us to process and make sense of the chaotic swirl of phenomena we encounter. Being able to function within a culture is largely a matter of being familiar with its central stories. Suspicion, in this light, is one of the stories literary scholars think by, one of the ways in which they orient themselves toward the texts they teach and analyze. What interests me, in this chapter, is not the interpretation of narrative but *interpretation-as-narrative*—the means by which a critical sensibility spins out story lines that connect understanding to explaining. What are the guiding affinities between suspicion and storytelling?[7]

There is a notable irony at work here. After all, in literary and film theory, narrative has often been targeted as an archenemy. Stories, critics charge, strive to simplify and shortchange a world of infinite possibility; they ride roughshod over the complexity of phenomena; they impose schemata that push characters down predetermined paths and block other options from view. Narrative, in short, has been hailed as a mechanism of cultural coercion, one of the ways in which readers are inveigled into certain ways of acting and thinking. This critical distrust of plot draws its strength from a deepening historical sense of the artificial and arbitrary nature of structure. For early twentieth-century modernists, for example, narrative no longer expressed the truth of a natural or historical order but was felt to impose such an order onto a world in flux, falsifying more subtle and elusive forms of connection.[8]

And yet the critic who mistrusts plot is also a plotter extraordinaire, a consummate spinner of stories. What D. A Miller identifies as a stratagem of power in realist novels—elaborate networks of causality that connect one seemingly trifling detail to another—is also the MO of the suspicious-minded critic, who is convinced that things are worse than they appear and that what seems arbitrary or unconnected is being steered by a covert logic of causality.[9] (Think of the popularity of the phrase "it is no coincidence that" or "it is no accident that" in contemporary academic prose; for the practitioner of critique, it often seems, there *are* no coincidences.) Djelal Kadir channels the sensibility of many scholars in the humanities when he writes of being in "an age and place in which alertness and insight have to be self-conscious practices cloaked in reflexivity and suspicion, lest we be had or taken."[10] This fear of "being had" inspires the critic to take defensive measures by sniffing out connections invisible to others and choreographing incidental details into disturbing constellations of meaning. He is braced for bad news and assumes that someone or something— however elusive or difficult to pin down—must be to blame. In short, critical thinking, even as it questions narrative, is addicted to narrative, weaving together clandestine connections and exposing subterranean structures. The literary critic, like a good police investigator, must spin a story that allows her to identify a guilty party.[11] While the previous chapter dealt with literary critics as readers, we now consider critics as writers of certain narrative scripts.

For the most part, the impact of such plot patterns is subliminal; we direct our attention to the propositions that our fellow critics lay before us rather than the narratives that these statements sustain. And critics, of course, are not free to make up any kind of stories they please. If they are commenting on a literary text, they are expected to refer back to this text at frequent intervals and anchor their claims in evidence. The role of these source texts is to offer a plenipotentiary of traces, clues, or symptoms; the job of the critic is to interpret these clues by situating them within larger structures of meaning (a procedure that is refined, but, as we will see, by no means abolished in deconstructive readings).

Suspicious criticism, in this sense, asks much the same questions as the whodunit; both partake of what Carlo Ginzburg calls a conjectural paradigm: poring over signs, moving from an effect to the reconstruction of a cause, from observation to explanation, from what has been done to the identification of a doer. Ginzburg's influential essay situates the modern notion of the clue within a long history of interpreting signs. Thousands of years ago, hunters learned to decipher animal tracks, tufts of hair, bent twigs, and entangled feathers; to sniff out, interpret, and classify. Such practices are the long-distant predecessors of modern forms of knowledge and regimes of truth: the art historian, the psychoanalyst, and the detective all pounce on the insignificant trace as the gateway to a hidden reality.[12] In the rubbish heap of overlooked detail lie secret treasures that disclose themselves, via the magic of the inspired hunch, to the gaze of the expert investigator. The present-day critic thus joins a transhistorical community of interpreters, decoders, and sign readers.

One patent difference between detective fiction and academic critique: in the latter, the wrongdoer is not an anomalous individual— a deranged village vicar, a gardener with a grudge—but some larger entity targeted by the critic as an ultimate cause: Victorian society, imperialism, discourse/power, Western metaphysics. The picture of transgression in classic crime fiction has attracted disapproving comments from literary critics. They decry its focus on the individual

criminal as a shameful cop-out, a denial that wrongdoing is systematic and widespread, in cahoots with the law rather than at odds with
the law. "Detective fiction," declares Franco Moretti, "exists expressly
to dispel the doubt that guilt might be impersonal and therefore collective and social."[13] The practice of critique takes the opposite tack,
insisting that guilt is always collective and social—the result of un-
ethical structures rather than immoral persons. Policing and politics
(and often a strong dose of philosophy) come together to shape the
narrative drive of a suspicious hermeneutic.

This chapter takes its title from a play by the British dramatist J. B.
Priestley: a much-loved staple of amateur dramatics and secondary
schools in England, though less well known in the United States. *An
Inspector Calls* is an enthralling drama of detection in the service of
social goals, a striking exemplum of policing as politics. A mysterious police officer descends on the home of a prosperous Edwardian
family and draws out, via an interrogation of each of its members,
their mutual complicity in the recent death of a young working-class
woman. Ignoring their outraged protestations of innocence, the inspector calmly tears aside the façade of bourgeois respectability. Like
an avenging angel, he lays bare the consequences of the actions of
an upper-middle-class family and weaves together a social narrative
in which all of them are implicated. He is the quintessential suspicious reader, combing history against the grain in order to tease out
unnoticed connections and hidden causes: those who seem furthest
from wrongdoing turn out to be deeply implicated in the creation of
social suffering. The inspector's searching questions, as if by magic,
draw forth stuttering confessions and sheepish admissions of complicity, exposing the festering sores and cankers that lie hidden at the
heart of bourgeois life. He weaves a story in which everything is connected, everyone is culpable and no one—including members of the
audience—is let off the hook.[14]

In similar fashion, the present-day inspectors of literary studies
arrive on the scene intent on transmuting apparent innocence into
political guilt. Like Priestley's protagonist, they stomp their muddy
boots through the drawing rooms of culture while laying bare its complicity in a history of wrongdoing. The method of critique, with its inspired blend of deduction and politics, calls forth a narrative about a

crime and the extraction of a confession. Literary criticism mimics the methods of detection—not just in its deciphering of clues but also in its commitment to tracking down a guilty party. The plot line of suspicion takes on a life of its own, priming readers to approach a text in a spirit of heightened mistrust and to search for signs of reprehensible activity. Let us consider how a suspicious hermeneutic organizes reading and reasoning along certain lines and then consider what else—beside the righteous impulse to call out a wrongdoer—is at stake in such acts of storytelling.

CRIMES, CLUES, CRIMINALS

A handy starting point is the building blocks of the detective novel: the criminal, the clue, the crime. What is the role of these three elements, and how are they bound together to create a certain constellation of meaning? How is this pattern redrawn when the investigator turns out to be a literary critic rather than a detective? What kind of changes do these elements undergo? How is the structure of critique analogous to the structure of crime fiction? And in what sense is critique's reliance on narrative intertwined with the making of moral judgment?

That the detective novel is a plot-driven form seems self-evident. The lure of the genre lies in the artfulness and ingenuity with which it arouses and then slakes our curiosity. In its essence, declare Glenn Most and William Stowe, "the detective novel is almost pure narrative."[15] To read such a novel is to yield to a tantalizing tempo of withholding and unfolding, of progression and digression. In the manner of a cerebral striptease, details are dangled before us, red herring piled on red herring, information doled out fragment by painstaking fragment, until the veils are finally lifted and the truth is laid bare. After Poirot has ushered the assembled cast of characters into the drawing room and ceremoniously explained who did what to whom, the loose ends are tied up and the shadows dissipate. The death that is turned into narrative is a death that has been stripped of its uncanniness, a mystery that has been solved.

Detective fiction, moreover, relies on not a single but a double plot;

it tells the story of the crime versus the story of the investigation. In the words of Tzvetan Todorov, the former is absent but real, the latter is present but insignificant.[16] That is to say, the detective novel is organized around the disinterment of a hidden history: an original act of violence that sets the text in motion and the explanation of which is its telos or purpose. Nothing significant happens in the classic detective novel that is not tied to this first act of transgression, this purposefully omitted prelude. What distinguishes the genre is its retrospective mode of narration; it proceeds from an effect (the corpse) to the deduction of a cause (the killer). The job of the detective is thus to reason backward in order to bring a constellation of past events to light.

A similar double structure defines the work of the critical reader, who shares the detective's concern to expose hidden connections by moving from effects to causes—here, the hidden social forces that lie behind the puzzling or contradictory features of the literary text. Through a process of interpretation, the critic solves an intellectual puzzle, enlightens the reader, and traces out a movement from obfuscation to understanding. In both criticism and crime fiction, then, the piecing together of clues creates knowledge in the present via the explanation of the past.

Yet there are differences in how this pattern plays out in the experience of reading. The chronology of the classic detective novel follows a sequence of *crime-clues-criminal*. We are confronted, at the start, with the brute fact of death: the splayed, blank-eyed corpse is the jarring event that sets the plot in motion, hiding on its person the tantalizing secret of how and why the victim died. The discovery of the crime triggers the search for clues, for the seemingly insignificant detail—a mislaid button, a torn ticket stub, a scattering of cigarette ash—that will yield up its hidden message to the expert gaze. Detective fiction turns the random scraps and detritus of daily life into hieroglyphs that glint with mysterious meaning. It is these clues that sustain the scaffolding of the sleuth's deductions and that pave the way for the final exposure of the murderer, who can be anyone in principle but must be someone in particular.

While the clues are scattered everywhere, the murderer is nowhere to be found. In a classic detective novel, the identity of the criminal is withheld until the closing pages; it must be withheld, given that an eagerness to find out "whodunit" compels us to turn the pages. To acquire this knowledge ahead of time—thanks to a hint dropped by a friend or a careless reviewer—is to have one's reading pleasure spoiled. As readers, we expect to be kept in the dark about the inner workings of the detective's mind—the narrator often being a slow-witted sidekick (Watson, Hastings) who shares our own befuddlement and perplexity.

When we turn to the practice of critique, however, things look rather different. The role of narrator and investigator merge in the academic critic, and the reader eavesdrops on the process of reasoning and deduction as it takes place. In contrast to the detective novel, there is no experience of breathless suspense, no sly withholding of crucial information. Nor is there a "double hermeneutic," a game of wits in which the reader strives to compete with, or to outguess, the expert investigator. Indeed, critics often let the cat out of the bag at the very start by invoking a guilty party. The identity of the criminal is rarely a mystery, preceding the specifics of any individual crime.

In a hard-hitting critique of Henry James, for example, Mark Seltzer observes on the second page that there is a "criminal continuity" between techniques of literary representation and technologies of power—that the novel is guilty not only of exercising power but of doing its utmost to conceal this fact.[17] "One reason for suspecting this link between art and power," he continues, "is that James works so carefully to deny it." The more emphatically the text protests its innocence, the more vigorously it thrashes about in the sticky web of its own falsehoods and reveals its culpability. This trick of turning into a denial into a tacit confession owes a debt to the Freudian methods discussed in the last chapter, but it also borrows from techniques of detection, with their transmutation of seeming innocence into ultimate guilt. As we will see, the paradigm of the clue provides the critical reader with a rationale for demonstrating that texts mean something quite different than what they appear to mean. The culprit is thus unmasked at the very start of the argument, and the more typical sequence is that of *criminal-clue-crime*.

In this sense, the key question posed by scholarly criticism is less "whodunit" than *how* it was done. The interest of readers is not triggered by any burning curiosity about the identity of the villain—a genre, discursive structure, or social system whose failings are already, for the most part, quite familiar to fellow critics. Academic essays are not known for their nail-biting denouements, and the revelation of the guilty party is rarely a surprise. Rather, we are captured—in the best-case scenario—by the ingenuity and inventiveness of critics' interpretations, the agility and artfulness with which they weave connections between text and world.

The offending party, we should note, is often a text, genre, or linguistic structure, rather than, for example, a particular writer. Several decades ago, Chinua Achebe declared, in a well-known essay, that Conrad was a racist, and there are certainly critics willing to take authors to task for their political views. Many scholars of literature, however, prefer to keep biographical criticism at arm's length, insisting that the meanings of a text spill far beyond the aims and intentions of its creator. This inclination received a boost from structuralist and poststructuralist theories that stressed the formative power of language rather than consciousness, repudiating any form of author-centered criticism as the last gasp of a discredited humanism. As a result, the role of the individual—an essential point of reference for both the law and detective fiction—is frequently minimized or denied.

At the same time, the story line of detection, with its presumption of a guilty party, triggers a search for agents who are bent on doing harm. Moral judgments are tied up with presumptions of motive: a key element, as we've seen, in a suspicious hermeneutic. As a result, personification is common in literary studies, with critics imputing intentions, needs, or desires to nonhuman forces. Linguistic or social structures are endowed with many of the qualities of the flesh-and-blood human beings they are supposed to replace; literary texts serve as protagonists or quasi-persons in an unfolding drama of incrimination and indictment.[18] The act of reading thus stages a struggle between the critic and a personified agent—power, the unconscious, ideology, textuality—who plays the role of secret malefactor in the drama of detection. Interpretation becomes a moral as well as a political exercise in the detection of guilt.

In her influential book *Critical Practice*, for example, Catherine Belsey emphasizes that she is interested not in indicting specific authors but in showing how the formal structures of literature serve political ends. One of her aims is to deflate the truth claims of nineteenth-century fiction; literary realism, she declares, is an ideological project that seeks to railroad the reader into accepting the naturalness and inevitability of a particular world view. "The realist text," she explains, "is a . . . structure which claims to convey intelligible relationships between its elements" and seeks "to create a coherent and internally consistent fictive world." That is to say, realist works of literature strive to deceive their readers by pretending to offer plausible accounts of the way things really are. Realism is part of a system of ideology "masquerading as coherence and plenitude" by seeking to conceal its own political agendas. It diverts attention from its own incomplete and inconsistent accounts of reality by presenting them as Truth. The stories of Sherlock Holmes serve Belsey as an ideal example of this manipulation; their project is "to dispel magic and mystery, to make everything explicit, accountable, subject to scientific analysis."[19] These stories thus paper over their own evasions and omissions by appealing to the pseudo-objectivity of reason and science. It is precisely because the work of fiction is "ostensibly innocent" that it can be "ideologically effective."

This façade of innocence is pierced by the critic, who, in imputing intention to the text, treats it as a quasi-person equipped with a desire to deceive. The realist work is charged with fraudulence and fabrication, with masking social contradictions by pulling the wool over the reader's eyes. And yet—and here the critical narrative spirals into a quasi-tragic form that traces out a recurring scenario of failed ambition—this deception is doomed to fail. The schism between intention and effects, between surface and depth meanings, between what the text says and what it cannot admit or face up to, means that the ideologies of the text can be unraveled by the expert reader-interrogator. Thus, according to Belsey, Jules Verne's *The Secret Island* contains an "unpredicted and contradictory element" that has the effect of disrupting the "colonialist ideology which informs the conscious project of the work." In a similar manner, while "the project of the Sherlock Holmes stories is to dispel magic and mystery, to make everything explicit, accountable, subject to scientific analysis," this intention is undercut by the shadowy and mysterious women in the margins of the text who subvert its conscious embrace of patriarchal rationality. The text is condemned out of its own mouth in an involuntary confession, blurting out its "incoherences, omissions, absences and transgressions."[20]

The critic thus assembles a line of argument that correlates textual clues to larger social conditions that the work is anxious to paper over. As we saw in the last chapter, the motif of repression has the effect of turning what look like contingent associations into buried connections via a narrative logic of cause and effect.[21] Nothing is random or accidental; every textual detail harbors a hidden purpose and pulsates with fateful meaning. And yet the text's culpability precedes any specific act of interpretation; it is the presumption of guilt that allows absences or omissions to be transformed into suspicious evasions. The critic does not uncover guilt so much as generate it out of the axioms of her own interpretative practice. Thus the truth contained in the Sherlock Holmes stories is not any kind of truth about human or social reality but "the truth about ideology, the truth which ideology represses, its own existence as ideology itself."[22]

In such appeals to ideology the culpability of the text is acknowledged yet also qualified. The individual work does not act alone, as it were, but is steered by larger forces working silently behind the scenes. The scenario conjured up by such plotting transports us from the pastoral world of the murder at the vicarage to the shadowy scenes of hard-boiled crime fiction or film noir, with their endemic violence and widespread corruption. Behind the single miscreant is arraigned a murkier and more menacing power: politicians in cahoots with organized crime, sleazy bigwigs with their cordon of thugs and hit men. Suspicion, remarks Fredric Jameson, saturates the atmosphere of Raymond Chandler's novels, present not only in the attitude of the private eye but also in the watchful glances of the rooming house manager, the servant, the casual bystander.[23] A similar mood of watchfulness permeates the critical theory seminar: a conviction that no text is innocent and every sentence has something to hide. Like Holmes or Poirot, literary critics use techniques of interpretation and ratiocination to suss things out; like Philip Marlowe, they know that crime is ubiquitous and inescapable, soaking deep into the social fabric.

What, then, is the offense with which the text is being charged? In some cases the allegation is one of deception; the work of literature seems to ignore what it cannot help but know. In turning a blind eye to the inequities of the status quo, it tacitly condones the misdeeds of others. The text is not, in the first instance, responsible for structures of domination that the critic lays at the door of material forces. And yet, in tolerating such inequities without confronting them—opting to whitewash, overlook, or ignore unpleasant realities—it plays the role of an invidious accomplice. It is a collaborator in wrongdoing, an associate partner in crime.

In other cases, however, the allegation is not just of deception but also of active duress. No longer a complicit onlooker, the literary text is charged with being an active perpetrator. This ratcheting up of culpability can be explained by the rise to prominence of theories that cast language in the role of a determining, even dictatorial, power. Rather than serving as a medium of communication or self-expression, language was charged with circumscribing thought and dictating the boundaries of what could be said. It was a primary agent in the enforcing of hierarchies, the imposition of social wounds, the peremptory silencing of the excluded or marginalized. Giving voice to this perception of language as a form of symbolic violence, Barthes could declare, in the late 1970s, that to speak is not to communicate but rather to subjugate.[24]

Foucauldian critics drove home the point by insisting that power was not something wielded autocratically by individuals or social groups. Rather, it was diffused throughout society via undetectable capillaries of control: a micropolitics of discourse that molded the contours of personhood all the way down. In one of the most influential examples of such analysis, D. A. Miller asked: "How does the novel—as a set of representational techniques—systematically participate in a general economy of policing power?" "Policing" now extends well beyond the institutions of the law to describe processes of cultural regulation and surveillance that know no bounds. The Victorian novel, via its deployment of various techniques—the panoramic gaze of an all-knowing narrator, the explanatory mechanics of plot, its representations of the domestic and the deviant—is stealthily engaged in regulating and disciplining its readers, schooling them in modes of appropriate conduct. The effectiveness of this strategy lies above all in its skilful self-effacement; the novel denies any connection with policing, posturing as a power-free zone, a redemptive sphere of freedom, imagination, even lawlessness. Disciplinary power, remarks Miller, "is the policing power that never passes for such, but is either invisible or visible only under cover of other, nobler, or simply blander intentionalities—to educate, to cure, to produce, to defend."[25]

Invisibility is key; it is a premise of critique that the act and fact of coercion are camouflaged and kept from view. The suspiciously minded scholar differs from others not just in an ability to solve the crime but, more fundamentally, in *knowing that a crime has taken place.* The egregious acts perpetuated by literary texts—in contrast to the hard-to-miss cadaver spread-eagled on the drawing room carpet—fly below the radar of lay readers as well as old-school scholars and aesthetes. Where others remark on an exquisite prose style or a probing exploration of human experience, practitioners of critique are alert to systematic cover-ups and hidden dramas of malfeasance. Such wrongdoing, they insist, is not anomalous but endemic, propping up the structural inequities of the status quo. Another key difference between classic detective fiction and academic critique: in the former, crime is visible and anomalous; in the latter, it is *invisible yet ubiquitous.*

How does this recognition affect our third category, the clue? Simon Stern offers an admirably succinct definition: a clue is a significant detail that does not come into visibility until it is recognized and interpreted by an expert.[26] That it is only a detail—something minor, tangential, seemingly incidental—explains why it is easily overlooked by the ordinary onlooker or the lay reader. Clues are not obvious; they do not leap to the eye or impose themselves on consciousness. Hiding in plain view, they call for a dexterous wielding of the magnifying glass or the jeweler's loupe. We find ourselves in the realm of the micrological and the infinitesimal; as Watson says to Holmes, "You have an extraordinary genius for minutiae."[27] Of course, not every detail counts as a clue; it is only under certain conditions that the former will metamorphose into the latter. And here the status of the interpreter is salient; the detail needs the imprimatur of professional knowledge in order for its truth to unfold. The clue is a product of specialized knowledge—a hieroglyph to which the expert holds the key.

We can see here why the parallels between detection and literary criticism prove so tempting. For who is the detective but a fellow reader, a critic in another guise for whom the world of mundane objects and everyday actions—a discarded match, a spot of ink, a broken glass, a slip of the tongue—serves as a primary text? The device of the clue has the effect of coating mundane or irrelevant details with a sheen of supercharged significance. "If you are looking for clues," writes Moretti of the reader of detective fiction, "each sentence becomes significant, each character interesting; descriptions lose their inertia; all words become sharper, stranger."[28] Reading-as-detection, in engendering a deep-seated suspicion of everyday reality, also has the effect of rendering that reality newly gripping and worthy of attention; every detail is pregnant with potential purpose, haloed with a heightened, even hallucinatory, intensity of meaning.

Is Moretti also referring, consciously or not, to his own history as a Marxist critic? For such a critic, likewise, there are no dead passages, no yawn-inducing descriptions to be skipped over, no pesky subplots unworthy of attention. Instead, every literary detail quivers with a secret import; every phrase harbors a potential double meaning; any minor character can suddenly spring to the fore as a clinching proof of a text's hidden agenda. Even silences can be made to speak; that certain topics are not mentioned only confirms the ubiquitous denials and disavowals of capitalist ideology. A similar attentiveness to occluded subtexts can be found in the work of postcolonial critics intent on excavating the anxieties of empire. In a recent book, for example, Yumna Siddiqi speaks directly to the themes of this chapter by embracing the parallel between sleuth and postcolonial scholar; "the work of analysis undertaken here," she writes, "can be likened to the process of detection. My methodology . . . is that of the detective who investigates culture by reading clues and reconfiguring the literary and historical facts of the case into an intelligible whole."[29]

As Siddiqi goes on to acknowledge, this procedure has potential risks: a use of inappropriate categories, a forcing of explanations, a jumping to conclusions. Her goal, she writes, is to steer clear of such pitfalls by following the example of Sherlock Holmes, keeping her nose to the texts and making "conjectures about anxieties of Empire on the basis of the evidence they provide."[30] Siddiqi is admirably lucid and self-conscious about her own procedures, yet we are left with some sticky and unresolved questions about the status of evidence. As we will see, the meaning of the clue is far from straightforward in detective fiction. It seems even murkier in the case of symptomatic reading—where an absence is easily alchemized into a presence and textual details can be read against the grain to support the critic's prior convictions about large-scale psychic or social structures. This is what Lawrence Grossberg dubs the "world in a grain of sand" method of reading: the belief that individual texts serve as microcosms of a larger social whole and that if read correctly, they will yield the hidden truth of that whole. The infinitesimal clue thus bears a much heavier burden of proof, as a sign of systemic rather than individual wrongdoing.[31]

We should note, moreover, that the kinship between critic and detective has become frayed in recent years. Present-day critics are less likely to think of investigators as allies and kindred spirits than as symptoms in need of demystification. Holmes, especially, has come in for some rough treatment. That he is an amateur rather than a professional, an eccentric bohemian rather than a staid bourgeois, no longer sways or mollifies his critics. Rather, in a line of argument that we examine more closely in the next chapter, his apparent deviation from social norms merely reinforces his deep complicity with those norms. The techniques of Holmesian detection are seen as foreshadowing the features of a modern carceral society bent on recording and tracking the movements of its citizens. The detective, declares Moretti, is the figure of the state, and detective fiction "is a hymn to culture's coercive abilities. . . . Every story reiterates Bentham's Panopticon idea: the model prison that signals the metamorphosis of liberalism into total scrutability."[32] The state and the detective join forces to decipher every detail of individual existence, turning the body of the suspect—and we are all suspects—into a legible text. Mark Seltzer chimes in with a similar line of argument: "Crime, in Holmes' sense, has been redefined to include an expanding range of activities, a shift that moves toward the placing of every aspect of everyday life under suspicion."[33] No longer an oddball or a charismatic outsider, Holmes is now seen to foreshadow the techniques of phone tapping, videotaping, and data mining that characterize our own society of surveillance.

This altered perspective springs from a growing critical disenchantment with the machinery of the law—the political realization that matters of law often have very little to do with matters of justice. Meanwhile, Foucauldian thought inspired a new and painful self-consciousness about the ways in which expert knowledge can serve as a mechanism of power. The relations between critic and detective, rather than being one of solidarity and fellow feeling, shifts to one of disapproval and active disidentification. Instead, the critic may prefer to side with the figure of the criminal, taking the part of the various crooks and outlaws who are scattered through the pages of detective fiction. At the level of content, then, she shifts her allegiance from the detective to the transgressor—and yet, at the level of method, *she continues to read like a sleuth.* That is to say, she refuses to take meanings at face value and pounces on the overlooked yet revelatory detail; the text, like the criminal suspect, must be interrogated and made to yield its hidden secrets. What suspicious critics question in stories of detection—placing everything under scrutiny and surveillance, so that the most trifling detail is potentially incriminating—is also the heart and soul of their own method. Ordinary readers, like the hapless Watson, are fooled by the evidence before their eyes: they see but they do not observe. The structures of fiction are masked, declares Moretti, and its deeper meanings are off-limits to authors as well as ordinary readers. It is only the expert interpreter who can press below distracting surfaces to the concealed meanings of signs, who is able to trace out a chain of reasoning that points inexorably to a guilty party. Both detectives and critical readers, to quote Bloch once more, make it their goal to "ferret things out."[34]

Ferreting, I've been suggesting, is a matter of storytelling, of creating a compelling narrative. The detective must reason backward, from an effect to a cause, from a corpse to a killer, weaving disparate scraps of information into a coherent sequence. The clue is indispensable to this process, and yet clues speak with many voices and their messages are sybilline and often opaque. As Pierre Bayard points out, "What constitutes a clue for one person may be meaningless to another. And a clue is named as such only when it serves as part of a more general story."[35] Indeed, clues only come into view as clues—rather than as dull or distracting details to be brushed away like flies—once the beginning of an explanation is already in place. A clue, in

Bayard's words, is a choice: a decision to zero in on certain things while ignoring other virtual clues that hover at the margins of one's attention—clues that could add up to a very different explanation. (In his book, Bayard puts these ideas into practice by reopening the case of the Hound of the Baskervilles, explaining, tongue placed firmly in cheek, exactly how and why Holmes got things wrong.)

In both detection and criticism, then, the story dictates what counts as a clue as much as the clues determine the shape of the story. It is narrative that turns signs into clues; only when the detective already has some inkling about the nature of the crime or a possible criminal does a potential clue hove into view. Via a technique that Peter Brooks describes as "retrospective prophecy," the sleuth reasons backward from a presumed conclusion to find clues that point to the inevitable nature of such a conclusion.[36] Much the same holds true of the cultural critic whose presumption of a guilty party accompanies or precedes the deciphering of textual details. It is hardly surprising, then, that these clues will yield up their anticipated meanings, alerting us to the hidden cogs and opaque workings of the social machine. The paradigm of the clue, as Elisabeth Strowick puts it, turns suspicion into a method of knowledge.[37]

A short story by Witold Gombrowicz nicely captures this circular quality of suspicious interpretation. "The Premeditated Crime" is told from the viewpoint of a magistrate who travels to the countryside for a business meeting, only to discover that the man he was supposed to meet has just died of a heart attack. He becomes increasingly suspicious of the members of the deceased's family, convincing himself that a terrible crime is being covered up. After all, he points out, the idea of a corpse rhymes perfectly with the idea of an investigating magistrate: each needs and calls for the other. It is his job, he insists, to "link the chain of facts, to create syllogisms, spin threads and search for evidence." Pushing beyond appearances and spurning what seems to be obvious, he sets about tracking down signs of guilt. That the man has indisputably died of a heart attack is a minor detail that can be peremptorily brushed aside. "I raised my finger and frowned. 'A crime does not come of its own accord, gentlemen; it must be worked upon mentally, thought through, thought up—dumplings don't cook themselves.'"[38] Browbeating the dead man's son into leaving his fingerprints on the throat of the corpse, the magistrate finally succeeds in turning an accidental death into evidence of a cunningly planned murder. His professional duty is now fulfilled to his own satisfaction. Suspicion conjures up a never-ending stream of signs-to-be-read and conclusions-to-be-drawn; crime is premeditated not only by the criminal but also by the industrious and ever-vigilant investigator!

METASUSPICION

Is the practitioner of critique, then, doomed to play detective? Is it possible to read critically without investigating, interrogating, and indicting? As we've seen, poststructuralism instigated a heightened sensitivity about the power-laden language of interpretation: a rueful realization that suspicious reading was imputing the very signs of guilt it claimed to discover. In response, various critics rallied to literature's defense, eager to establish its innocence and clear its name, to protect it from appropriation and to safeguard it from the accusations of overzealous interpreters. While the literary work is exonerated and granted immunity from prosecution, it is now *criticism itself that becomes the crime.*

Let us turn to Shoshana Felman's virtuoso and much-cited reading of prior readings of Henry James's *The Turn of the Screw.* In her essay, Felman draws on deconstructive and Lacanian styles of thought in order to skewer the very method of interpretation-as-detection. Her point of departure is the well-known Freudian analysis of James's story by Edmund Wilson: exhibit A in her exposé of suspicious reading. Wilson famously explained the ghosts of *The Turn of the Screw*—the apparitions of the disreputable servants Peter Quint and Miss Jessel—as the feverish hallucinations of the young governess who serves as its narrator. Whereas previous critics had taken these supernatural aspects of the text at face value, Wilson recasts the meaning of *The Turn of the Screw* in one stroke, transforming it into a case study in neurosis and sexual repression. What seem to be ghostly manifestations turn out to be nothing more than the hysterical projections of a repressed young woman infatuated with her employer.

Felman, however, remains unpersuaded and unmoved. Such an

interpretative gambit on Wilson's part, she declares, is an egregious example of psychoanalysis seeking to gain mastery over literature by translating it into the categories of its own hermeneutic code. The Freudian critic is a protodetective who is intent on solving a mystery, nailing down answers, explaining away literary ambiguity through the deciphering of signs. He is the quintessential example of the suspicious reader intent on tripping up the text and forcing it to blurt out its shameful secrets.

Felman drives home, over and over again, how this attempt to acquire mastery over the text is doomed to fail, how the work of literature dupes the Freudian critic who prides himself on not being duped. "*The Turn of the Screw*," she writes, "constitutes a trap for psychoanalytical interpretation to the extent that it constructs a trap, precisely, for suspicion." That is to say, the sophisticated reader who reads against the grain of the text to ferret out its repressed meanings is outflanked by James's novella, which offers a running commentary on the folly of such acts of decoding. Its central protagonist, after all, is the quintessential suspicious reader; refusing to take anything on trust, she scrabbles frantically to get to the bottom of the baffling events taking place around her. "As a reader," writes Felman, "the governess plays the role of the detective: from the outset she tried to detect, by means of logical inferences and decisive proofs, both *the nature of the crime* and the identity of the criminal."[39] Yet this frenzy of detectivelike questioning brings no satisfying resolution; instead, James's story ends in catastrophe with one of the governess's young charges expiring in her arms. For Felman, this concluding scene crystallizes the patent perils of critical interpretation. *The Turn of the Screw*, she points out, explicitly warns against the very method of reading that Wilson imposes upon it—even as he remains oblivious to its admonitions.

In her reading of James's story, then, Felman assumes the role of defense rather than prosecution. She bends over backward to do justice to the vertiginous richness and many-layered ambiguities of the literary text. She demonstrates repeatedly that *The Turn of the Screw* is a conundrum that cannot be solved, an artifact of language that exceeds the bounds of rational apprehension and analytical argument, a labyrinthian hall of mirrors in which readers can only lose their bearings. We may think we "know" what *The Turn of the Screw* is about, but our confidence is premature; it turns out that James's text is already far ahead of us, offering a prescient reading of its own critical readings, running rings around the clumsy maneuvers of the dunderheaded critic. Its words flow over, under, and around the categories we seek to impose upon it, escaping the net of our analytical concepts. Graced with a surfeit of linguistic subtlety and sophistication, literature is cleared of all wrongdoing.

Here Felman's deconstructive approach marks its difference from orthodox Freudianism as well as the tradition of ideology critique. And yet suspicion is not eliminated or eradicated but ratcheted up a few more notches and applied with renewed zeal to a fresh target. It is no longer the text that is charged with criminal activity but the exegesis of the text. In Felman's own words, "It is nothing other than the *very process of detection* which *constitutes the crime.*" A moral and juridical language of culpability is now directed at the practice of criticism itself. Psychoanalytical critics are charged with seeking to "'explain' and *master* literature," censured for "killing in literature that which makes it literature." In pressing the text to confess its secrets, Edmund Wilson commits an act of egregious violence, a willful annihilation of the text's otherness. Freudian interpretation, Felman declares with a rhetorical flourish, is "a peculiarly effective murder weapon."[40]

What lies behind this emphatic, even melodramatic, association of the act of reading with the act of murder? Why does the deconstructive critic take on the role of homicide detective? Like a diligent cop, Felman digs out clues to support her allegations, yet her reading of these clues is dictated by her assumption that a crime has taken place. The parallel she constructs is seductive in its symmetry: inside the text, the truth-crazed governess murders her charge; outside the text, the truth-crazed Freudian critic kills literature. And yet the ending of *The Turn of the Screw* is more cagey about the circumstances of Miles's death than this reading suggests, remaining purposefully mute as to cause and culpability. Felman, however, supplies the missing link, pinpointing a cause, a wrongdoer, and a motive. The governess is guilty, thanks to an overriding desire to get to the bottom of things that leads to the death of her own charge. The search for truth is condemned by its own hand; rationality is exposed as dangerous and destructive; James's text shows us that "a child can be killed by the very act of understanding."[41] As the governess kills Miles, so Freudian criticism—and, Felman suggests, any form of reading for meaning—wreaks deadly violence on the literary text. Interpretation is not just blundering but brutal.

Thus, even as Felman insists on the radical indeterminacy of literature, the effect of her commentary is to transpose James's story into a moral allegory about the violence of interpretation. Her essay remains fixated on the fundaments of detective fiction: Who did it, and who is guilty?[42] In spite of its strictures against interpreting, it engages in a whirlwind of hermeneutic activity, plumbing the depths of the scholarly commentary on James's novel in order to bring to light a hidden drama of misrecognition and murder. Felman constructs a moral drama—a melodrama—of guilt and innocence, of accusation and judgment. Suspicion thus yields to what could be called metasuspicion: a stringent reckoning with the history of critical interpretation.

Deconstructive and Foucauldian critics have been especially drawn to such metacritical strategies. Stories about the depredations of reading have proliferated over recent decades, as critique turns a gimlet gaze on its own history, scrutinizing its own motives in a self-reflexive loop of spiraling distrust. The prosecutor now finds himself in the dock; the hermeneutics of suspicion is placed on trial. The critic's explanations are unmasked as flimsy rationalizations: rather than illuminating a work of art, critique is accused of strong-arming it into submission, bullying it into blurting out its secrets. The history of criticism bristles with neologisms—logocentrism, epistemophelia—that portray critical reason as nothing more than a stealthy exercise in coercion and domination. In encouraging suspicious styles of reading, declares Elisabeth Strowick with a Foucauldian flourish, the human sciences are complicit with a society of surveillance and "act as agents of the micro-physics of power."[43] The critic-detective now stands exposed as the ultimate wrongdoer.

The larger implications of such a "critique of critique" will need to await the next chapter, but we can glimpse the weirdly paradoxical and self-canceling nature of this line of argument. If suspicious reading is a matter of "looking behind" the text, what is the rationale for looking behind the looking behind? Does putting the screws on suspicion disable it or infuse it with fresh vitality and strength? The more vigorously critique is interrogated, after all, the more we seem to reinforce the very style of thinking we are trying to avoid. Metasuspicion does not mitigate mistrust but augments and intensifies it. The hermeneutics of suspicion thus turns out to be an exceptionally hardy beast—one that seems remarkably impervious to direct attack. Seemingly indestructible and invulnerable, it burrows deep into the flesh of its most implacable opponents; like a fabulous hydra, it sprouts new heads as quickly as critics lop them off.

THE ART OF CRITIQUE

A change of tactic is clearly called for. As we saw earlier, Ricoeur distinguishes between a hermeneutics of suspicion and a hermeneutics of trust, between a reading that demystifies and a reading that restores. Perhaps we can gain a better handle on suspicious reading by treating it with a degree of generosity, bestowing upon it some of the sympathy it is inclined to withhold from others. Rather than trying to get behind it, let us face squarely up to it and consider the meanings and motives it makes manifest. Phenomenology, Ricoeur observes, is a method well suited to such an approach, expressing itself in a care or concern for phenomena, a preference for description over explanation, a willingness to attend rather than to analyze. To engage in a phenomenological account is not to expose a subterfuge or puncture an illusion but to try to figure out how things mean and how they matter.

Much work in the phenomenology of reading, however, is a strangely bloodless affair, drained of affect and intensity. Interpretation is treated as a purely cerebral exercise, a question of filling in gaps, imposing schemas, and deciphering ambiguities, akin to doing a leisurely Sunday morning crossword puzzle. But what of that sudden manic surge of exegetical energy, the drawn-out agony of banging one's head against an impervious wall of words followed by the bliss of that *aha!* moment when things fall into place? Reading—even academic reading—is a less dry and dispassionate activity than it is often made out to be. "Nothing whets the intelligence more than a passionate suspicion," writes Stefan Zweig in his wonderful novella *Burning Secret*, reminding us that suspicion is not opposed to passion but is a kind of passion, which shadows and sustains intellectual obsessions of many kinds.[44]

Some years ago, for example, I found myself struggling to articulate a critique of a certain idea of femininity (as artifice, performance, a play of veils) that was embraced by male artists and intellectuals of the fin de siècle. For several weeks, I circled fruitlessly around the same questions, brooding over an intractable corpus of texts in a fog of anxious curiosity and heightened irritability. My objections could not, as it were, take hold; the works I was poring over seemed, like the smooth surface of a glacier, to repel every attempt to establish a foothold. And then that longed-for moment finally arrived when a coherent interpretative schema, without forewarning, suddenly fell into place. It is the sheer exhilaration of such moments—the delirious triumph of hitting the jackpot after strenuous effort—that helps keep critique in business. In Freudian accounts of interpretation, the desire for knowledge is linked to a sublimated sexual curiosity or an unconscious drive for domination. I want, however, to attend to pleasures that are in plain sight: the satisfying click of seeing an idea slot into place; the all-engrossing nature of an intractable textual puzzle; the intoxicating experience of "flow" when work and play fuse magically into one.

The hermeneutics of suspicion, in short, offers the promise of pleasure as well as knowledge. What draws the critic to this way of reading? Some possible answers: the intellectual kick of detecting figures and designs below the text's surface, the delight of crafting ingenious and counterintuitive explanations, the challenge of drawing together what seems disparate and disconnected into a satisfying pattern. The hermeneutics of suspicion is an art as much as a science: a piecing together of signs to create new constellations of meaning, a patient untangling and reweaving of textual threads. Its conjectures owe much to inventiveness, leaps of faith, and inspired hunches; suspicious reading, at its best, is not an arid analytical exercise but an inspired blend of intuition and imagination. Conjecture, remarks Ginzburg, is not so far from divination, and the deciphering of clues blurs the line between reason and irrationality. When Edmund Wilson ventures that a story about ghosts is really an allegory of frustrated female sexuality, when D. A. Miller insists that heartwarming stories of Victorian domestic life are bent on disciplining and punishing their readers, it is the heart-stopping boldness of such claims that ensures their impact. The effect is that of a gestalt switch, a jolt in perspective that allows previously unsuspected patterns to come into view.

Acknowledging the art and artfulness of critique does not mean denying other influences and pressures. These include, as we've amply seen, a certifying of expertise; critique functions as a form of academic credentialing, a "clerkly skepticism" that defines itself against the more artless and breathless pleasures of lay reading.[45] Yet such practices would not "take"—would not entwine themselves so deeply into our repertoires of thought—if they did not also succeed in generating attachments. Their impact is phenomenological as well as sociological. We get caught up in stories of suspicion; they animate and motivate us, they give us ideas, they get under our skin. And "once stories are under people's skin," Arthur Frank remarks, "they affect the terms in which people think, know, and perceive. Stories teach people what to look for and what can be ignored; they teach what to value and what to hold in contempt."[46]

A primary value associated with the story line of critique is political: its challenge to the traditional hierarchy of writer and reader. In a famous essay, Roland Barthes declared that the author's death frees up the reader to make of the text what he wishes, to cast off, in revolutionary fashion, the repressive yoke of God-given, author-sanctioned meaning. For Michel de Certeau, this reader is akin to a savvy poacher, stealing and reinterpreting the words of others, making raids on property he does not own. This picture of the reader as a rebellious iconoclast and outlaw is a tad starry-eyed, yet it is hard to dispute the satisfactions of reading texts against the grain. Refusing obligations of reverence and fidelity, critics assert their right to fashion something new out of the words on the page, to reframe and repurpose them in the light of their own commitments. Such rewriting is never entirely free of hubris in its claim to know the text better than it knows itself, but it also promises a creative remaking that allows unexpected insights to unfold. Suspicious reading can provide a new purchase on old texts—an especially appealing strategy for feminists, postcolonial critics, queer theorists, and other latecomers to the academy. As Kate McGowan puts it, echoing the views of many other critics, "The value of unrelenting interrogation is the value of resistance."[47]

This political payoff is considered in more detail in the following chapter, but there are other motives at work than are captured by such higher-order rationales. While often wary of pleasure, suspicious reading generates its own pleasures: a sense of prowess in the exercise of ingenious interpretation, the striking elegance and economy of its explanatory schemes, the competitive buzz of inciting the admiration and applause of fellow scholars. The delight it engenders is in part a ludic delight, a pleasure in creating complex designs out of textual fragments, conjuring inventive insights out of overlooked details. For many critics, such reading is not just a professional mandate but an avocation, an irresistible invitation to test their wits and exercise their skills. Interpretation-as-detection offers a form of engrossing, high-level, intellectual stimulation— offering the promise of what Holmes famously calls "mental exaltation."

Critique, in other words, is a form of addictive and gratifying play: a language game in a quite literal sense. Like most games, it combines rules and expectations with the possibility of unexpected moves and inventive calculations. To read in this way is to maneuver against an imagined opponent, to engage in determinate and precise calculations of strategy, to perform a role equipped with certain requirements. Such gamelike qualities do not void other dimensions of reading, but they are often especially salient in an academic context, where scholars are rewarded for ingenious forms of puzzle-making and puzzle-solving. Elizabeth Bruss draws out the qualities of such a way of reading:

> In a gaming situation, communication must be viewed as a tactic, an attempt to constrain another player's expectations. One must then respond to it tactically, with guarded skepticism, treating narrative devices or the total range of reference in a work as evidence of an opponent/collaborator's resources. . . . One becomes engrossed in a literary game without "believing" in it. Its excitement does not depend on empathy or illusion but on the challenge of strategic dilemmas: when to trust, what to trust, whether to trust at all, and how to proceed with reading in the light of such risk and uncertainty.[48]

Works of metafiction (*Pale Fire*) openly advertise and revel in these gamelike features of interpretation, but all texts can be read along similar lines by being treated as imaginary opponents to be bested rather than voices to be trusted. We scan the text for weak spots and vulnerable areas that will yield to our critical probes and pliers. The payoff of such an approach includes the delight of deploying skills and plotting strategy; critics strive to devise intellectual moves that fit the protocols of academic reading while also looking for new ways to outwit an adversary. They engage in a series of moves that fuse convention and innovation, striving to become ever more skillful players, to outfox not only the text but also other critics. What drives such maneuvers is not just an allegiance to ethical or political values but also aesthetic criteria of adroitness, ingenuity, sophistication, intricacy, and elegance. The critic, as Matei Calinescu remarks, is "involved in a competitive game in which he or she wants to be the first to have made certain interesting, subtle, compelling, and quotable observations."[49]

Game theory, however, is flawed by its tendency to conceive of players as purely rational actors. In a recent survey of Victorian criticism, Anna Maria Jones wonders why the field has been so overrun by Foucauldian styles of suspicious reading. Her answer: a hermeneutics of suspicion is also a hermeneutics of sensation. That is to say, a critic's sifting of textual clues and ferreting out of hidden truths offers pleasures that not only intellectual but also emotional. Suspicious reading generates a gripping story line in which the experience of suspense is followed by the ultimate pleasures of revelation and explanation. Here, Jones proposes, criticism borrows not only from detective fiction but also from the Victorian sensation novel, a genre that triggered emotional and visceral responses in its readers. Foucauldian critics, like the nineteenth-century texts they analyze, take delight in the revelation of shocking secrets, the pursuit of guilty parties, and the detection of hidden crimes. In both cases, the most obvious answer is never the right one, and the counterintuitive explanation is the one most highly rewarded. We write and read suspiciously not only in the hope of acquiring more critical knowledge but because we are addicted to the charge of narrative suspense and revelation. Uncovering the hidden import of seemingly inconsequential clues drives the pleasure of both fiction and criticism.[50]

As we are coming to see, the tone of suspicious reading is mixed and multihued, its motives often ambiguous and equivocal. On the one hand, the practice of critique harbors an unmistakable kernel of antagonism, as we proceed to arm ourselves against imagined adversaries to whom we impute malicious or hostile intent. Critical prose may take on a triumphalist cast, as we take pride in casting off our former naïveté, congratulate ourselves on our newly acquired perspicacity, feel sharper, shrewder, more knowing, less vulnerable. Suspicious reading, as Sedgwick remarks, pivots on a sense of prideful self-vindication, a trust in the inherent merits of critical exposure. We may even indulge in bouts of gloating and hand-rubbing: thanks to our critical labors, the text finally receives its comeuppance.

And yet such antagonism also leaves room for a tribute to our object of attention, an admission that it contains more than meets the eye. There is, after all, only a meager satisfaction to be found in pointing out the prejudices of an openly biased or tendentious work. Like Holmes squaring off against Moriarty at the Reichenbach Falls, we seek to pit our wits against a worthy opponent, to dig out cunningly concealed rather than self-evident truths, to engage in a strenuous battle of wills from which we hope to emerge triumphant. A skillful suspicious reading is, in this sense, also a close reading, requiring intimate knowledge of its object. Indeed, the words we are dissecting may be words that once seduced and entranced us, at an earlier moment in our reading history. We must inhabit the text, come to know it thoroughly, explore its every nook and cranny, if we are to succeed in drawing out its hidden secrets.

The schematic opposition of critical detachment and amateur enthusiasm, in other words, fails to do justice to the mixed motives and complicated passions that drive academic argument. Robert Fowler puts it well: "Many of us have found in *criticism* our revelation or our ecstasy, because for the first time, with the obtaining of critical distance, we could see the features of the text that had hitherto read us, and we were enchanted and liberated by what we saw."[51] Suspicious reading affords its own moments of pleasure and passion, without which it could never have achieved such prominence. Rather than becoming immersed in a text, critics become immersed in techniques of deciphering and diagnosing a text, are enamored of the very act of analysis. There can be a real enjoyment in embracing a discipline and being disciplined; there can be pleasure in retrieving recondite information and engaging in meticulous and fine-grained interpretation.[52] Critical reason, to anticipate the arguments of the next chapter, is often infused with moments of enchantment, and suspicion turns out to be not so very far removed from love.

CRITIQUE IS NOT A CAPITAL CRIME
(ONLY A MISDEMEANOR . . .)

Let me, finally, attempt a nimble two-step without tripping over my feet, both agreeing and disagreeing with my fellow critics of suspicious reading. Yes, the ubiquity of suspicion is unfortunate; no, critique is not a capital crime. Yes, we need to dial down the frequency of interrogation and cross-examination; no, suspicious reading is not an act of unconscionable violence. That acts of interpretation rely on storytelling is not a cause for concern—but without a doubt, we are deluged by too many scholarly narratives that adhere to the same formula and format.

According to W. H. Auden, "The interest of the detective story is the dialectic of innocence and guilt."[53] We have traced out a similar interest as it shows itself in the policing and self-policing work of criticism. In his commentary on Marx's *Capital*, Althusser famously declared that there is no such thing as an innocent reading, observing that we must therefore "say what reading we are guilty of." As the quintessential suspicious reader, Althusser refuses to exonerate himself from suspicion and shuffles willingly into the ranks of the accused. He is prepared, he says, to take responsibility for his justified crime and to defend his way of reading by proving its necessity.[54] In his wake, various critics have brooded over the inevitable guilt of reading, calling for a scrupulous inventory of one's own interpretative sins. But why, we might wonder, must reading always be a matter of guilt and innocence, crime and complicity? Such wording suggests a secular spin on Christian doctrine: we are all stained by the original sin of interpretation. Guilt no longer accrues to specific words, thoughts, or actions but is held to be intrinsic and inescapable—an existential state imposed by the fallen condition of language. Critique first sniffs out the guilt of others, only to engage, finally, in an anguished flurry of breast-beating and self-incrimination, a relentless rooting out of concealed motives and impure thoughts. Mea culpa, mea culpa, mea maxima culpa—except that, in contrast to Christian theology, there is no hope of final salvation!

That literature and art have often been created in unjust social circumstances is indisputable; that specific works may articulate points of view that deserve to be challenged is uncontroversial. Yet it does not follow that the main task of criticism should be to decry art's complicity, to engage in what T. J. Clark—himself no slouch as a social critic—calls "a constant, cursory hauling of visual (and verbal) images before the court of political judgement."[55] We may gain a temporary upper hand over the texts we interrogate, but at the cost of ever being surprised, stirred, reoriented, replenished, or called to account by the words we encounter. Our gain, in this respect, is also our substantial loss. Meanwhile, our detective skills are less impressive than we think: we uncover the guilt that we imputed at the very start.

And yet, conversely, there are also reasons to balk at the harsh charges and heated accusations that are now being leveled at a hermeneutics of suspicion. When critics vilify critique, claiming that it does untold violence to literature by decimating its otherness, they treat the text—as we saw in Felman's essay—as if it were a person. A similar line of argument is pursued by other deconstructively minded thinkers; Sarah Kofman, for example, laments the brutality of a Freudian method that tortures, mutilates, dissects, and dismembers literary works.[56] Recent work on the ethics of reading has intensified this inclination to think of texts as fragile quasi-persons that should be handled with kid gloves. Yet such metaphorical thinking can lead us astray. Texts, after all, are neither mortal nor sentient, and not even the most ruthless or reductive analysis can destroy an object made out of words that survives unscathed to be read anew by other readers. Like the perky plastic rodents in a carnival game of Whac-A-Mole, the text pops back up again after we bash it with our rubber mallet.

The worry, to be sure, is about damage of a less literal kind—a fear that the spread of critique has diminished or disabled our appreciation of works of art. Blinkered by their suspicion, the argument goes, trigger-happy critics are rendered oblivious to beauty and complex design; bristling with indignation, they dispatch any text that offends their sensibilities to the dustbin of history. Yet the effects of critical reading are more equivocal than such complaints would suggest. When it comes to matters of survival, as we'll see in the final chapter, it is often far better to be attacked than to be ignored. In most cases, a suspicious hermeneutics is unlikely to remove a text from circulation or cause it to go out of print. Indeed, it often has the opposite effect, endowing it with fresh vitality and excitement by hooking up to new agendas, debates, and audiences. Animus can inspire a fervid and concentrated attention on one's adversary, an exceptionally diligent focus on the object that is being interrogated. Edward Said's reading of *Mansfield Park* as an allegory of imperialism, for example, made the work of Jane Austen newly intriguing and worthy of attention to a community of postcolonial critics who might otherwise have paid her writing scant heed.

This is not to say that we can ignore or brush aside the question of what constitutes a fair or responsible reading. I find myself disagreeing with Richard Rorty when he expresses his wholehearted admiration for the critic "who simply beats a text into a shape which will serve his own purpose," who "is in it for what he can get out of it, not for the satisfaction of getting something right."[57] We cannot afford to be quite so cavalier about the differences between finding things out and making them up, between imposing our ideas on a text and learning something from a text. And while not even the most unkind or obtuse commentary can "do violence" to a text, it can certainly do harm to the text's author or to a community of readers who cherish it. Reading, in this sense, indisputably has an ethical dimension. The overwrought language of some literary theory, however, raises the stakes of interpretation to an almost comical level. If misreading, overreading, or bad reading is a fault, it is one that we are all prone to commit on a regular basis: more like a traffic violation rather than a capital crime.

The danger that shadows suspicious interpretation, I propose, is less its murderous brutality than its potential banality. For several decades it has served as a default option in literary studies. Its gestures of demystification and exposure are no longer oppositional but obligatory; its claims to intellectual novelty or political boldness are ever harder to sustain. Unchecked by counterforces, locked into a self-confirming circle of argumentation, a hermeneutics of suspicion dissipates its problem-solving powers and loses much of its allure. It no longer tells us what we do not know; it singularly fails to surprise.

Suspicious reading is also, I've been arguing, a style of interpretation that has paid scant attention to its own aesthetic and affective qualities, conceiving itself as an austere exercise in demystification. Once we acknowledge that suspicious interpretation is not only thought-driven but also pleasure-driven, not just a critique of narrative but also a type of narrative, its exceptional status is diminished. Critique can no longer pride itself on being so very different to the texts that it subjects to scrutiny. To some critics, such a downsizing of oppositional thought may seem like a loss. Yet this diminution may also turn out to be a liberation, freeing us up to try out other styles of criticism, to explore ways of reading less invested in inspection, interrogation, and the pursuit of the guilty.

· 4 ·

Crrritique

By now my more patient readers may be getting restive. (The rest will have long since tossed this book aside in a fit of exasperation.) "Yes, yes," they mutter testily, "it's all very well to say that critical reading is a matter of a certain orientation or stance—one that takes the form of a metaphorical act of 'digging down' or 'standing back.' And we are willing to grant you the point, more or less, that critics sometimes act like cops hell-bent on nailing down a suspect and solving a crime. But aren't you overlooking something? These rhetorical devices and figures of speech are there for a reason; scholars are using them to make important arguments. Isn't it time you stopped beating about the bush and tackled the substance of these arguments? Let's not forget that critique is a philosophical and political idea—one that enjoys wide respect and boasts an impressive intellectual lineage!"

Now that we are armed with a better grasp of the rhetoric of critique, we can roll up our sleeves and set about scrutinizing its key tenets. The preceding chapters have, I hope, captured something of the texture and taste, the tone and timbre, of certain styles of reading and reasoning. Critique is often feted in the humanities as a cure-all for dogma and orthodoxy, but it is less frequently pondered in all its mundane particulars—as a hotchpotch of figures of speech, turns of phrase, moral dramas, affective nuances, stylistic tics and tricks. It is invoked rather than examined, brandished to ward off enemies and cast a protective shield over one's endeavors. It is synonymous with

intellectual rigor, theoretical sophistication, and noncompliance with
the status quo. For many scholars in the humanities, it is not just one
good thing but the only conceivable thing.

The role of critique, declare Janet Halley and Wendy Brown, is to
"dissect our most established maxims and shibboleths." According to
Robert Davis and Ronald Schleifer, critique "terrorizes received ideas"
and is "*always* questioning culture."[1] Who would not want to be seen
as dissecting shibboleths? Is it not the fundamental job of intellectuals to question culture? And why would anyone want to be associated with the bad smell of the uncritical? Critique, it must be said,
is gifted with an exceptionally talented press agent and an unparal-
leled mastery of public relations. Occupying the political and moral
high ground in the humanities, it seems impervious to direct attack,
its bulletproof vest deflecting all bursts of enemy fire. Indeed, as we'll
see, even those most eager to throw a spanner into the machinery of
critique—those gritting their teeth at its sheer predictability—seem
powerless to bring it to a halt. The panacea they commonly prescribe, a
critique of critique, might give us pause. How exactly do we quash critique by redoubling it? Shouldn't we be trying to exercise our critique-
muscle less rather than more?

The phrase "hermeneutics of suspicion" has thrown a different
light on our object by alerting us to two key elements: an ambient attitude or sensibility and ways of reading that flip between what I have
called "strong" and "second-level" hermeneutics. Critique, I have argued, is not especially well attuned to the specifics of its own makeup,
presenting itself as an austere, even ascetic, intellectual exercise. And
yet it turns out to be a motley creature, a mash-up of conflicting parts:
not only analytical but affective, not just a critique of narrative but
also a type of narrative (even, on occasion, a stirring melodrama), not
just a stance of stern and uncompromising vigilance but an activity
equipped with its own pleasures and satisfactions.

We have also considered critical or suspicious reading as a genre—
that is to say, a constellation of rhetorical patterns and templates of
thought that are frequently repeated and easily identified. As David
Bordwell points out, "Pay less attention to what critics say they do and
more attention to their actual procedures of thinking and writing—
do all this, and you will be led to nothing but a body of conventions

no less powerful than the premises of an academic style in painting or music."[2] This fact is not, in itself, intrinsically alarming or a cause for embarrassment—not, at least, if you hold to the view that all communication relies on conventions, frames, and forms of taken-for-granted knowledge. It is, however, a potential blow to the self-image of critique, which tends the flame of its estrangement from the commonplace. To be critical is to be at odds with or opposed to reigning structures of thought and language. Yet, for younger scholars at least, critique is the main paradigm in which they have been trained; while buffing and polishing its role as agent provocateur to the intellectual mainstream, it *is* the mainstream. What happens to critique once it is entrenched as a professional protocol and a disciplinary norm in its own right?

Here we may be reminded of the once-vociferous debates in the art world about the death of the avant-garde. In both cases, the rallying power of a concept hinges on its antagonism to a larger social field that is pictured in spatial as well as temporal terms. Thus the imagined location of critique/the avant-garde is *elsewhere*: outside, below, in the margins, or at the borders. If it were to occupy the center, it would be something other than itself, estranged from its essence. And critique, like the avant-garde, is conjured in the future tense; spurning tradition, rupturing continuity, it strains forward rather than backward. The tradition of critique, as Gianni Vattimo points out, has close ties to a progressive philosophy of history that envisions humanity moving toward ever-greater emancipation.[3] While such sweeping stories of historical betterment have been undermined in recent decades, critique retains a strong affinity with the "not yet" of the future and strains impatiently against the drudgeries of the already known.

In short, critique, like the avant-garde, imagines itself taking a crowbar to the walls of the institution rather than being housed within them, barreling toward the future rather than being tugged back toward the past. What happens once this self-image flickers and fades and the euphoria of its iconoclastic ambitions begins to wane? For some scholars, the consequences look impossibly bleak; convinced that the last loophole for action has been closed, the only sound they hear is that of the prison door slamming shut. Yet the malaise of critique could also free us up to reassess our current ways of reading and

reasoning: to experiment with modes of argument less tightly bound
to exposure, demystification, and the lure of the negative.

. . .

Crrritique! The word flies off the tongue like a weapon, emitting a
rapid guttural burst of machine-gun-fire. There is the ominous caw-
ing staccato of the first and final consonants, the terse thud of the
short repeated vowel, the throaty underground rumble of the accompanying *r.* "Critique" sounds unmistakably foreign, in a sexy, mysterious, pan-European kind of way, conjuring up tableaus of intellectuals
gesturing wildly in smoke-wreathed Parisian cafés and solemn-faced
discussions in seminar rooms in Frankfurt. Its now ubiquitous presence in close readings of Conrad and Coetzee testifies to the mingling
of intellectual bloodlines associated with the rise of "theory"; a word
once closely associated with the recondite realm of European philosophy is now part of the lingua franca of anyone teaching freshman English. And yet its appearance also reminds us that we remain within
the boundaries of a certain intellectual milieu. We are all capable of
criticizing what we don't like, but it is only under certain conditions
that we think of ourselves as engaged in something called "critique."

Why has this two-syllable word achieved such a commanding position? On what grounds has it proved so seductive and self-sustaining?
What is the mystique of critique? Like any complex sign, the word
contains multitudes—long histories of use, sediments and layers of
association, densely compacted meanings. In what follows, I draw out
the most salient of these associations by making a stab at a definition.
The aim is not to deliver an intellectual history of critique or to dwell
on the lengthy disputes about norms and foundations that have occupied political theorists and philosophers.[4] In keeping with the ambitions of the book as a whole, I retain a focus on how the concept of
critique has been deployed in the recent history of literary studies and
related fields.

Let us shuffle forward slowly, then, keeping our eyes peeled and
our noses close to the ground, attending to the obvious as well as the
overlooked, considering how sentences are formed, evidence is provided, and paragraphs are assembled. The goal, once again, is not to

unmask critique by exposing the hidden structures that determine it. Rather than look through critique, let us look squarely at it, viewing it as a reality rather than a symptom, a many-sided object rather than a beguiling façade. Let us treat it, in short, as a major rhetorical-cultural actor in its own right.

There are, I propose, five qualities that come into play in the current rhetoric of critique:

1. *Critique is secondary.* A critique is always a critique *of* something, a commentary on another argument, idea, or object. Critique does not vaunt its self-sufficiency; it makes no pretense of standing alone. It owes its existence to a prior presence. It could not exist without something to respond to, without another entity to which it reacts. Critique is symbiotic; it does its thinking by responding to the thinking of others.

All words, to be sure, connect up to other words. No text is an island; no phrase can fend off the countless other phrases that crowd in from all sides. Yet in the case of critique, this state of dependency is its raison d'être; it is unabashedly oriented toward words that come from elsewhere. In literary studies, this secondary state often shows itself in the practice of extended quotation. Paraphrase, long considered heretical, still remains risky; critics are expected to make their case via judicious citation and scrupulous attention to the words on the page. Here, critique links up, etymologically and historically, to criticism and a long history of textual exegesis and commentary. These connections help clarify why critique is so easily absorbed into the everyday routines of literary studies; the crafting of words about other words, after all, is built into the DNA of the discipline.

Yet critique also emphasizes its difference from criticism, defined, in René Wellek's words, as the study of concrete works of literature with an emphasis on their aesthetic evaluation. Critique is not literary criticism, in the traditional sense; indeed, it is often emphatically defined as its adversary and opposite. One function of critique, declares the Marxist critic Drew Milne, "is to criticize the functions that criticism is made to serve."[5] It is not that critique avoids judgment—as we will see, it is tangled up in it—but that it draws its criteria from other domains. Philosophy, politics, history, psychoanalysis—the perceived rigor of such fields is counterposed to wishy-washy forms of aesthetic judgment. Raymond Williams puts the case forcefully in his *Keywords*: "Criticism becomes ideological not only when it assumes the position of the *consumer*, but also when it masks this position by a succession of abstractions of its real terms of response (as *judgement, taste, cultivation, discrimination, sensibility; disinterested, qualified, rigorous*, and so on)."[6] Criticism, it is argued, teems with hidden interests and rationalizations, concealing its motives behind a curtain of pure aesthetic criteria. Practitioners of critique, by contrast, spurn this language of duplicity and scorn the traditional role of the literary critic as arbiter of taste. They reserve a special ire for any type of aestheticism or formalism that strives to liberate literature from the chains of context—though critique, as we will see, is by no means bereft of ambitions toward transcendence.

While secondary, critique is far from subservient. Rather, it seeks to wrest from a text a different account than it gives of itself. In doing so, it assumes that it will meet with, and overcome, a resistance. If there were no resistance, if the truth were self-evident and available for all to see, the act of critique would be superfluous. The goal is not the reconstruction of an original or intended meaning but a willful or perverse counterreading that brings previously unfathomed insights to light. Nevertheless, critique cannot stray too far from its object without endangering the plausibility of its claims. It must show that the meanings it imputes were there all along, discernible to those who have eyes to see and ears to hear. With a conjuror's flourish, the critic yanks the rabbit out of the hat and shows that the work of art harbors the seeds of its own self-criticism. By "interrogating" a text, he causes it to stutter out its errors, missteps, derelictions, oversights, lapses, and miscalculations. This, I think, is what Robert Koch means when he writes that critical discourse "preserves its object, leaves it intact, but hollows it out from inside so that the object speaks with a voice that is not its own. . . . The object betrays itself."[7] Critique ventriloquizes those concealed or counterintuitive meanings that the text is reluctant to own up to. It thereby establishes its sovereignty over the words it deciphers, allowing it to turn a text inside out and to know that text better than it knows itself.

The secondariness of critique is not just a conceptual issue—critique presumes the existence of an object to be critiqued—but also

a temporal one. Critique comes *after* another text; it follows or succeeds another piece of writing: a time lag that can span decades, centuries, even millennia. Critique, then, looks backward, and in doing
so it often presumes to understand the past better than it understood
itself. Hindsight is translated into insight; from our later vantage
point, we feel ourselves primed to see better, deeper, further. "We don't
read such criticism to attach ourselves to the past," observes the film
scholar Tom O'Regan. " "The past shows us what not to do, what not to
be, where not to go."[8] The belatedness of critique is also a source of its
iconoclastic strength. Scholars of Greek tragedy or Romantic poetry
may mourn their failure to fully inhabit a vanished world, yet this historical distance is also a productive estrangement that allows insight
to unfold. The tomes gathering dust in the libraries must yield to our
analytical judgments—even if we occasionally stumble across embry-
onic versions of our own ideas lurking in their margins and corners.
Whatever the limitations of our perspective, how can we not know
more than those who have come before? We moderns leave behind us
a trail of errors, finally corrected, like a cloud of ink from a squid, remarks Michel Serres.[9] Critique likes to have the last word.

The last word in relation to what? Works of literature can be found
wanting for reasons that crop up with ceremonial regularity: the
tyranny of dualisms and dichotomies, speciously unified and coherent models of character, teleological narratives that turn identity into
destiny, the euphemistic or evasive treatment of social injustice. The
practice of critique is, in this sense, often synonymous with a strong
contextualization; texts are scanned for signs of sociohistorical fractures and traumas that they studiously suppress. Contained within
a historical moment, they are held to account for the structures of
domination that define that moment. Dickens is reproached for his
complicity with the visual regimes of commodity culture; Milton is
scrutinized for signs of his implication in the history of colonialism.[10]
Critique cuts into a work at a judicious angle in order to expose its
hidden interests and agendas, wielding the scalpel of "context" to rep-
rimand "text."

Moreover, distrust is often directed with equal force at the history
of criticism—at scholarship that masquerades as a purely aesthetic or
literary affair and thus fails to be properly critical. The hermeneutics

of suspicion is a triangular structure, involving not just a critic and a text but also the past history of a scholarly field, including its luminaries, sages, academic stars, and éminences grises. Defined by its distrust of authority (see point 4 below), critique is obligated to take up arms against ideas as soon as they are grist for the academic mill of Routledge primers and Norton anthologies. In the current intellectual landscape, however, the goalposts can shift with disconcerting speed, and it is often a matter of dispute which positions are "hegemonic" and which others "marginal"—leaving plenty of room for a host of differing parties to feel aggrieved. The stakes are especially high in such arenas as feminism, postcolonial studies, or queer theory, where the devastating charge of "being insufficiently critical" can lead to a sense of being excommunicated from the field.

In American studies, for example, arguments are commonly made by bestowing or withholding the sobriquet of the critical. In his survey of the field, Liam Kennedy notes that Americanists "commonly approach America with suspicion, fear, even anger; we view it as a powerful duplicitous force to be denounced or mystified."[11] This volatile mix is also directed at the history of American studies itself, as each wave of scholarship reproaches its predecessors for failing to be critical enough of its object. In the last few decades, the "myth and symbol" approach of the 1950s and '60s has been excoriated for its humanism and conservatism; the subsequent "new Americanism," centered on the experiences of women and people of color, lambasted for its essentialism and naïve identity politics; and the most recent trend, transnational American studies, reproached for its embrace of globalization and sugarcoating of empire. Whatever the ambitions of individual critics, it is hard to dodge the bullet of the accusation that they are shoring up the very ideology of American exceptionalism they call into question. Critique serves as a ubiquitous device for diagnosing the various missteps that hinder the realization of the field's radical promise.[12]

And yet the symbiotic status of critique also means that its prose is never pure and unadulterated, that it speaks, whether voluntarily or involuntarily, in more than one voice. It strives to enfold a prior text, to assert its sovereignty over the words of others—but these same words may stubbornly protrude like awkward or ungainly limbs, poking holes in the fabric of the larger argument. A striking or ambiguous quotation, for example, can overshadow the words that surround it, throwing into doubt the claims that it was summoned to serve. Positioned in close proximity, text and commentary may rub against each other in surprising or unanticipated ways, generating a friction that thwarts the larger argument. Words from the past may spring back to life, acquiring fresh vigor and vitality, buttonholing and beguiling readers and short-circuiting the negative judgment they were drafted to support. And textual examples or quotations may serve as trip wires that interrupt or derail the larger arc of a conceptual argument, creating a multi-voiced rather than single-voiced piece of writing. Critique, in short, cannot entirely protect itself from the possibility of being undone by its own object.[13]

What, in this light, should we make of the distinction between transcendent and immanent critique—a distinction often deployed in order to champion the merits of one form over the other? The practitioner of transcendent critique, according to Adorno, assumes an Archimedean standpoint above the blindness of society; he censures and condemns the object of his attention; he wishes to wipe everything away as with a sponge. Such a critic, in short, seeks to haul himself by his bootstraps out of the miasma of confusion and bad faith in which his fellows are immersed. Brooding over his estrangement from the world, he rules out any possibility of commonality or kinship. Immanent critique, by contrast, operates in a more stealthy and circuitous fashion, immersing itself in those thoughts and ideas that it opposes. It temporarily "takes on" these ideas in order to test them out; it criticizes them in their own terms by adopting their criteria and teasing out their internal contradictions. Rather than seeking an external vantage point of theoretical or political purity, it is happy to get its hands dirty so as to better know its object. The distinction between transcendent and immanent critique is thus the difference between a "knowledge which penetrates from without and that which bores from within."[14]

Adorno no sooner develops this opposition between transcendental and immanent critique than he impatiently brushes it aside, as a too-tidy dichotomy. And here our prior reflections on the secondary status of critique proves all too pertinent. Given this status, how can critique ever exist above or outside its object? How could it be squeaky clean and scrubbed free of foreign contaminants? The genre of critique, as we have seen, is symbiotic, relational, and thus intrinsically impure; it feeds off the ideas of its adversaries, is parasitic on the words that it calls into question, could not survive without the very object that it condemns. While definitions of "critique" often cite its origins in the Greek word *krinein*—meaning to separate, to distinguish, to judge—the subject and object of critique are more closely intertwined than such definitions admit. However high we lift up our feet, that pesky wad of chewing gum remains stuck to the bottom of our shoe.

Yet, at the same time, critique opens up a gap between itself and its object; it affirms its difference from what it describes and asserts its distance from the voices that it ventriloquizes. In this sense, it harbors an impulse toward transcendence, reaching beyond the limits it perceives in the words of others. There is much wrangling in political theory about whether the idea of critique needs a normative foundation or universal ground. Perhaps we should imagine the transcendent or quasi-transcendent impulse of critique differently: not as a grounding but as an opening. In contrast to the image of a stable foundation resting firmly beneath one's feet, the metaphor of an opening—the shaft of light falling through a window-slit; the bright patch of blue sky amidst gathering storm clouds—captures the sense of an alternative that is glimpsed but not yet fully visible. It is less a matter of invoking a solid and unshakable ground than of gesturing toward something that is immanent with, yet also irreducible to, present experience.[15] By describing its object in words this object would not have chosen, critique pushes back against prevailing pressures and opens up a possibility of thinking differently.

In some cases, of course, the clash between the values of a text and the norms of the critic is impossible to miss; the work is interrogated, judged, and sentenced without further ado. Increasingly, however, scholars have become wary of norms-and-values talk and leery of appealing to alternative theories that lend themselves to a further round of interrogation. They take to heart Foucault's injunction that we should challenge what exists rather than provide alternatives. As a result, the impulse toward transcendence manifests itself in other ways: in a charismatic image of the critic's dissident, risk-taking persona, or an embrace of self-reflexivity and knowingness as the ultimate good. As we have seen, critique takes on the guise of an ethos or disposition—an attitude of restless skepticism, irony, or estrangement—rather than a systematically grounded theoretical framework. In this way, the critic carves out a distance from the words and worlds of others, espousing a stance irreducible to the tyranny of the given— a stance of what Alan Liu calls "detached immanence."[16]

The status of critique, in short, cannot be resolved by championing a "good" immanent critique against a "bad" transcendent critique— or indeed the other way round.[17] Transcendent and immanent are not names for two mutually exclusive classes or groups of criticism. Rather, they crystallize a tension that lies at the heart of critique as a genre.

2. *Critique is negative.* To use the language of critique is to make a judgment of a less than favorable kind. Critique is, in one way or another, a negative act (even though it is not purely or exclusively negative: there is always, as Adorno points out, an affirmative residue).[18] To engage in critique is to grapple with the oversights, omissions, insufficiencies, or evasions in the object one is analyzing. It is to tabulate a limit, to discern a lack, to heave a sigh of disapproval or disappointment. Raymond Geuss remarks that the idea of critique possesses "unambiguously negative connotations." Robert Koch writes that "critical discourse, as critical discourse, must never formulate positive statements: it is always 'negative' in relation to its object." And Diana Coole notes that "negativity and critique are thus intimately related."[19]

Negativity, however, can be spun in a variety of ways. Emotional or affective tone can express a writer's state of mind: encountering a certain kind of critical prose, we conjure up a picture of its author as outraged, disillusioned, or out of sorts. But negativity is also a matter of rhetoric, conveyed via acts of deflating or diagnosing that have less to do with individual attitude than with a shared grammar of language, a field of linguistic conventions and constraints. Even the most chipper and cheerful of graduate students, on entering a field in which critique is held to be the most rigorous method, will eventually master

the protocols of professional pessimism. And finally, of course, negativity is also an idea — an enduring theme in the history of philosophy
that has preoccupied many thinkers and theorists.

One common strategy of negative argument among literary and
cultural critics can be dubbed "deflation via inversion." This rhetorical
trick of the trade follows a two-step rhythm: the critic dangles an en-
ticing or promising prospect before the reader, only to whisk it away
and replace it with its opposite. A rise is followed by a fall; an idea is
expressed only to be negated; a hopeful "before" gives way to the cold
shower of an "after." Harkening back to the Marxist idea of critique
as an "inversion of an inversion" (bourgeois ideology perceives reality
upside down, argues Marx, so that it must be flipped right side up
to arrive at the truth), this verbal strategy is a staple of current criticism. As a result, we are primed to expect bad news, to assume that
any positive state of affairs is either imaginary or evanescent, to steel
ourselves for the worst. The positive turns out to be a temporary way
station en route to the negative, whose sovereignty is rousingly re-
affirmed. The rose-colored glasses are yanked from our eyes as we
are apprised, one more time, of the absurdity of any vestigial shred
of optimism.

Thus the animal studies scholar Cary Wolfe opens his discussion
of a recent novel by Michael Crichton by observing that it seems to
"radically question the discourse of speciesism." Any nascent hopes we
might have, however, are quickly dashed, as Wolfe serves up the bad
news: in spite of its apparent progressiveness, Crichton's novel "leaves
intact the category of the human and its privileged forms of accom-
plishment and representation in the novel: technoscience and neo-
colonialism."[20] Acknowledging that the television show *Queer as Folk*
differs from previous dramas in offering "uncompromisingly realis-
tic images of gay life," Giovanni Porfido then flips things around to
claim that this visibility is less desirable than it might seem; it is linked,
we learn, to the "commodification of social identities and neoliberal
forms of visual govermentality."[21] Along similar lines, we are regularly
apprised that what looks like difference is yet another form of sameness, that what appears to be subversion is a more discreet form of
containment, that any attempt at inclusion spawn yet more exclusions.

While the terminology fluctuates, what remains constant is a rhetorical sequence that raises hope only to deflate it. "You may think you are beholding X," declares the critic, "but you are really seeing Y!" Y turns out to be not just different from Y but its antithesis; it does not supplement or modify it but cancels it out. The bad news looks even worse in being contrasted to what might have been.

The point is not that the current state of animal rights discourse or the politics of gay and lesbian inclusion are beyond criticism. No doubt self-congratulatory stories of social progress (Look how far we've come!) can become exceptionally grating. But we cannot oppose such a "myth" of progress to the critic's bleak-eyed assessment of how things really are—as if the negativity of critique were somehow beyond rhetoric or misinterpretation or prejudice or narrative, a nose-to-nose encounter with the gritty textures of truth. It is not a matter of fiction versus reality but a matter of weighing up the pros and cons of different dispositions. And here "criticizability" is itself created, to a greater extent than scholars acknowledge, by a practice of reading that is geared to detect flaws and document disappointment. Critique's fundamental quality is that of "againstness," vindicating a desire to take a hammer, as Bruno Latour would say, to the beliefs and attachments of others. Faith is to be countered with skepticism; illusion yields to a sobering disenchantment; the fetish must be defetishized, the dream world stripped of its powers. Like an upscale detox facility, critique promises to flush out the noxious substances and cultural toxins that hold us in their thrall. It demonstrates, again and again, that what might look like hopeful signs of social progress harbor more disturbing implications. In this sense, there is a logic of perfectionism or absolutism at work: not just impatience with the slowness of incremental change but a conviction that such change is actively harmful in blinding us to what remains undone. Disguising a failure to root out structural inequality, it only promotes complacency and shores up the forces of liberal optimism. Piecemeal change thus turns out to be worse than no change at all.

Yet the negativity of critique, like Baskin-Robbins ice cream, also comes in various flavors; it is not just a matter of fault-finding, scolding, censuring, and correcting. Indeed, quite a few scholars are eager to back away from the rhetoric of denunciation, a posture short on sty-listic subtlety as well as philosophical nuance. The nay-saying critic all too easily brings to mind the finger-wagging moralist, the thin-lipped schoolmarm, the Victorian patriarch, the glaring policeman. The act of negating is tangled up with a long history of prohibition and inter-diction and burdened with a host of unattractive associations. It can all too easily come across as contemptuous, vengeful, heartless, or vit-riolic. In recent years, it has often been tied up with stereotypes of killjoy feminists, embittered minorities, and other resentment-filled avatars of "political correctness."[22]

In response, present-day defenders of critique often downplay its associations with negative judgment and what they call a juridico-repressive paradigm of punishment. Critique, they insist, is not a matter of castigation or a categorical thumbs-down; rather, it takes the form of a more judicious and considered assessment. A preferred idiom is that of "troubling" or "problematizing," of demonstrating the ungroundedness of beliefs rather than diagnosing false conscious-ness. And the prevailing tone is ironic and deliberative rather than angry and accusatory. The role of critique is no longer to castigate but to complicate, not to engage in ideas' destruction but to expose their cultural construction. Judith Butler, for example, declares that critique has little to do with negative judgment; it is, rather, an "ongoing effort to fathom, collect, and identify that upon which we depend when we claim to know anything at all."[23] This is a model of argument cast in the mode of Foucauldian genealogy rather than old-style ideology critique: critique not as a denunciation of error and a hunt for mis-laid truths but as an inquiry into the way knowledge is organized that seeks, as far as possible, to suspend judgments. Along similar lines, Barbara Johnson has argued that a critique of a theoretical system

> is not an examination of its flaws and imperfections. It is not a set of criti-cisms designed to make the system better. It is an analysis that focuses on the grounds of the system's possibility. The critique reads backwards from what seems natural, obvious, self-evident, or universal in order to show that these things have their history, their reasons for being the way they are, the effects on what follows from them and that the start point is not a (natural) given, but a (cultural) construct, usually blind to itself.[24]

Yet it seems a tad disingenuous to describe this version of critique as being untouched by negative judgment and the examination of flaws. Isn't an implicit criticism being transmitted in the claim that a cultural construct is "usually blind to itself"? And the adjectival chain "natural, obvious, self-evident, or universal" strings together, as we saw in chapter 2, some of the most negatively weighted words in contemporary criticism. Detachment, in other words, can easily convey an implicit judgment, especially when it is used to expose the deepseated convictions and heartfelt attachments of others. In this respect, the ongoing skirmishes between ideology critique and poststructuralist critique do not override their commitment to a common ethos: a sharply honed suspicion that goes behind the backs of its interlocutors to retrieve counterintuitive and unflattering meanings. "You do not know that you are ideologically driven, historically determined, or culturally constructed," declares the subject of critique to the object of critique, "but I do!"[25]

How, then, do we parse these differing shades of negativity—vehement acts of disputing or denouncing, on the one hand, and a more measured yet skeptical technique of putting into question, on the other? The political theorist Diana Coole has drafted a helpful survey of various facets of the negative in modern thought. When scholars talk about *negation*, they are often intent on refuting a particular idea, argument, or text; the idea of *negativity*, by contrast, embodies a more general process of undoing or unraveling that is not tied to a single act of judgment. The first of these terms, we might say, often negates an identity, whereas the second gestures toward a nonidentity. This latter idea is associated with such themes as the limits of discourse, the margins of meaning, the experience of the limit, and the status of the unrepresentable—themes that Coole traces through the work of Nietzsche, Derrida, Adorno, and Kristeva. Negativity is associated with the language of "gaps, hiatus, lacunae, discontinuities, undecidables, confusions, ambiguities, inconsistencies, transgression, contradictions, antinomies, unknowables."[26] It is, in sum, not a specific defect but a structural limit of language and knowledge.

Contemporary styles of critique are divided between negation and negativity. Negation—the explicit act of rebuttal, refusal, or rejection—displays the bracing qualities of moral clarity and rhetorical force, demanding that we speak out against injustice, condemn prejudice, expose fallacious or meretricious lines of reasoning. Our moral makeup, proposes the philosopher Susan Neiman, includes the need to "express outrage, the need to reject euphemism and cant and to call things by their proper names."[27] Negation, in short, speaks to the expectation that we take a stand and take a side on the issues that matter. What looks like a hard-hitting indictment to some scholars may, however, seem like *plumpes Denken* (crude thinking) to others — those apprehensive that the act of saying no, in its blithe confidence and sense of certainty, may simply be the mirror image of a yes. Is it really the case that reason can so easily be marshaled to correct unreason? Doesn't the act of denouncing the errors of others risk shoring up the critic's own smugness and superiority? And isn't there something intemperate about such a rush to judgment — as if the critic were being propelled by a mind-fogging sense of outrage that precludes judicious reflection?

Negativity, by contrast, correlates to a more nonchalant, if still vigilant, attitude — a wariness of general principles or normative claims. It is, we might say, less a matter of *taking a stand* than of *assuming a stance*: of looking skeptically at the procedures through which truths are established and edging away from the perceived naïveté of positive propositions. The role of the critic is now to hone and sharpen an awareness of the limits of language and thought. "Negativity," writes Coole, "conveys a restlessness that disturbs the slumbers of the given, that undermines any reified plenitude, presence, power or position."[28] The negative, in other words, is now at war with the normative. It is not about laying down the law through a language of prohibition or punishment but about resisting the law. Negativity is not tied to a particular object but floats free of specific causes and catalysts, as an ethos of perpetual agitation that is commendable for its own sake. The literary critic Stephen Ross speaks admiringly of "critique as a fundamentally negative energy, and process of incessant disruption and challenge" that avoids the mistake of offering concrete alternatives to what is challenged.[29] The critic is now the one who dismantles, disassembles, and takes apart, who, like a latter-day Penelope, unravels the threads of explanation, justification, and judgment woven during the previous day.

Critique is associated, in this sense, with what Koch calls the pathos of failure; brooding over the inevitable derailments of thought and disappointments of action, it is driven by a gnawing dissatisfaction that comes within striking distance of a full-blown pessimism. Anticipating the worst, preoccupied with not being conned, it takes its cue from The Who's "We Won't Get Fooled Again." And yet this negativity also acquires a heroic spin; scorning placebos and consoling fictions, critics position themselves against the mentality of the mainstream. "Critique is risky," as one account has it; "it can be a disruptive, disorienting, and at times destructive enterprise of knowledge."[30] This embrace of subversion gives rise to a halo effect, an aura of ethical and political virtue that burnishes its negative stance with what Coole calls a "normative glow."[31]

Talk of halos may call to mind Baudelaire's well-known prose poem "The Lost Halo." On being spotted by a startled friend in a den of ill repute, a poet explains that his halo fell from his head while he was dashing across the Paris boulevards. Rather than mourning its loss, however, he experiences a sense of great relief at being deprived of his sanctity. Now, he declares, he can finally move through the world as one flawed, imperfect, and ordinary creature among others. Marshall Berman seizes on this poem as an exemplary depiction of the "primal scene of modernity." What Baudelaire gives us, he argues, is a picture of a transformed world. Thrown into the maelstrom of the city streets, dodging the chaos and confusion of oncoming traffic, the poet finds himself in a milieu that has been pulled up by its roots and thoroughly desanctified. The lost halo testifies to a world in which hierarchies are leveled, where the poet no longer enjoys the status of a prophet and the artwork itself is stripped of its numinous and God-given powers. It symbolizes, in short, the irreversible loss of the sacred.[32]

This view of modernity as a one-way slide into disenchantment is one that we have had some occasion to query. In fact, the concluding words of Baudelaire's poem suggest that the halo is not lost for good but will probably be picked up and reused—even if only, the speaker declares, by a "bad poet." This lapidary judgment is endorsed by Berman: if haloes are not yet obsolete, this is simply a sign of the persistence of antimodern impulses, the regressive-nostalgic longings of those unwilling to face up to the ambiguities and ironies of modern life. But is it quite so self-evident that the halo is destined for the dustbin of history? It is not just that critique has failed to eradicate the desire for the sacred and to root out magical, mystical, and mythological thinking, which flourish in both old and new guises. We might also consider that critical thinking conjures up its own forms of enchantment; the faith in critique is no different, in certain respects, from other forms of faith. It involves an attachment to certain precepts and practices that can be experienced with an almost primordial intensity, that is often impervious to counterarguments, and that is relinquished painfully and with difficulty. Faith, in this sense, is less a matter of conscious assent to a series of propositions than a gradual easing into an overall orientation and way of thinking. When one is truly enchanted by critique, it feels entirely reasonable, logical, even inevitable.[33]

That critique has its sacred texts, rites of passage, and articles of faith is not a deplorable lack or shameful failing—something to be corrected by an industrial-strength dose of yet more critique. It is a timely reminder, however, of the blurred lines between the secular and the sacred, the modern and the premodern, and thus of the limits of any vision of critique as disruptive negativity. And here we might look to Ian Hunter's history of critique, which revises the usual account of its Enlightenment origins. Far from being a purely secular phenomenon forged in the fire of Cartesian doubt and political revolution, critique has its roots, according to Hunter, in a religious tradition of pastoral pedagogy and self-examination. It is here that a certain idea of the person comes into being, one whose sense of selfhood and ethical purpose is formed through a state of watchfulness and self-regulation. There are, Hunter suggests, striking parallels between the practice of relentless self-scrutiny that typifies the workings of the Protestant conscience in the seventeenth century and the culture of critical self-reflexivity that reigns in present-day humanities departments. Like Nietzsche, Hunter connects modern suspicion to a history of spiritual self-examination. Critique, he proposes, has become the medium of a secular holiness, the preferred rhetoric of today's "spiritual intelligentsia."[34] The halo dropped by the poet—now dented, dirty, a little lopsided, but still emitting a faint steady glow— has been picked up by the critic.

3. *Critique is intellectual.* Everyday practices of assessing and evalu-

ating, such as the experience of debating the merits of a movie with a friend, usually fall under the rubric of "criticism." What, then, is the difference between "criticism" and "critique"? Is it really the case, as scholars have argued, that criticism is just a matter of fault-finding and putting down, while critique—as an academic practice—justifies its judgment by offering rationales and justifications?[35] Surely ordinary acts of criticism also leave room for justifying and explaining. A first response, perhaps, may take the form of an intemperate outburst or peremptory verdict: "That was a god-awful film!" we mutter irritably to our companion while making our way out of the movie theater. If pressed for a further explanation, however, we can usually come up with one: "The different parts of the film didn't hang together, its portrayal of women was utterly retrograde, and I've always hated that director's work anyway!" When talking to others, we often provide reasons for our judgments, defend our perspectives, and describe our feelings. It seems misleading to claim that critique differs from criticism in being "intellectually serious"—as if the realm of everyday interaction were entirely deprived of such seriousness.

One difference between criticism and critique is, surely, rhetorical or performative—that is to say, the distinction is realized and enforced in the speaker's choice of words. When we describe ourselves as engaged in critique, we imagine ourselves taking part in a particular kind of conversation. We tacitly link ourselves to a larger history in which figures such as Kant, Marx, and Foucault loom large; we situate our ideas in relation to a distinguished tradition of theoretical reflection and intellectual dissent. In this context, critique is drawn, as we have seen, toward self-reflexive thinking. Its domain is that of second-level observation, in which we reflect on the frameworks that form and inform our understanding. The critical observer is a self-observer; the goal is to objectify one's own thought by looking at it from outside, so as to puncture the illusion of any spontaneous or immediate understanding. Contemporary critique is irresistibly drawn to the "meta": metafiction, metahistory, metatheory. Even if objectivity is an illusion and truth is a chimera, how can critical self-consciousness not trump the alternatives? Self-reflexivity is the holy grail of contemporary thinking: widely hailed as an unconditional good. "Critical theory," states a popular introduction to the field, echoing the sentiments of countless other primers, "aims to promote self-reflexive exploration": its purpose is to "question the legitimacy of common sense or traditional claims made about experience, knowledge, and truth."[36]

This questioning of common sense is also a questioning of ordinary language. Contemporary critique is often mistrustful of a prose style that aspires to be clear, simple, and direct—qualities that it holds to be inherently ideological. "Clarity," declares the critic and filmmaker Trinh T. Minh-ha, "is a means of subjection, a quality both of official taught language and of correct writing, two old mates of power: together they flow, together they flower, vertically, to impose an order."[37] Trinh worries that the demand for clarity is detrimental, even dangerous, turning language into a tool for the conveying of the already known. As such, it remains squarely on the side of the conventional and closed-minded, policing what counts as acceptable communication. It cannot hear the sounds of difference or strangeness; it is oblivious to the rhythm of the eccentric and the offbeat; it peremptorily dismisses what cannot be voiced in logical argument and straightforward prose.

This suspicion of clarity leads to a preference for intricate syntax and specialized idioms that call attention to the snares of language. Self-reflexivity, in short, becomes a matter of the form as well as the content of academic prose. This phenomenon of so-called difficult writing has triggered volleys of accusations and counteraccusations that sometimes shed more heat than light. Lamenting the ascendancy of an "awkward, jargon-logged, academic prose," the philosopher Denis Dutton declares that its torturous neologisms and convoluted syntax mask a lack of substance. "The pretentiousness of the worst academic writing," he writes, "betrays it as a kind of intellectual kitsch" that promises but never delivers genuine insight.[38] For Dutton, the difficulty of this writing is a surface effect. Bullying the reader into submission, it announces its importance through the obfuscatory weight of its words rather than the genuine complexity of its thought.

Dutton's salvo has triggered sharp responses from poststructuralist critics who query the self-evident merits of accessibility and chafe at the very notion of a "common language." If the goal of critique is to challenge the taken-for-granted, they declare, it must put pressure on the form as well as the content of expression. Jonathan Culler and

Kevin Lamb invoke the history of literary modernism and its use of language to estrange perception. Like modernism, they suggest, "critical prose must draw attention to itself as an act that cannot be seen through"; it must resist being consumed, digested, swallowed up. In doing so, it can undermine or unwrite the prevailing discourses that make up our world.[39] Paul Bové adopts a similar line of argument, testifying to a "tradition that insists upon difficulty, slowness, complex, often dialectical and highly ironic styles," as an essential antidote to the "prejudices of the current regime of truth: speed, slogans, transparency, and reproducibility."[40] Critique, in short, demands an arduous working over of language, a refusal of the facile phrase and ready-made formula.

Intervening in these debates, Judith Butler invokes the precedent of Adorno. His worry, she notes, was that to "speak in ways that are already accepted as intelligible is precisely to speak in ways that do not make people think critically, that accept the status quo, and that do not make use of the resource of language to rethink the world radically." The communication of truth pivots on the structures through which it is conveyed. If these structures are already known, they will only protect the reader's ignorance, shoring up complacency and parochialism. What does it say about me, Butler wonders, when the only knowledge I value is one that answers my need for the familiar, that does not make me pass through what is isolating, estranging, difficult, and demanding?[41] New thought, in short, demands a language that spurns convention and the pablum of the already known, even at the risk of a certain isolation from collective life. Here Butler flips Dutton's account of the link between style and sensibility on its head. Difficult language is no longer a sign of entitlement or obfuscation but conveys a certain humility—in contrast to the danger of dogmatism that haunts the champion of lucid and legible prose.

We must also keep in mind, however, that the quality of being either pedestrian or perplexing is embedded not in words themselves but in how readers receive and respond to these words. A style of writing cannot be difficult in itself, only in relation to the expectations of a given audience. And academics are, for the most part, primed to expect abstruse or opaque formulations and to appreciate lengthy cascades of qualifications. As Ien Ang points out, in spite of the political weight given to practices of defamiliarization, they take place within the confines of academic communities to whom such practices are already very familiar.[42] A way of writing that seems opaque or recondite to outsiders also promotes in-group belonging and socialization into a scholarly milieu. There is no reason why scholars should not use specialized terminology or an exacting style to communicate with their peers; some ideas, after all, can be challenging and complicated, and not all scholarship needs to be accessible to the person on the street. But its close ties to modes of professionalization and scholarly gatekeeping make it hard to sustain the claim that there is something intrinsically radical or resistant about difficult writing.

In short, defamiliarization, as Michael Warner observes, does not work all by itself, and we need to think in more specific terms about how what we say is heard, misheard, or ignored in public life.[43] Moreover, if we accept Latour's idea that the impact of ideas is directly correlated to the strength and the length of their networks, disdain for accessibility may be misplaced—even while our arguments will be transported, transformed, and often misunderstood as they move through public space. The charge, moreover, that everyday language is "commodified" fails to acknowledge that critical theory is also a form of cultural capital and a prestige-driven commodity—though in neither case does this commodity status tell us very much about how words are being used in different situations, and to what end. Meanwhile, the creation of a great divide between critique and common sense condemns everyday language to a state of slow-wittedness and servitude while condescending to those unschooled in the patois of literary and critical theory. That individuals do not engage in "critique" does not mean that they must be uncritical.

All too often, remarks Bruno Latour, intellectuals—he is speaking of sociologists, but the point holds more generally—"behave as if they were 'critical,' 'reflexive,' and 'distanced' enquirers meeting a 'naïve,' 'uncritical,' and 'unreflexive' actor."[44] Critical thinking is restricted to one side of the intellectual encounter, and everyday thought is pictured as a zone of undifferentiated doxa. Against this trend, the pragmatic sociologists Luc Boltanski and Laurent Thévenot have sought to redefine critique as routine rather than rarefied. In their influential work *On Justification*, they analyze a variety of what they call *cités*:

spheres of value that structure the realm of everyday experience.[45] Society, far from being a homogeneous whole, consists of ongoing conflict between these differing spheres and their languages of justification. (The characteristic values of family life, for example—personal attachments, cross-generational obligations, work that is hard to measure and quantify—collide with those of the office or the factory floor.) As people move between these differing worlds and adjudicate their claims, they must engage in acts of assessment, justification, and disputation. Critical thinking, in this light, is rooted in the everyday lives of individuals negotiating their relationship to competing spheres of value. There is no presumption here that the nature of ordinary language gets in the way of such thinking. "The social world," declares Boltanski, "does not appear to be the site of domination endured passively and unconsciously, but instead a space shot through by a multiplicity of disputes, critiques, disagreements."[46] In a spin on Raymond Williams's comment that "culture is ordinary," we can say that for Boltanski and Thévenot "critique is ordinary."

We might wonder why these practices of arguing and questioning need to be dubbed critique—as if the only way for scholars to take such practices seriously is to slap an honorific academic label on them. Why redescribe everyday language as a form of critique when "critique" is not a term of everyday language? Here, however, we must give the vagaries of translation their due; *critiquer* includes both critique *and* criticism, even though the English translation must resolve this ambiguity in a specific direction. What is attractive about this line of thought, in any event, is its more capacious and democratic vision of what counts as thoughtful reflection. This is not to lapse into the populist mind-set that sometimes afflicts cultural studies: the contention that "ordinary people" are inherently savvier, sharper, more intuitive, more authentic, or more radical than the academics who write about them. (A weirdly self-hating and self-canceling form of argument!) It is rather to think of theory not as a fundamental estrangement from ordinary language but as being in dialogue with ordinary language: to reject the premise of a radical asymmetry between academic and everyday thought. Is it not time to ditch the dog-in-the-manger logic of a certain style of argument—where scholars assign to themselves the vantage point of the tireless and vigilant thinker while refusing to extend this same capacity to those unreflecting souls of whom they speak?

4. *Critique comes from below.* Negative judgments can come from many different sources, but not all these sources seem equally salient to our topic. Take the examples of a father reproving his misbehaving child, the politician lamenting the shortsighted interests of her constituents, the teacher taking a red pen to the errors of his students. Why does the term "critique" not seem quite right here? No doubt because we think of critique as emanating from below, as a blow against authority rather than the exercise of authority. In his essay "What Is Critique?" Foucault draws out this association of critique with the struggle against subjugation. The critical attitude, he argues, arises as a response to new forms of regulation that emerge in the fifteenth and sixteenth centuries, while also connecting back to the religious attitudes and spiritual struggles of the Middle Ages. It is an expression of the desire not to be governed, or at least not to be governed quite so much. Critique is iconoclastic in spirit; it rails against authority; it seeks to lay bare the injustices of the law. It assumes an emphatically political as well as moral weight. It is the "art of voluntary insubordination, that of reflected intractability."[47]

Politics and critique are often equated in literary studies and elsewhere. As Kimberly Hutchings points out, the idea of critique as an exemplary politics haunts the history of modern thought.[48] But what kind of politics is being alluded to? And who gets counted as a proponent of critique? The term "conservative critique" is bandied about in the media, yet many scholars in the humanities would balk at such a phrase. The neoconservative pundit who weighs in on the failures of affirmative action is certainly making a political argument, but his discourse, in their eyes, would not qualify as critique. There is, admittedly, a strong strain of conservative cultural thought (*Kulturkritik*) that spurns the degradations of modern capitalism and the tawdriness of the marketplace and turns its face toward the past.[49] But that this strand of thought is usually translated as "cultural criticism" clinches the point: "critique" is a term commonly associated with a progressively oriented politics—one allied, in some way, with the interests of traditionally subordinate groups: the working class, women, racial or sexual minorities. (The precise construal of "in some way" is, as we will see, a source of some contention.)

This vision of critique can be traced back to Marx—who sprinkles the word copiously through his book titles—and is cemented in the tradition of critical theory associated with the Frankfurt School. In a well-known essay written in the 1930s, Max Horkheimer defines "Critical Theory" in opposition to what he calls "Traditional Theory"—by which he means the narrowly focused, "can't see the woods for the trees" research of stereotypical academics holed up in their offices or laboratories. Burying their heads in the sand, the specialists collating arcane scraps of knowledge are oblivious to their position in a larger capitalist system. By contrast, Horkheimer contends that critical theory "has society itself as its object." Rather than striving to better the functioning of elements in the structure, it aims to question the very existence of the structure. Critique is, in short, an openly committed form of scholarship that makes no pretense to neutrality, objectivity, or detachment. Critical theory aims not just at an increase in knowledge but, as Horkheimer declares with a dash of brio, at "man's emancipation from slavery."[50]

We see here a vision of critique that will inspire a subsequent history of literary and cultural studies—not just its Marxist variants but a spectrum of political approaches, from feminism to cultural studies, from queer theory to postcolonialism. Cultural studies, for example, often champions the popular music and movies that Horkheimer and Adorno excoriate, but it holds fast to two key tenets of critical theory: a claim to offer a comprehensive view of society and a casting of politics in the register of opposition.[51] Critique, its advocates insist, transcends the narrow purview of the disciplines; it reaches beyond the plodding positivism of the social sciences as well as the belletristic chitchat of traditional criticism. What interests critique is the big picture, a.k.a. the political picture. Scoffing at specializations, disdaining conventional divisions of thought, critique connects the dots by bringing together what has been artificially separated.

There is also a political epistemology built into the idea of critique: a conviction that those at odds with the status quo see better and farther than others. While society's defenders reel off the reasons why we live in the best of all possible worlds, practitioners of critique skewer this bad faith and expose its naked self-interest. Their advocacy of resistance springs from a sharpened consciousness of the insufficiencies and injustices of the present. According to David Couzens Hoy, "Critique is what makes it possible to distinguish emancipatory resistance from resistance that has been co-opted by the repressive forces."[52] In this sense, critique is not just a tool but a weapon, not just a form of knowledge but a call to action.

But who gets to claim the mantle of opposition? And how is critique's status as a discourse of intellectuals (point 3) to be reconciled with its claims to emanate "from below" (point 4)? These questions have acquired fresh urgency in recent decades, thanks to the changing demographics of the academy and the explosion of new fields of research. In the US academy especially, fields ranging from African American and women's studies to postcolonial studies and queer theory have been drawn to critique. It is often a premise of such fields that the subjugated knowledges of the disenfranchised alienate them from the status quo, offering them a unique vantage point of critical insight and skeptical judgment. There is what seems like a natural flow or progression from the experience of marginality to the espousal of certain styles of thinking and reading. Critique is authorized by being rooted in the experiences of those who have been historically deprived of authority: the traditions of vernacular suspicion noted in chapter 1.

To those outside of academia, however, critique may look like a somewhat different creature: one whose claims to speak from below are overshadowed by its debt—in language, rhetoric, and method of argument—to scholarly conventions and academic idioms (a.k.a. "professional suspicion"). Such idioms, with their connotations of expert knowledge and accompanying status, can inspire feelings of resentment and trigger complaints of being inaccessible or irrelevant to larger communities of the oppressed. Wendy Brown and Janet Halley observe that

> critique is variously charged with being academic, impractical, merely critical, unattuned to the political exigencies at hand, intellectually indulgent, easier than fixing things or saying what is to be done—in short,

either ultraleftist or ultratheoretical, but in either case without purchase on or in something called the Real World.[53]

These words call to mind a history of often rancorous disputes between feminist theorists and a broader women's movement, as well as the more recent standoffs between activists campaigning for gay marriage and a vanguard of queer theorists opposed to such attempts—as they see it—to normalize dissident sexualities. No doubt complaints about the out-of-touch logic of critique echo especially loudly in the fields of legal and political studies where Halley and Brown are located—fields where academics are more likely to run a gauntlet of impatient activists and campaigners. But the question of the larger political payoff of critique is posed, if anything, even more poignantly in literary studies, where it is often far from evident how a postcolonial reading of Jane Austen published in an undersubscribed academic journal has much bearing on the global struggles to which it alludes.

In a well-known essay, Nancy Fraser remarks that critical theory possesses a "partisan though not uncritical identification" with oppositional social movements.[54] On the one hand, its commitments are unashamedly political; critical theory, she declares, channeling the well-known words of Marx, "is the self-clarification of the struggles and wishes of the age."[55] On the other hand, as underscored by Fraser's insertion of the phrase "not uncritical," critique also guards its independence and reserves the right to query the actions and attitudes of the oppressed as well as the oppressors. Its ability to say no to the world, to refuse obligations and affiliations, to carve out a space of negative freedom, remains vital to its own sense of mission. Critique, in this sense, is the quintessential form of unhappy consciousness, forever torn between its intellectual and its broader political allegiances.

This sense of being divided or torn plays itself out with special vigor in literary and cultural studies. On the one hand, as we have noted, critique can inspire passionate affinities and call into being groups and collectivities that did not previously exist. Not only did it help pave the way for new fields of study organized around race, gender, and sexuality—where urgent questions could be posed and texts read afresh—but it also drew scholars into intellectual communities where ideas were debated, books recommended, and syllabi shared.

Critique not only "detaches from" but also "connects to." Pitting one-self against common obstacles is a powerful way of forging connection and friendship; a sense of solidarity arises out of a shared experience of struggling against antagonists and oppressors. The distinction between friend and enemy, as Chantal Mouffe insists, lies at the very heart of the political.

At the same time, these intellectual communities often cast a skeptical or jaundiced gaze at more popular forms of minority expression. Thanks to the models of language current in literary and cultural theory, forms of ordinary self-understanding are often held to be laden with metaphysical residues and essentialist assumptions. In a thoughtful essay, for example, Sue-Im Lee describes the ratcheting up of critique in Asian American studies to question the very success of Asian American fiction—now seen as a sign of its pandering to middlebrow expectations and dominant US values. Popular novels by Maxine Hong Kingston, Amy Tan, and others are reproached for en-dorsing a "vision of normative progress toward wholeness"; the very deployment of a language of Asian-American identity is seen as a sign of complicity vis-à-vis prevailing regimes of thought. Any affiliation with a broader minority community here collides with the intellec-tual's allegiance to the principle of critique, which triggers more pas-sionate and intensely felt attachments.

How, then, can critique reconcile its intellectual commitments with its political claims to speak "from below"? One increasingly favored strategy is to shift from specific others to a general or abstract prin-ciple of otherness—as exemplifying whatever is repressed, marginal, and therefore noncomplicit with power. For example, the language of "radical alterity" has come to the fore in poststructuralist thought, as a way of countering the potentially paralyzing effects of negativity and skepticism. Ewa Ziarek defines and defends this notion of alterity as encompassing whatever lies beyond the scope of Enlightenment thought and a subject-centered philosophy. There is, for Ziarek, a vital affinity between this "other" of reason and the works of such writers as Beckett, Kafka, and Gombrowicz.[56] Alterity turns out to be a con-cept well suited to the study of literary texts and especially the more enigmatic, opaque, or haunting works of literary modernism—those defined by a linguistic intricacy and allusiveness that escapes definitive interpretation.

This appeal to a nonspecific otherness can give critique a shot in the arm, infusing it with a powerful dose of energy and ethical substance. Like the leftist tradition of utopian thought to which it bears obvious affinities, it holds open the possibility of a radically different future. One risk of fixating on the "radically other" and vesting one's hopes in a "future to come," however, is rendering whatever currently exists as simply more of the same. If we stare for too long at the bright patch of sky, our eyes struggle to readjust to our immediate surroundings; dazzled by the light, we no longer perceive distinct objects but only a vague and confused blur. In like fashion, a rhetoric of radical otherness can blind us to the differences, variations, contradictions, and possibilities in social conditions as we find them. The multiple hues of the present are flattened into a monotone shade of gray.

What, in this light, should we make of the often-heard complaints about the "domestication" of critique? The phrase is striking because it suggests that critique was once wild and untamed—a gaunt, hungry wolf roaming across the tundra, its eyes gleaming in the darkness. Displaced from the wilderness to the feminine space of the domus, it has traded freedom for food and been made docile and biddable by human contact. A domesticated critique is a critique that is defanged. The reproachful ring of the phrase stems from a still-resonant ideal of the critic as a vagabond and outsider, living a life of heroic unpredictability away from the obligations and compromises of the mainstream. It captures the ideal of what Bruce Robbins calls a "roving, unattached criticism" that steers clear of entangling or compromising loyalties.[57]

Robbins takes aim at this myth of the unattached critic, suggesting that a programmatic animus toward institutions, combined with a misguided embarrassment about their status as professionals, has hindered scholars from thinking clearly about the politics of intellectual work—a politics that will, of necessity, take place within structures of higher education rather than outside them. The ethos of critique, I've been suggesting, often encourages this conviction that connection is synonymous with co-option and that social and institutional bonds are signs of bondage—a conviction that often remains in place even while critique is being called into question. In a recent essay, for example, Robyn Wiegman assails the hopes of American studies scholars (including her former self) who see their solidarity with oppressed groups as some kind of challenge to the status quo. The performance of such a critical stance, she points out, has become virtually obligatory for those anxious to appear in the pages of *Critical Inquiry* or *American Quarterly*. In other words, the appeal of progressive scholars to a political principle *outside* their academic field only confirms the extent of their immersion *within* this field and their co-option by its professional norms and values. In the language used by Wiegman, the scholar's performance of a stance of "critical non-complicity" both cements and conceals her actual complicity—not just with the conventions of an academic discipline but also with the larger structures of economic and political injustice that sustain them. Suspicion gives way to metasuspicion, critique to the critique of critique.[58]

At issue here, I would suggest, is the ultimate traction of critique's spatial metaphors and consequent political vision: the categories of outside and inside, center and margin, complicit and noncomplicit. As long as such categories remain in place, the critic is destined to ping-pong between moments of hubristic defiance and crestfallen despair. The defiant proclamations of critique, once they are embraced, reproduced, and disseminated, are automatically downgraded and devalued as a sign of co-option. Whatever looks like success is a sign of failure; that particular ways of thinking are widely adopted and institutionally ratified only confirms that they were not radical enough to begin with. As a result, critique finds itself caught in a logic of constant self-excoriation, reproaching itself for the shame of its own success in attracting disciples and generating attachments. It is permanently tormented by the fear of not being critical enough.

The elaboration of an alternative framework must await the next chapter, but it will take its inspiration from Latour's observation that "emancipation does not mean 'freed from bonds,' but *well*-attached."[59] In this line of thought, we are always already entangled, mediated, connected, interdependent, intertwined; the language of "exteriority" and "noncomplicity" expresses not just an unrealized idea but a fun-

damentally unrealizable one. Some of these bonds prove more helpful or enabling than others, and some mediations may empower while
others limit or constrain, but the condition of being "linked in" is not
an option. Nor can we come to grips with the workings of institutions
by portraying them as purely coercive structures, with all attempts at
change waved away as reformist illusions—a form of thinking that
clings, as Mouffe remarks, to a remarkably essentialist view of institutions.[60] What is needed, in short, is a politics of relation rather than
negation, of mediation rather than co-option, of alliance and assem-
bly rather than alienated critique.

5. *Critique does not tolerate rivals.* Critique often chafes at the presence of other forms of thought, whose deficiencies it spells out in emphatic tones. Unwilling to admit the possibility of peaceful coexistence or even mutual indifference, it concludes that those who do not
embrace its tenets must therefore be denying or disavowing them.
In this manner, whatever is different from critique is turned into a
photographic negative of critique—evidence of a shameful lack or culpable absence. To refuse to be critical is to be uncritical; a judgment
whose overtones of naïveté, bad faith, and quietism seem impossible
to shrug off. In this line of thinking, critique is not one path but the
only conceivable path. Drew Milne pulls no punches in his programmatic riff on Kant: "To be postcritical is to be uncritical: the critical
path alone remains open."[61]

Joan Scott also rallies to the defense of critique, which she sees as
being threatened by an increasingly conservative academic climate.
As evidence of this conservatism she cites a growing eclecticism—
that is to say, a tendency among scholars to draw on diverse methodologies, including empirical ones, rather than rally around the flag
of poststructuralism. This shift, she ventures, is a defensive strategy
adopted by younger scholars to placate their elders rather than a sign
of any genuine weariness with a hermeneutics of suspicion. Scott takes
pains to emphasize that she is not opposed to change or the cross-
pollination of intellectual vocabularies. She contends, nevertheless,
that such eclecticism, thanks to its refusal to address theoretical or
political conflict, can only be "conservative and restorative." Urging a
return to the practice of rigorous interrogation epitomized by decon-

struction and poststructuralism, Scott concludes that the role of critique is "to unsettle received wisdom and so provide an irritant that leads to unforeseen ideas and new understanding."[62]

Scott and Milne are in distinguished company; over the years, many scholars have swooped in to champion critique as the only way of carving out a space of freedom from forces pressing in from all sides. Appealing to Nietzsche and Marx as guiding lights, Paul Bové declares that a criticism that does not engage in rhetorical and institutional critique "is the worst sort of metaphysics." Those fail to practice this style of critique, he warns, render themselves useful to the dominant social order, though most "liberal educators and critics serve a function of which they are at best only partially aware."[63] They are, not to put too fine a point on it, stooges of the status quo.

Here again, we see the halo effect of critique, its radiant promise of political as well as intellectual legitimacy. In consequence, even those most disenchanted with critique seem unable, finally, to wriggle free of its grip. The British sociologist Michael Billig, for example, casts a jaundiced eye on the current state of his discipline. He points out that critique thinks of itself as battling orthodoxy yet is now the reigning orthodoxy—no longer oppositional but obligatory, not defamiliarizing but oppressively familiar. "For an increasing number of young academics," he remarks, "the critical paradigm is the major paradigm in their academic world."[64] Unlike their elders, who turned to critique in order to break free of the disciplinary norms they had inherited, these younger scholars have spent their intellectual lives deconstructing, interrogating, and speaking Foucauldian.

How, then, can scholars cast off this mantle of compulsive criticality? What alternatives could we imagine? What new dispositions or methods might we embrace? The solution proposed by Billig is a "critique of the critical." Critique, in other words, is not to be abandoned but intensified; critique is to be replaced by critique squared. If critique is diagnosed as the problem, how can it also be hailed as the solution? The problem with critique, it turns out, is that *it is not yet critical enough.* That is to say, the guiding values of critique—the merits of interrogating and cross-examining, the single-minded pursuit of the guilty, and the conviction that "no sign is innocent"—remain in place. These tenets, however, are now turned on critique itself in order to lament its transformation into a shopworn convention and a pedagogical cliché. The objections to critique are still part and parcel of the critique-world; the value of the critical is questioned only to be emphatically reinstated.

Similar issues emerge in a recent debate on the question "Is Critique Secular?" While postcolonial studies has served as a major arena of critique, it has also fielded some important challenges to a rhetoric of demystification that is ill equipped to engage the religious commitment and consciousness of most of the world's populations. Talal Asad, for example, expounds persuasively on the corrosive and colonialist dimensions of critique, citing its ignorance of faith, its disdain for piety, its inability to enter imaginatively into a lived experience of the sacred. "Like iconoclasm and blasphemy," he observes, "secular critique also seeks to create spaces for new truth, and, like them, it does so by destroying spaces that were occupied by other signs."[65] Critique, he contends, has become doxa, bolstering the West's sense of its superiority vis-à-vis non-Western cultures mired in dogmatic faith (the occasion of the debate was a response to the furor over the Danish cartoons lampooning the prophet Mohammed). Asad points out that critique is now a quasi-automatic stance for Western intellectuals, promoting a smugness of tone that can be harshly dismissive of the deeply felt beliefs and attachments of others. He writes: "I am puzzled as to why one should want to isolate and privilege 'critique' as a way of apprehending truth."[66] And yet Asad concludes his compelling argument by calling for a critique of critique—reinvoking the concept that his essay has so painstakingly dismantled.

Why do these various protestations against critique end up re-embracing critique? Why does it seem so excruciatingly difficult to conceive of other ways of arguing, reading, and thinking? We may be reminded of Eve Sedgwick's comments on the mimetic aspect of suspicious interpretation: its success in encouraging imitation and repetition. It is an efficiently running form of intellectual machinery, modeling a style of thought that is immediately recognizable, widely applicable, and easily teachable. Critique is contagious and charismatic, drawing us into its field of force, marking the boundaries of what counts as serious thought, so that the only conceivable response to the limits of critique seems to be the piling up of yet more critique.

Casting the work of the scholar as a never-ending labor of distancing, deflating, and diagnosing, critique rules out the possibility of a different relationship to one's object. It seems to grow, as Sedgwick puts it, "like a crystal in a hypersaturated solution, blotting out any sense of the possibility of alternative ways of understanding *or* things to understand."[67]

In consequence, other ways of reading are presumed, without further ado, to be sappy and starry-eyed, compliant and complacent. A substantial tradition of modern thought that has circumvented or challenged the logic of critique—ranging from the work of Wittgenstein, Cavell, and Polanyi to more recent avatars such as Latour and Rancière—drops out of sight. We are led to believe that the only alternative to critique is a full-scale surrender to sentimentality, quietism, Panglossian optimism, or—in literary studies—the intellectual fluff of aesthetic appreciation. In short, critique stacks the cards so that it always wins.

Refusing to participate in this language game would make room for a richer variety of affective as well as intellectual orientations; it would allow us to be surprised by what our colleagues have to say; it would encourage us to pose different questions as well as discover unexpected answers. And here, as Richard Rorty points out, the best way of redirecting an established line of thought is not to take up arms against it (via the technique of "critique") but to come up with inspiring alternatives and new vocabularies. What if we refused to be railroaded into the false choice between the critical and the uncritical? How might argument and interpretation proceed if critique were no longer our ubiquitous watchword and ever-vigilant watchdog? What other shapes of thought could we imagine? And how else might we venture to read, if we were not ordained to read suspiciously?

"Context Stinks!"

"So what are you proposing, then?" The badgering voices can no longer be ignored. No more hedging—an end to equivocation! If we abstain from critique, if we swear to renounce the temptations of suspicion, what stars will guide our path? And what will save us from perdition, what will keep us from committing all those sins we've been warned against since we were bright-eyed neophytes: naïve reading, sentimental effusion, impressionistic judgment, fuzzy-headed amateurism, and mere "chatter about Shelley"? Can we be postcritical—as distinct from uncritical?

Eve Sedgwick's essay, we will recall, contrasts paranoid reading to "reparative reading"—a stance that looks to a work of art for solace and replenishment rather than viewing it as something to be interrogated and indicted. In recent years, various critics have explored the possibility of a more affirmative or engaged aesthetic response. Michael Snedeker, for example, offers a stirring defense of optimism against the fixation on melancholia, shame, and self-shattering in queer theory, striving to rescue the idea of happiness from reflexive imputations of naïveté and complacency. Lamenting the "grim seriousness that passes for high theory," Doris Sommer affirms the importance of the play drive and the broad-based seductions of art as a way of inspiring and sustaining civic engagement. Meanwhile, there is talk of a broader "eudaimonic turn" in literary studies: a disenchantment with disenchantment and a new willingness to embrace such themes as joy, hope, love, optimism, and inspiration.[1]

Little is gained from a shift in sensibility, however, if prevailing world pictures and modes of argument remain intact. Mood is not synonymous with method, even though it has implications for method. As Sedgwick notes, suspicious reading is a strong theory that risks tautology in its determination to find its own bleak prognoses confirmed over and over again. What would a less strong theory look like—one that leaves room for the aleatory and the unexpected, the chancy and the contingent? That does not trace textual meaning back to an opaque and all-determining power, while presuming the critic's immunity from the weight of this ubiquitous domination? Such a framework would need to clarify how agency is distributed among a larger cohort of social actors; to refuse dichotomies of inside versus outside, transgression versus containment; and to more fully acknowledge the coimplication and entanglement of text and critic. Rethinking critique, in this sense, also means rethinking our familiar ideas of context.

"Context stinks!" declares Bruno Latour in his book *Reassembling the Social*, channeling the words of the architect Rem Koolhaas: "It's a way of stopping the description when you are too tired or lazy to go on."[2] Latour's challenge to sociological thinking is also a provocation to those literary and cultural critics who have placed their bets on the explanatory force of the C-word. Admittedly, context has often been queried in literary studies, whether we think of the Russian formalist case for the autonomy of literary form or Gadamer's insistence that the work of art is never just a historical artifact. And in recent decades, deconstructive critics have assailed any notion of history or context as a stable ground. Not only are our ideas about what counts as relevant context steered by rhetorical devices, not only do we pluck certain contexts out of the air while ignoring countless others, but such attempts at explanation, they contend, spring from a misguided desire to nail down a final or ultimate meaning.

And yet these arguments have had little success in halting the tsunami of context-based criticism. One reason, perhaps, is that the questioning of context can convey a fastidiousness of tone that squares poorly with the democratic ambitions of contemporary thought. Scholars sometimes draw a firm line between "exceptional texts" that exceed or speak beyond their historical moment and "conventional" or "stereotypical" texts that remain trapped within it—a distinction that can seem empirically tenuous as well as theoretically dubious. Alternatively, the repudiation of context can result in a single-minded fixation on details of language and style that seems overly precious and rarefied, too far removed from the messy, mundane realities of how and why we read. (That a questioning of context, done differently, allows for *greater* attention to such realities will be one of the counterintuitive claims of this chapter. It is not just the work of art that is shortchanged when a description ends too soon but also everything that surrounds it.)

Critics thus find themselves zigzagging between dichotomies of text versus context, word versus world, internalist versus externalist explanations of works of art. Literary studies seem destined to swing between these two ends of the pendulum, with opposing sides rehashing the same arguments. "How absurdly naïve and idealistic you are!" scold the contextualizers. "Your myopic focus on the words on the page blinds you to the inescapable impact of social and ideological forces!" "How reductive and ham-fisted you are!" retort the formalists. "Sermonize about social energies or patriarchal ideologies until you turn blue in the face, but your theories of context are tone-deaf to what makes a painting a painting, a poem a poem!" There are different historicisms and many types of politics, to be sure, but the task of doing justice to the distinctiveness of art works is a recurring thorn in their flesh. Jean-Paul Sartre's quip that Valéry was a petit-bourgeois intellectual but that not every petit-bourgeois intellectual was Valéry retains its power to sting. And yet we know perfectly well that art works are not heaven-sent, that they do not glide like angels over earthly terrain, that they cannot help getting their shoes wet and their hands dirty. How, then, can we do justice to both their singularity and their sociability, their distinctiveness and their wordliness?

It is here that actor-network theory offers another view of works of art *and* of the social constellations in which they are embedded. It is no longer a matter of championing text over context, or vice versa, but of rethinking the fundaments of analysis. In this chapter, then, I draw on insights from actor-network-theory to lever the following propositions.

1. *History is not a box*—that is to say, standard ways of thinking about historical context are unable to explain how works of art move across time. We need models of textual mobility and transhistorical attachment that refuse to be browbeaten by the sacrosanct status of period boundaries.

2. Literary texts can be usefully thought of as *nonhuman actors*—a claim that, as we'll see, requires a revision of common assumptions about the nature of agency. A text's ability to make a difference, in this line of thought, derives not from its refusal of the world but from its many ties to the world.

3. These ideas lead, finally, to a notion of *postcritical reading* that can better do justice to the transtemporal liveliness of texts and the coconstitution of texts and readers—without opposing thought to emotion or divorcing intellectual rigor from affective attachment.

HISTORY IS NOT A BOX

After a long period of historically oriented scholarship, scholars of literature and art are returning to aesthetics, beauty, and form. Are we not missing something crucial, they ask, when we treat works of art as nothing more than cultural symptoms of a historical moment, as moribund matter immured in the past? In recent decades, there has been much talk of a New Aestheticism, a New Formalism, a return to beauty—signs of a readiness to embrace once-taboo topics.[3] And yet this wave of criticism shows scant interest in the puzzle of how texts resonate across time. Focusing on formal devices or the phenomenology of aesthetic experience, it simply brackets rather than resolves the problem of temporality. We cannot close our eyes to the historicity of art works, and yet we sorely need alternatives to seeing them as transcendentally timeless on the one hand and imprisoned in their moment of origin on the other.

The flimsiness of our temporal frameworks can be contrasted to the rich resources available for conceptualizing space. Postcolonial studies, especially, has transformed our ways of thinking about how ideas, texts, and images migrate. Challenging notions of the discrete, self-contained spaces of nation or ethnicity, scholars have developed a rich language of translation, creolization, syncreticism, and global flows. Similar models might help us explore the mystery of transmission across time. Why is it that we can feel solicited, buttonholed, stirred up, by words that were drafted eons ago? How can texts that are inert in one historical moment become newly revealing, eye-opening, even life-transforming, in another? And how do such flashes of transtemporal connection and unexpected illumination cut against the grain of the progress narratives that drive the rhetoric of critique?

Postcolonial studies, to be sure, troubles our models of time as well as space by messing up the tidiness of periodizing categories, showing how historical schemes often prop up the complacency of a West-centered viewpoint. The task of "provincializing Europe," in Dipesh Chakrabarty's well-known phrase, invites us to rethink, from the ground up, how we historicize and contextualize, and to what end. A similar restiveness with historicism is beginning to make itself felt across the spectrum of literary studies. Though we cannot as yet speak of a posthistoricist school, a multitude of minor mutinies and small-scale revolts are under way, triggered by scholars mulling the question of "time after history." Queer theorists call for an "unhistoricism" open to the affinities between earlier times and our own that does not blanch at proximity and anachronism. Scholars of the Renaissance are reclaiming the term "presentist" as a badge of honor rather than a dismissive jibe, unabashedly confessing their interest in the present-day relevance rather than the historical resonance of Shakespeare's plays. Literary critics advertise their conversion to the iconoclastic work of Michel Serres, who urges us to think of time not as a straight arrow but as an undulating snake or even a crumpled handkerchief. And in the background hovers the beatific figure of Walter Benjamin, the patron saint of all those wary of periodizing schemes, chrononological containment, and progressive histories.[4]

These arguments all take issue with the prevailing picture of context as a kind of historical container in which individual texts are encased and held fast. The historicist critic assigns to the period-box a list of attributes—economic structure, political ideology, cultural mentality—in order to finesse the details of how they are manifest in a specific work of art. This work may be afforded a "relative autonomy," but only in relation to a larger field of forces. This macrolevel holds the cards, calls the tune, and specifies the rules of the game; the individual work, as a microunit encased within a larger whole, can only react or respond to these preestablished conditions. History, in this light, consists of a vertical pile of neatly stacked boxes—what we call periods—each of which surrounds, sustains, and subsumes a microculture. Understanding a text means clarifying the details of its placement in the box, highlighting the correlations and causalities between text-as-object and context-as-container.

New Historicism, to be sure, has struggled mightily against the iron grip of the text/context distinction. Testifying, in an oft-cited phrase, to the historicity of texts and the textuality of history, it strives to muddy and muddle the boundaries between word and world. Works of art, in a New Historicist argument, no longer loom like mighty monuments against a historical backdrop that is materially determining but semiotically inert. Instead, history itself is revealed as a buzzing multiplicity of texts—explorers' diaries, court records, child-rearing manuals, government documents, newspaper editorials—that underwrite the transmission of social energies. By the same token, a literary work does not transcend these humdrum circumstances but remains thoroughly entangled in fine-meshed filaments of power, one more social text among others. It is no longer a matter of treating literature as foreground and context as background, but a systematic leveling of such distinctions.

In a frequently cited phrase from *Shakespearian Negotiations*, Stephen Greenblatt declared his desire to speak with the dead. Much work in the New Historicist vein, however, leans toward diagnosis rather than dialogue, treating texts as historically distant artefacts and underscoring the distance between past texts and present lives, between "then" and "now." Historicism serves as the equivalent of cultural relativism, quarantining difference, denying relatedness, and suspending—or less kindly, evading—the question of why past texts matter and how they speak to us now. It has become a commonplace that we cannot know the past as it really was, that history is always, at least in part, the history of the present. And in their introductions, preambles, and afterwords, scholars testify to their present-day passions and expound on their existential or political commitments. Yet these avowals rarely translate into the testing out of transhistorical methodologies or the tracing of cross-temporal networks. Instead, the literary object remains cooped up in the conditions that preside over the moment of its birth, yoked to other texts, objects, or structures of the same moment, indelibly stamped as an early modern, eighteenth-century, or Victorian artifact. This is the domain of what Wai Chee Dimock calls "synchronic historicism," in which phenomena are stuck fast to neighboring phenomena in the same slice of time.[5]

This "slice of time" approach is a reaction against earlier forms of historical thinking that sought to make sense of the past via a single sweeping story—usually a story of inexorable improvement headed by a collective agent such as Western civilization, the human spirit, or the working class. Such stories—what in the heyday of postmodernism were called "grand narratives"—cannot help but simplify and distort the relations among past events, while relegating most of humanity to the sidelines and backwaters of history. The backlash against such historical narratives, however, has had less happy consequences: any form of cross-temporal thinking—tainted by the guilt of association—has fallen out of favor. Instead, we are inculcated, in the name of history, into a remarkably static view of meaning, where texts are corralled amidst long-gone contexts and obsolete intertexts, incarcerated in the past, with no hope of parole.

For Latour, by contrast, there is no historical box and no society, if we mean by this term a bounded totality governed by a predetermined set of structures and functions. Society does not stand behind and steer human practices, as if it were outside of and ontologically distinct from these practices, akin to a shadowy, all-seeing, puppet master. Rather, what Latour calls the social is just the act and the fact of association, the coming together of phenomena to create assemblages, affinities, and networks. It exists only in its instantiations, in the sometimes foreseeable, sometimes unpredictable ways in which ideas, texts, images, people, and objects couple and uncouple, attach and break apart. We are no longer afforded a panoramic vision of the social order: to do actor-network theory is not to soar like an eagle, gazing down critically or dispassionately at the distant multitudes below, but to trudge along like an ANT, marveling at the intricate ecologies and diverse microorganisms that lie hidden among thick blades of grass. It is to slow down at each step, to forgo theoretical shortcuts and to attend to the words of our fellow actors rather than overriding them—and overwriting them—with our own. The social, in other words, is not a preformed being but a doing, not a hidden entity underlying the realm of appearance but the ongoing connections, disconnections, and reconnections between multiple actors.

These interconnections are temporal as well as spatial; woven out of threads crisscrossing through time, they connect us to what comes before, enmeshing us in extended webs of obligation and influence. Time is not a tidy sequence of partitioned units but a profusion of whirlpools and rapids, eddies and flows, as objects, ideas, images, and texts from different moments swirl, tumble, and collide in ever-changing combinations and constellations. New actors jostle alongside those with thousand-year histories; inventions and innovations feed off the very traditions they excoriate; "the past is not surpassed but revisited, repeated, surrounded, protected, recombined, reinterpreted, and reshuffled."[6] The trick is to think temporal interdependency without telos, movement without supersession: pastness is part of who we are, not an archaic residue, a source of nostalgia, or a return of the repressed. Latour's claim that we have never been modern does not deny that our lives differ in obvious ways from those of medieval peasants or Renaissance courtiers. It insists, nonetheless, that these differences are exaggerated and overdrawn, thanks to our fondness for stories about the disenchantment of the world, the radicalism of modern critique, and other testimonies to our own exceptional status.

Along similar lines, Jonathan Gil Harris takes issue with what he calls a "national sovereignty model of time" that is endemic in literary and cultural studies. The idea of period, he points out, serves much the same function as the idea of nation; we assign texts and objects to a single moment of origin in much the same way as we tether them to their place of birth. Both period and nation serve as a natural boundary, determining authority, and last court of appeal. The literary work, it is assumed, can only be a citizen of only one historical period and one set of social relations; scholars work overtime as border guards, and any movement across period boundaries is heavily policed. The past remains a foreign country, alien and inscrutable, its strangeness repeatedly underscored. "What do we do," Harris wonders, "with things that cross temporal borders—things that are illegal immigrants, double agents, or holders of multiple passports? How might such border crossings change our understanding of temporality?"[7] Cross-temporal networks mess up the tidiness of our periodizing schemes; they force us to acknowledge affinity and proximity as well as difference, to grapple with the coevalness and connectedness of past and present.

This line of thought obviously jars with a Foucauldian criticism that envisions the past as a series of self-contained epistemes, priming the critic to scrutinize the beliefs and attitudes of earlier times with cool-eyed neutrality. Detachment gives way to implication and entanglement. Instead of absolute temporal difference and distance, we have a hotchpotch and rich confusion, a spillage across period boundaries in which we are connected to the historical phenomena we describe. Actor-network theory is equally bemused by a modernist vision of time as a break with the shackles of the benighted past. Not only is the classic model of revolution rendered incoherent by the ubiquity of cross-temporal networks, but so is the ethos of the vanguard—those anointed few who, by dint of their intellectual farsightedness, political convictions, or artistic sensibility, propel themselves out of the swirling mists of confusion and bad faith in which others are immersed. History is not moving forward, and none of us are leading the way.

Why, in short, are we so sure that we know more than the texts that precede us? The advantage of our hindsight is compensated for by their robustness, resilience, and continuing resonance. Their temporality is dynamic, not fixed or frozen; they speak to, but also beyond, their own moment, anticipating future affinities and conjuring up not yet imaginable connections. In a lucid reckoning with historicism, Jennifer Fleissner invites us to read nineteenth-century novels as living thought rather than embodiments of past cultural work, as voices that speak back to our own axioms and convictions.[8] Context does not automatically or inevitably trump text, because the very question of what counts as context and the merits of our explanatory schemes are often anticipated, explored, queried, expanded, or reimagined in the words we read. The detachment of historical explanation is ruffled, even rattled, once we recognize that past texts have things to say on questions that matter to us, including the status of historical thinking.

This busy afterlife of the literary artifact refutes our efforts to box it into a moment of origin, to lock it up in a temporal container. Of course, the moment of a text's birth places obvious limits on theme, form, or genre: we look in vain for signs of modernist spleen in Attic verse, for Dadaist decoupage in eighteenth-century landscapes. And yet these constraints do not rule out possibilities of transtemporal connection and comparison—allowing Karl-Heinz Bohrer, for example, to expand on the echoes and affinities between Baudelairean verse and Greek tragedy across the chasm of historical difference.[9] Texts are objects that do a lot of traveling; moving across time, they run into new semantic networks, new ways of imputing meaning. What Wai Chee Dimock calls "resonance" is this potential to signify and change across time, to accrue new meanings and associations, to trigger unexpected echoes in unexpected places. Resonance, she declares in an important essay, puts the temporal axis at the center of literary studies.[10]

Dimock, to be sure, does not address the role of institutions in influencing literary longevity. Certain texts persist while others fall from view not simply because particular texts resonate with individual readers but also due to structures of gatekeeping and evaluation, of selection and omission. These screening processes, enacted in discussions over what to publish, where to allot marketing funds, or how to revise the undergraduate curriculum, allow some works to circulate more widely than others. From this point of view, transtemporal mobility is at least partly a result of institutional inertia. Citations generate more citations; graduate students go on to teach the texts they were themselves taught; canons—whether of fiction or of theory—reproduce themselves over time. Indeed, even as new texts filter into the classroom and as ways of reading change, it seems impossible to imagine education without some level of baseline continuity and transmission of prior knowledge. But this is only to reinforce what I take to be Latour's fundamental points: that we cannot, by sheer act of will, sever our ties to the past and that the impact of art works—an argument I turn to shortly—depends on their social embedding rather than being opposed to it.

Arguments about what counts as "real" context, moreover, spill well beyond the boundaries of theoretical disputes into the everyday realities of what and how we teach. In English departments, especially, identification with period remains the marker of professional expertise, announced in the books that are footnoted, the conferences attended, the jobs advertised. Everything reinforces the idea that the original historical meaning of a text is its most salient meaning; suspicions of dilettantism hover over those scholars who range across several periods rather than settling down in one. "The period," declares Bruce Robbins, ". . . should perhaps be seen as a sort of pseudo-anthropocentric norm that has been adopted for a long time out of laziness. It is one level of magnification among others, no less valid than any other, but also no less arbitrary."[11] Robbins proposes "genre" as an equally salient category around which to organize the teaching of literature, one that is much more hospitable to theorizing transtemporal connections, repetitions, and translations. There is, in short, no compelling intellectual or practical reason why original context should remain the final authority and the last court of appeal.

To argue for greater attention to transtemporal affinities and connections is not to deny historical differences—any more than the rise of transnational studies implies the disappearance of Poland or Peru. It is, however, to make the case for a less hemmed-in and less rigidly constricted model of meaning that gives texts more room to breathe. Persuaded—for a host of good reasons—that texts are not eternal, universal, or ahistorical, critics have placed all their bets on the time-boundedness of the artwork. The invocation of original context has become an ethical and political duty: a sign that one is on the right side, fighting the good fight against the retrograde ranks of aesthetes and litterateurs mumbling into their sherry glasses.[12] And yet that texts move across time is an everyday intuition reconfirmed whenever we see someone on the subway absorbed in the pages of *Pride and Prejudice* or *The Adventures of Sherlock Holmes*. Art works may not be timeless, but they are indisputably—in their potential to resonate in different moments—time-full.

ART WORKS AS NONHUMAN ACTORS

Some of what I've said so far seems quite consonant with the tradition of Birmingham-style cultural studies. Both cultural studies and actor-network theory are wary of theoretical shortcuts and the temptations of sociological reduction. Both schools of thought insist that phenomena cannot be reduced to epiphenomena of invisible structures, that texts, ideas, and people disconnect and reconnect in differing and often unpredictable ways, and that we cannot know in advance what the political effects of artistic or cultural texts will be.[13] Cultural studies, moreover, puts the act of reception at the heart of its model of culture. In principle, it encourages a polytemporal view of textual meaning as remade over time by new audiences: the performance of *Macbeth* in early seventeenth-century London would thus boast no special priority or privilege compared to the play's many afterlives on the stages of New York or New Delhi, Sydney or Singapore. In practice, however, this infrequently turns out to be the case. As taken up in US literature departments, for example, cultural studies has often encouraged an entrenchment of historicism and a solidifying of "slice of time" approaches, as seen in coinages such as "Victorian cultural studies" or "medieval cultural studies." The transtemporal, in this light, remains a path not taken.

Moreover, the difficulty of context-talk lies not just in a bias toward historical origins but also in its ways of conceiving agency and causality. The cudgel of context is commonly wielded to deprive the artwork of influence or impact, rendering it a puny, enfeebled, impoverished thing. And this tendency is magnified in a cultural studies tradition that sees contextualization as the ultimate virtue. ("For cultural studies, context is everything and everything is contextual," writes Lawrence Grossberg.)[14] Context is inflated, in short, in order to deflate text; while newly magnified social conditions dispose and determine, the art work grows dim and fades from view. We pound home the importance of social fields, discursive regimes, or technologies of power—and yet fail to reckon with the fact that the "artwork is one of the actors involved in the drama of its own making."[15]

Why are the producers or recipients of culture afforded such exceptional powers and the individual text granted virtually none? How much light do such theories shed on why people are willing to drive hundreds of miles to listen to a band playing a certain song, or to spend years in graduate school agonizing over a single novel? The terminology of "cultural capital," "the hegemonic media industry," or "interpretive communities" goes only so far in clarifying why it is this particular tune that plays over and over in our heads, why it is Virginia Woolf alone who becomes an object of obsession. We explicate the puzzle of our attachments by invoking veiled determinations and covert social interests—while paying scant attention to the ways in which these objects solicit our affections, court our emotions, and feed our obsessions.

Of course, the siren calls of *Mrs Dalloway* or "Brown-Eyed Girl" do not echo in a void; no account of their appeal can omit the high school clique that finally convinced you of the genius of Van Morrison, the parents whose rapturous praise of your second-grade assignments propelled you toward graduate school, the vocabularies propagated by *Critical Inquiry* or *Rolling Stone* that gave you a language through which to articulate and justify your obsession. But what exactly do we gain by stripping down the number of agents and influences at play, by boosting the power of "context" at the expense of "text" in the name of some final reduction? Why downplay the role of art works in ensuring their own survival? Why overlook the ways in which they weasel themselves into our hearts and minds, their dexterity in generating attachments?

Perhaps Latour's idea of the nonhuman actor can clear a path. What, first of all, are nonhuman actors? Speed bumps, microbes, mugs, baboons, newspapers, unreliable narrators, soap, silk dresses, strawberries, floor plans, telescopes, lists, paintings, can openers. To describe such disparate phenomena as actors is not to overlook the salient differences between things, animals, texts, and people, nor is it to impute intentions, desires, or purposes to inanimate objects. Rather, an actor, in this schema, is anything that modifies a state of affairs by making a difference. Nonhuman actors do not determine reality or single-handedly make things happen—let us steer well clear of any technological or textual determinism. And yet, as Latour points out, there are "many metaphysical shades between full causality and sheer inexistence," between being the sole source of an action and being utterly inert and without influence.[16] The "actor" in actor-network theory is not a solitary self-governing subject who summons up actions and orchestrates events. Rather, actors only become actors via their relations with other phenomena, as mediators and translators linked in extended constellations of cause and effect.

Nonhuman actors, then, help to modify states of affairs; they are participants in chains of events; they help shape outcomes and influence actions. To acknowledge the input of such actors is to place people, animals, texts, and things on a similar ontological footing by emphasizing their interdependence. Speed bumps, to take Latour's well-known example, cannot entirely prevent you from gunning your car down a suburban street, but the presence of these "sleeping policemen" (as the French call them) makes such acts of derring-do much less likely. The literary device of the unreliable narrator can always be overlooked or misunderstood—and yet it has also schooled countless readers in how to read against the grain and between the lines. The salience of speed bumps or storytelling techniques derives from their distinctive properties, their nonsubstitutable qualities—all of which go by the board if they are dissolved into a larger social theory and seen only as bearers of predetermined functions. If a single cause is used to explain a thousand different effects, we are left no wiser about the nature of these effects. To treat the relationship between silk and nylon as an allegory for divisions between upper- and lower-class taste, as Latour writes in a dig at Bourdieu-style sociology, is to reduce these phenomena to illustrations of an already established scheme, to bypass the indefinite yet fundamental nuances of color, texture, shimmer, and feel that inspire attachments to one fabric or the other.[17] Silk and nylon, in other words, are not passive intermediaries but active mediators; they are not just channels for conveying predetermined meanings but compose and configure these meanings in specific ways.

Here we might note the idea of "affordance"—a word gaining traction in literary studies to help explain how meanings are coconstituted by texts and readers. Coined by the psychologist James J. Gibson to explain how animals interact with their environment, affordance offers a helpful way of thinking about the properties of a substance in relation to those who make use of them (thus a knee-high surface, for example, affords the possibility of "sitting-on").[18] Especially salient for the present argument is that affordance is neither subjective nor objective but arises out of the interaction between beings and things. C. Namwali Serpell has recently picked up on this idea to discuss the experience of reading in ways that account for the agency of both texts and readers, for the tension between "measurable form and experiential dynamism." Like buildings, literary works "make available" certain options for moving through them, and yet these possibilities are also taken up in wildly varying ways by empirical readers.[19]

What would it mean, then, to acknowledge poems and paintings, fictional characters and narrative devices, as actors?[20] How might our thinking change? Clearly, the bogeyman in the closet is a tradition of high-minded aestheticism—the fear that acknowledging the agency of texts will tip us back into the abyss of a retrograde religion of art and allow a thousand Blooms to flower. Once we start talking about the power of art to make us think and feel differently, can the language of eternal transcendence and the timeless canon be far behind? "Every sculpture, painting, haute cuisine dish, techno-rave and novel," remarks Latour, "has been explained to nothingness by the social factors hidden behind them. . . . And here again, as always, some people, infuriated by the barbarous irreverence of social explanations, come forth and defend the inner sanctity of the work against barbarians."[21] From the standpoint of actor-network theory, as we are starting to see, neither perspective holds water. The glory of the "text" is not to be defended by rescuing it from the slavering jaws of "context." There is no zero-sum game in which one side must be crushed so that the other can triumph. We are no longer held captive by the vision—sentimental and blood-stirring, but hopelessly off target!—of a no-holds-barred battle between David and Goliath: where poems and paintings resist the social order or, if we lean toward pessimism, are co-opted by the nefarious forces that surround them.

The ANT viewpoint, then, is rather different: that art's distinctive qualities do not rule out social connections but are the very reason that such connections are forged and sustained. There never was an isolated self-contained aesthetic object to begin with; left to its own devices, this object would have long since sunk into utter oblivion rather than coming to our attention. Art works can only survive and thrive by making friends, creating allies, attracting disciples, inciting attachments, latching on to receptive hosts. If they are not to fade quickly from view, they must persuade people to hang them on walls, watch them in movie theaters, purchase them on Amazon, dissect them in reviews, recommend them to their friends. These networks of alliances, relations, and translations are just as essential to experimental art as to blockbuster fiction, even if what counts as success looks radically different.

The number and length of these networks prove far more salient to a text's survival than matters of ideological agreement. If you are an unrepentant avant-gardist making installations out of soiled diapers and statues of the Virgin Mary, your allies are not just the respectful review in the pages of *Artforum* but also the conservative pundit who invokes your example to lambast the state of contemporary art, amping up its visibility and talked-aboutness and generating a flurry of commentary, a slot on National Public Radio, and, a few years down the road, an edited collection of essays. Romantic visions of solitary subversion make it easy to forget that rupture vanishes without trace if it is not registered, acknowledged, and mediated—that is to say, made the object of new attachments and connections between actors. Art works must be sociable to survive, irrespective of their attitude to "society."

An indispensable element of this sociability—whatever other factors come into play—is a work's dexterity in soliciting and sustaining attachments. When we join an endlessly snaking line at the movie theater, when we devour the words of James Joyce or James Patterson deep into the night, it is because a certain text—rather than countless possible others—matters to us in some way. Of course, how it matters will differ, and forms of appreciation vary widely; the "questions for discussion" appended to the back of the typical book-club novel may trigger condescending chuckles in the English faculty lounge. But no fans, no enthusiasts, no aficionados—whatever their education or class background—are indifferent to the specialness of the texts they admire.

Still, this specialness is discounted in most current theories of reception, which boost context by downgrading text. The cultural studies scholar Tony Bennett, for example, stresses the power of what he calls "reading formations" or the "discursive and intertextual determinations that organize and animate the practice of reading."[22] How we react to works of art, he argues, is dictated neither by the internal features of the text nor by the raw social demographics of a reader's race, gender, or class but rather by the cultural frameworks we have absorbed. While our reading seems natural, we are nevertheless schooled—via family, education, and cultural milieu—to decode and decipher in certain ways. This line of thought is very helpful in highlighting the ways we absorb styles of interpretation (the practice of critique being, of course, one such "reading formation"). And yet the winner-takes-all logic that dogs contextual thinking leads Bennett to downplay the impact of texts—which, he declares, have no existence "prior to or independently of the varying 'reading formations' in which they have been constituted as objects-to-be read."[23]

This use of the passive voice conveys a view of the inertness and passivity of texts, as ineffectual creatures at the beck and call of external forces. As described here by Bennett, films and novels dissolve into the cultural assumptions and interpretative frameworks of their audiences; mute objects, they possess no force, no heft, no presence of their own. But what of those moments when the impact of a text is unforeseen, when it impinges on us in ways we cannot predict or prepare for? What about the song on the radio that unexpectedly reduces you to tears, the horror movie gore-fest that continues to haunt your dreams, the novel that convinced you to take up Buddhism or to get divorced? For Bennett, as for Stanley Fish, a literary work seems to be a blank screen on which groups of readers project their preexisting ideas and beliefs. We are thus hard-pressed to explain why any text should matter more than any other, why we can register the differences between individual texts so strongly, or how we can be aroused, disturbed, surprised, or brought to act in ways that we did not expect and may find it hard to explain. As Bennett himself acknowledges, the context of the reading formation trumps and transcends the power of the text.

We might note the puzzling dualism in evidence here: the frame of interpretation is taken to be "real"—to possess existential solidity and exceptional social power—whereas the literary text is denied any such reality. The difficult with such a dichotomy is that what counts as text and what serves as frame is more mutable and fluid than Bennett allows. No doubt we learn to make sense of literary texts by being schooled in certain ways of reading; at the same time, we also learn to make sense of our lives by referencing imaginary or fictional worlds. Works of art are not just objects to be interpreted; they also serve as frameworks and guides to interpretation. In this light, it seems impossible to sustain a strong distinction between a determining context and a passive and powerless text, given the ease with which literary works can migrate from one category to the other. Why freeze a single relationship between figure and ground, object and frame? Why not acknowledge that works of art can serve as cultural reference points for interpretation as well as objects to be interpreted?[24] Texts can *generate* criteria as well as be objects of criteria.

In fact, Bennett's practice turns out to be more flexible than some of his theoretical pronouncements might suggest, as we can see in a fascinating book coauthored with Janet Woollacott that grapples with the extraordinary success of the Bond franchise.[25] Why, the authors ask, did the James Bond novels and films sweep to worldwide success? How did they become participants in so many networks, attracting ever more intermediaries, until the entire globe seemed to be saturated with Bond films, paperbacks, advertisements, posters, T-shirts, toys, and paraphernalia? To be sure, the Bond phenomenon was shaped by the vagaries of reception; Fleming's novels, we learn, were associated with a tradition of hard-boiled crime fiction in the United States, while piggybacking on the popularity of the imperial spy thriller in the United Kingdom. But such explanations do not shed much light on why *this* particular series of novels marched toward worldwide visibility and prominence while countless others works of spy fiction languished like wallflowers in the cut-price piles and remainder bins. What was it about the James Bond novels *in particular* that attracted so many allies, fans, devotees, enthusiasts, fantasists, translators, dreamers, advertisers, entrepreneurs, and parodists? Surely their presence made a difference; they attracted coactors; they helped make things happen.

The notion of the nonhuman actor, moreover, assumes no particular measure of scale, size, or complexity. It can include not only individual novels or films but also fictional characters, plot devices, literary styles, filming techniques, and other formal devices that travel beyond the boundaries of their home texts to attract allies, generate attachments, trigger translations, and inspire copies, spin-offs, and clones. We are very far removed, in other words, from a mandarin aestheticism in which texts are sequestered away from the world's hustle and bustle, their individual parts relating only to each other. The appeal of Fleming's imaginary world, Bennett and Woollacott hypothesize, had much to do with his creation of a charismatic protagonist who moved easily into multiple media, times, and spaces and proved adaptable to the interests and emotions of different audiences. Characters from more rarefied milieus can be just as energetic and lively, triggering new connections as they travel across place and time: think of the worldwide enactment of Bloomsday or the long afterlife of Emma Bovary as a still-resonant touchstone for a particular kind of reader.

Most fictional characters, of course, are born only to expire with almost unseemly haste. In his essay "The Slaughterhouse of Literature," Franco Moretti conjures up the desolate reaches of the literary graveyard. Even while some works prove remarkably energetic, leapfrogging across time and space, the vast majority is soon lost from sight—99.5 percent, according to Moretti's estimate, even within the publishing milieu of Victorian England. Why do some texts survive and so many vanish from view? How do we explain the puzzle of durability? For Moretti, the answer lies in the force of form. Tracing the evolution of detective fiction, he argues that the invention of a formal device—namely the technique of the clue—explains the success of Sherlock Holmes and the rapid obsolescence of most of his fictional peers.[26] The clue, in other words, was an effective actor, attracting readers by generating new forms of interpretative pleasure. The reasons for the survival of Holmes were neither random nor purely ideological (if Conan Doyle was an apologist for patriarchal rationality, so, no doubt, were many of his fellow authors whose works vanished without trace). Whether our sample consists of Renaissance plays, modernist poems or Hollywood blockbusters, some examples will prove more mobile, portable, and adaptable to the interests of different audiences than others.

And yet the social makeup, buying power, and beliefs of audiences remain more salient to the equation than Moretti seems willing to concede. A text's formal properties cannot single-handedly control its cross-temporal reach, which pivots on the interplay of numerous factors as well as a hefty dose of serendipity. Literary works go in and out of vogue; what was once indispensable come to seem obsolete and old hat, while works overlooked on their first publication can acquire an energetic, even frenetic, afterlife. The reasons for these shifts are thematic and social as well as formal; that Hemingway's stock has gone down while Kate Chopin accumulates visibility and prestige is hardly a matter of literary devices alone. To reiterate our mantra: texts act not by themselves but with a motley assortment of coactors.

Digesting the implications of this idea means breaking with some of the usual ways of doling out agency via a text/context dichotomy. We have looked askance at the belief that literary works are stealthily engaged in coercing and conning their readers. In such scenarios, texts are awarded Superman-like powers with one hand only to have them whisked away with the other. A novel is charged and found guilty of manufacturing docile bourgeois subjects, but this jaw-dropping achievement turns out to be less impressive than it looks. The text, it turns out, is a reflex of larger systems of power steering the action behind the scenes, occult forces that determine without themselves being determined. In such a scenario, texts turn out to be passive intermediaries rather than active mediators—servile henchmen and obsequious bully boys that are at the beck and call of their shadowy yet omnipotent masters.

The insufficiencies of this scenario, however, should not drive us into the arms of a counteridiom of subversion, resistance, transgression, and rupture—those cardinal virtues of criticality. Literary works are not actors in this rugged, individualist sense, not lonely rebels pitted against an implacable status quo. If they make a difference, they do so only as coactors and codependents, enmeshed in a motley array of attachments and associations. The works that we study and teach—including the most antinomian texts of Beckett or Blanchot, Brecht or Butler—could never come to our attention without the work of countless helpers: publishers, advertisers, critics, prize committees, reviews, word-of-mouth recommendations, syllabi, textbooks and anthologies, changing tastes and scholarly vocabularies, and last, but not least, the passions and predelictions of ourselves and our students.

Some of these mediators, to be sure, may prove to be more helpful, generous, or respectful of their object than others, but the fact of mediation is not a regrettable lapse into complicity or collusion but an indispensable condition of being known. Unbought, unread, uncriticized, untaught, the works we admire would languish in limbo, forever invisible and impotent.

Nothing in this line of argument, moreover, prevents us from taking issue with what a work is saying, quarreling with its ideas, engaging in productive disagreement, whether on political or other grounds. There will certainly be times when a text, even after we have made our best effort to meet it halfway, will strike us as aesthetically uninteresting, politically retrograde, or in bad faith. Things go awry at the level of method, however, when this judgment is held up as sufficient or self-evident proof of a text's oppressive effects. We slide from close readings of works to causal claims about their social impact, as if these two activities were somehow synonymous.[27] Here we are gaining a free ride, as Latour would say, while failing to do the work of tracing the relevant networks, identifying the creation of new assemblies, or gathering empirical evidence for causal arguments. Politics, in the sense developed by actor-network theory, is no longer a matter of gesturing toward the hidden forces that explain everything; it is the process of tracing the interconnections, attachments, and conflicts among actors and mediators as they come into view.

One indispensable link in this chain of mediators is a reader whose response is never entirely predictable or knowable. It is here that literary studies need to steer clear of a vulgar sociology (where a reader is reduced to the sum of her demographical data) as well as of a one-dimensional theory of language (where a reader is a nodal point through which language or discourse flows). Readers are not autonomous, self-contained, centers of meaning, but they are also not mere flotsam and jetsam tossed on the tides of social or linguistic forces that they are helpless to affect or comprehend. When they encounter texts, they do so in all their commonality and quirkiness; they mediate and are in turn mediated, in both predictable and perplexing ways. If we need a sociology of the individual that does not reduce persons to mere effects of pre-existing structures, as Bernard Lahire has proposed,[28] we also need ways of thinking about individual readers that does not flatten and reduce them, that grasps their idiosyncrasy as well as their importance. Texts cannot influence the world by themselves, but only via the intercession of those who read them, digest them, reflect on them, rail against them, use them as points of orientation, and pass them on.

Here we can thank Derek Attridge for his helpful coinage "idioculture," which he defines as follows: "the singular, and constantly changing, combination of cultural materials and proclivities that constitute any individual subject . . . registered as a complex of particular preferences, capabilities, memories, desires, physical habits, and emotional tendencies."[29] The notion of an idioculture, in short, speaks to both the commonality and the uniqueness of personhood, to the labile mix of influences that makes us what we are. That our sense of self is fashioned, in large part, by the people we encounter, the ideas we stumble across, the experiences we embrace or submit to, does not render it any less salient or less real. Personhood is fashioned out of the dynamic push-and-pull of multiple influences rather than the imperious diktat of a single ideology. Even if we are all products of the cultural blender, each mixture of influences, vocabularies, memories, orientations, and temperament possesses a distinct and unmistakable flavor. We make ourselves out of the models we encounter; we give ourselves a form through the different ways we inhabit other forms. And we bring these differences to the event of reading, even as we are reoriented—sometimes subtly, sometime significantly—by the sum of what we read.

POSTCRITICAL READING

The question of reading can no longer be deferred. It is time to connect these comments on the mobility and agency of texts to current debates about interpretation. As we've seen, a number of critics are now casting around for alternatives to the fault-finding mentality of critique. Should we commit ourselves, as Timothy Bewes has argued, to the most generous reading possible, striving to read "with the grain" instead of "against the grain"? Should we be "just readers," as Sharon Marcus proposes, riffing off the double meaning of "just"

("mere readers," as opposed to overconfident theorizers and master-
ful explicators, yet also "ethical readers," seeking to do better justice
to the words we encounter)?[30] Should we resuscitate the notion of a
hermeneutics of trust associated with Ricoeur and Gadamer? Or rally
around Sedgwick's vision of reparative reading?

Hedging my bets, I prefer to stick with the broader term "postcritical reading." One advantage of this phrase lies in its relationship
to prior thought: the postcritical, to underscore the obvious, is not
to be confused with the uncritical. Like others, I find the vagueness
of the term to be also its singular strength, allowing it to serve as a
placeholder for emerging ideas and barely glimpsed possibilities. It is
a term that is gaining traction in various fields to denote pragmatic
and experimental modes of engagement that are not prefortified by
general theories.[31] The role of the term "postcritical," then, is neither
to prescribe the forms that reading should take nor to dictate the attitudes that critics must adopt; it is to steer us away from the kinds of
arguments we know how to conduct in our sleep. These are some of
the things that a postcritical reading will decline to do: subject a text
to interrogation; diagnose its hidden anxieties; demote recognition to
yet another form of misrecognition; lament our incarceration in the
prison-house of language; demonstrate that resistance is just another
form of containment; read a text as a metacommentary on the undecidability of meaning; score points by showing that its categories
are socially constructed; brood over the gap that separates word from
world.

So what does this leave? More than we might imagine. Let us concede, first of all, that a stress on the transtemporal movement of texts
and their lively agency is not entirely alien to the history of interpretation. If actor-network theory is a philosophy of relation, so, in its more
modest way, is hermeneutics, which casts texts and readers as cocre-
ators of meaning. Translated into ANT language, the reader-text connection becomes part of a network rather than a self-enclosed dyad—
yet a connection that remains vital to literary studies, especially in the
classroom. Reading, in this light, is a matter of attaching, collating,
negotiating, assembling—of forging links between things that were
previously unconnected. It is not a question of plumbing depths or
tracing surfaces—these spatial metaphors lose much of their allure—

but of creating something new in which the reader's role is as decisive as that of the text. *Interpretation becomes a coproduction between
actors that brings new things to light rather than an endless rumination
on a text's hidden meanings or representational failures.* Some of these
interpretations will "take" and help to spawn new networks, while
others will plummet out of sight without attracting disciples or generating durable attachments.

We now know that secular interpretation—even in the guise of
critique—has not stripped itself of its sacred residues and that reason
cannot be purified of all traces of enchantment. What of Hermes, then,
the figure often associated with hermeneutics? Hermes is, of course,
the fleet-footed herald and messenger of Greek myth, "the friendliest
of the gods to men."[32] He is the deity of roads, crossroads, thresholds,
boundaries—of translations and transactions across realms. Darting
from place to place, always on the move, he reminds us of the constant shuttling between text and reader, word and world, that defines
the hermeneutic enterprise. He is also the god of the windfall and of
chance—the deity to be thanked when one gets a lucky break or receives an unexpected gift. In this sense, too, he serves as an apt symbol for acts of interpretation—where understanding may come in a
quicksilver flash or an unexpected burst of insight. But Hermes is also
a guileful trickster and a thief, a master of cunning and deceit, a conjuror of illusion. He reminds us of our fallibility and vulnerability and
of the fact that the act of interpretation can make fools of us all.[33]

In 415 BC, the many statues of Hermes scattered throughout
Athens were vandalized in the course of a single night by unknown
perpetrators. This mysterious episode—linked to the murky history
of Athenian religious politics—foreshadows the feverish iconoclasm
of our own time. As we have seen, some critics are keen to knock
Hermes off his pedestal and spray-paint his shrine; they accuse his followers of being in cahoots with a reactionary metaphysics or a totali-
tarian politics. Hermeneutics has been diagnosed, deconstructed,
and denounced. Looking quizzically at this drive to demystify, we
have queried the various efforts to get "beyond" interpretation. Let
us embrace the divinities that watch over our work rather than try
to expunge them! The charismatic powers of Hermes will inspire
our endeavors and give wings to our thoughts. The qualities he em-

bodies—agility, nimbleness, spirited gaiety, mischievousness, ingenuity, mobility of action and thought—are ones we sorely need. Our
enemy is not interpretation as such but the kudzu-like proliferation of
a critical methodology that has crowded out alternative forms of life.
The ANT scholar Adam S. Miller puts it well: "The need for interpretation and translation is not the mark of a fallen world, it is the substance of life. To live is to interpret."[34]

There are no grounds, then, for concluding that interpretation is
at odds with actor-network theory. To be sure, Latour has no time for
a hermeneutic philosophy that brags about the interpretative ingenuity of the human subject vis-à-vis a mute and inert object world.
It is not a matter of rejecting interpretation, however, but of extending it: "Hermeneutics is not a privilege of humans, but, so to speak, a
property of the world itself."[35] That is to say, many different kinds of
entities are engaged in communicating, mediating, signaling, translating; the world is not a dead zone of reification but is as rife with ambiguity as any modernist poem. And yet, within this expanded frame,
how humans respond to poems or paintings still retains its salience,
as offering clues to art's specific mode of existence. Interpretation,
we might say, constitutes one powerful mode of attachment, whose
mechanisms are not well captured by the prevailing assumptions of
literary studies.[36]

Happily, France is now seeing something of a hermeneutic revival—a somewhat surprising event, given the invective often heaped
on the idea of interpretation in the heyday of poststructuralism. What
these new French critics take from the hermeneutic tradition is an
emphasis on the text's entanglement with its readers. This text is no
longer a monument to dead thought (*histoire*) nor a self-referential
web of linguistic signs (*écriture*). Rather, it springs to life via a mundane yet mysterious process in which words are animated by readers
and reanimate readers in their turn. Blending phenomenology and
pragmatics, Foucault and Fish, these critics offer a fresh take on questions of reading: one that embraces its affective as well as cognitive
aspects—employing the language of enchantment, incandescence,
and rapture without embarrassment—and that takes as axiomatic its
many connections to daily life.

Let us listen, for example, to Marielle Macé. "Works take their place in ordinary life, leaving their marks and exerting a lasting power," she writes. "Reading is not a separate activity, functioning in competition with life, but one of the daily means by which we give our existence form, flavor and even style."[37] In an important recent book, Macé traces out the means by which scraps and snatches of the books we read weave their way into the texture of our daily experience. This bleeding of literature into life is not the result of a naïve reading that requires a corrective slap on the wrist from the critical theorist. Rather, it is the means by which artistic models help to shape what Macé calls a stylistics of existence.

Reading, in this sense, is not just a cognitive activity but an embodied mode of attentiveness that involves us in acts of sensing, perceiving, feeling, registering, and engaging. (Here Macé's discussion also brings to mind Richard Kearney's stunning elaboration of a "carnal hermeneutics" that involves and intertwines body and thought, sensing and sense.)[38] To speak of a stylistics of existence is to acknowledge that our being in the world is formed and patterned along certain lines and that aesthetic experience can modify or redraw such patterns. In the act of reading, we encounter fresh ways of organizing perception, different patterns and models, rhythms of rapprochement and distancing, relaxation and suspense, movement and hesitation. We give form to our existence through the diverse ways in which we inhabit, inflect, and appropriate the artistic forms we encounter. Reading, Macé insists, is not simply a matter of deciphering content but involves "taking on" and testing out new perceptual possibilities.

We see here how literature's singularity and its sociability are intertwined rather than opposed. The text is not sequestered away in haughty or melancholic isolation; it is unmistakably worldly rather than otherworldly. That it is a social artifact, however, does not mean that its uses can be predicted by consulting the oracle of the critical theory textbook. The act of reading embodies a "pas de deux," an interplay between text and person that refuses the false choice of autonomous aesthetics or instrumental politics. We cannot simply oppose interpretation and use, Macé argues, as if we could somehow arrive at a way of engaging with the literary work that is scrubbed clean of our mundane needs, desires, and interests. This is the dream of transcendence, of reading and writing from nowhere, of engagement without the original sin of appropriation, that literary critics are often reluctant to relinquish.

Conversely, the uses of literature cannot be totted up via a one-note calculus of power: as if we read books only to shore up our social status; as if these books entice and seduce us only in order to bludgeon us into submission to the status quo. The effect of such theoretical shortcuts, to reprise a Latourian language, is to shrink and slash networks, leapfrog over coactors, and turn active mediators into passive intermediaries. They can only explain the work of literature by shoving it, eyes averted, into a premeasured box—without doing justice to the labyrinthian paths, unexpected detours, obscure motivations, and sheer happenstance by which "ways of reading," to quote Macé's title, connect up with "modes of being."

Here Macé shows a certain audacity in championing the figure of Emma Bovary. Rather than serving as a symbol of the pathologies of immoderate reading, Flaubert's heroine now embodies a certain universality in clarifying the vital role of projection, identification, and imaginary transformation in aesthetic experience. "This desire to read," Macé observes, "feeds on closeness. . . . We need to do justice to this passivity of the reader, the passivity of being seized by and abandoning oneself to models." What looks like mindless submission involves a more complex choreography, as a reader surrenders to a text so as to savor the pleasures of being estranged from ordinary consciousness. Such moments of self-forgetting allow us to try out other selves, explore fictional models, slip free, for an instant, of well-worn habits of thought. Emma thus stands for the sheer messiness and impurity of subjectivity. We need to stop opposing empathy and interpretation, suffering and acting, affective experience and hermeneutic distance, Macé declares.[39] Emotions are not mere icing on the cake—at best a pleasurable distraction, at worst a mystifying spell to be broken so that the work of hard-nosed analysis can begin. Rather, affective engagement is the very means by which literary works are able to reach, reorient, and even reconfigure their readers.[40]

Especially valuable in Macé's work is this refusal to disconnect affect from interpretation, her insistence—against antihermeneutic accounts of aesthetic experience—that these elements are intertwined rather than opposed. And here we can rope in another pertinent work of French criticism: Yves Citton's *Lire, interpréter, actualiser: Pourquoi les études littéraires?* Responding to a remark by President Sarkozy, who wondered why students destined to become counter clerks were reading *La Princesse de Clèves* rather than learning something practical, Citton unfolds an energetic defense of literary education and the present relevance of past works of art. Literary studies, he argues, should defend itself as a distinctively hermeneutic enterprise, as a matter of "*lecture*" rather than "*histoire*" or "*écriture.*" Advocating what he calls "*une lecture actualisante*" — where *actualiser* means to realize, to bring to life, but also to make contemporary — Citton insists that interpretation is not a matter of exhumation but one of reinvention, that attention to past context should not overshadow questions of transtemporal resonance and how literary works speak to us now.[41]

In a vigorous defense of an affective hermeneutics, Citton insists that reading is never just a matter of cognitive or analytical decoding. Emotional cues prompt inferences or judgments by conveying vital information about character and episode, style and world view; the affective and analytical aspects of meaning are closely intertwined. Meanwhile, textual details vibrate and resonate with special force when they hook up with our passions and predilections, our affectively soaked histories and memories. It is an axiom of hermeneutics that we cannot help projecting our preexisting beliefs onto the literary work, which are modified in the light of the words we encounter. This hermeneutic circle, however, includes not just beliefs but also moods, perceptions, sensibilities, attunements: not only do we bring feelings to a text, but we may in turn be brought to feel differently by a text.

But how, we might ask, is such talk of affect to be incorporated into literary studies as a scholarly subject and a form of academic credentialing? And what is to prevent the language of criticism from lapsing into subjective effusion or an idiosyncratic flurry of private associations? It is not a question of throwing critical analysis overboard, remarks Citton, but one of establishing a better balance between method and inspiration so as to enliven the dryness of our intellectual vocabularies. Meanwhile, the concern of hermeneutics is neither "the text itself" nor the lives of readers but the question of where and how the two connect. Our students are not let off the hook, in other words, in terms of acquiring the knowledge and analytical skills necessary to explicate a text's pertinent features. And yet Citton also urges us to be less shame-faced and sheepish about our inclinations, attachments, judgments, enthusiasms, devotions, obsessions. Why are we so hesitant to admit that studying literature can be, among other things, a way of fashioning a sensibility, redirecting one's affections, reevaluating one's priorities and goals?[42]

It is not that such affections are "innocent" or beyond reproach; no one would dispute that literary studies, like any and every other worldly activity, can include moments of misrecognition, overvaluation, self-congratulation, aggression, or self-delusion.[43] It is rather that, at a certain point, the practice of skeptical regress becomes intellectually uninteresting as well as counterproductive, especially in the light of the current erosion of public support for the humanities. Here we can circle back to the tenets of actor-network theory. "If you are listening to what people are saying," remarks Latour, "they will explain how and why they are deeply attached, moved, affected by the works of art that make them feel things."[44] We might well wonder why the legitimacy of literary studies requires condescending to such intuitions. Latour's work is a sustained polemic against the urge to purify: to separate rationality from emotion, to safeguard critique from faith, to oppose fact to fetish. In this light, the experience of the art work—like his examples of religious language or love talk—does not only convey information but produces a transformation.[45] The import of a text is not exhausted by what it reveals or conceals about the social conditions that surround it. Rather, it is also a matter of what it sets alight in the reader—what kind of emotions it elicits, what changes of perception it prompts, what bonds and attachments it calls into being.

One consequence of this line of thought is a perspective less dismissive of lay experiences of reading (which also precede and sustain professional criticism).[46] Instead of looking through such experiences to the hidden laws that determine them, we look squarely at them, in order to investigate the mysteries of what is in plain sight. To be sure, feelings have histories, and individual sensations of sublimity or self-loss connect up to cultural frames, but underscoring the social construction of emotion is often a matter of presuming the critic's immunity from the illusions in which others are immersed. What would it mean to halt this critical machinery for a moment? To treat experiences of engagement, wonder, or absorption not as signs of naïveté or user error but as clues to why we are drawn to art in the first place? To forge a language of attachment as robust and refined as our rhetoric of detachment? At the least, it would require us to treat texts not as objects to be investigated but as coactors that make things happen, not just as matters of fact but also matters of concern.

Let me offer a brief example of how some of these ideas might be brought into the classroom. A few years ago, I overhauled a class in literary theory that I had been teaching for well over a decade to bring it into closer alignment with my changing concerns and commitments. The first half of the course still resembles the standard survey course, introducing undergraduates to structuralism, psychoanalysis, Marxism, deconstruction, feminism, postcolonial studies, and so on, giving them a basic fluency in familiar theoretical idioms. In the second half, however, we turn our attention to topics usually given short shrift in such surveys: empathy and sympathy, recognition and identification, enchantment and absorption, shock and the sublime, the pleasures of fandom and connoisseurship as they shape how and why people read. These experiences are chosen for their everyday entailments as well as their continuing, if often subterranean, presence in academic criticism. I propose to my students that they are not ideological symptoms to be seen through but complex phenomena that we have hardly begun to look at. The wager of the course is that they can learn to think carefully about their attachments as well as cultivating detachment; that thoughtful reflection is not limited to the practice of critique; that we can move beyond the stultifying division between naïve, emotional reading and rigorous, critical reading.

The first part of the course—effectively an induction into various styles of suspicious interpretation—remains gratifying to teach. Besides introducing my students to current debates in literary studies, it is, for some of them, their primary exposure to Freud, Foucault, feminism, and other major strands of modern intellectual history. And yet I have come to feel that a course devoted entirely to critique is an exercise in bad faith in skirting or simplifying the question of why literature matters. Devoting the second half of the course to postcritical reading forces the class to grapple with tough questions. How do works of art move us, and why? Are certain features of texts more likely to trigger empathy or recognition, absorption or disorientation? What does it mean to talk about identifying with a character? (At least three distinct things, I propose: structural or formal alignment, moral allegiance, and emotional empathy.)[47] To what extent do our attachments work with or against our political or analytical perspectives toward texts? How do specifics of style, emplotment, viewpoint or mise-en-scène steer audiences toward particular reactions or moods? And how are our affective responses shaped by extratextual factors ranging from the idiosyncrasies of individual history to structures of expectation and preevaluation that shape collective practices of reading?

In his final essay for the course, one student chose to analyze a poem by James Wright in dialogue with recent accounts of empathy by Suzanne Keen and others, clarifying how poetic devices help bring about an education of emotion and a movement between self-elucidating and self-transcending forms of empathy. Another student investigated questions of enchantment in *The God of Small Things*, detailing the sensual and rhetorical seductions of its style and the absorptive dimensions of its literary world while developing a forceful argument against the rationalist mistrust of enchanted states. A third elucidated his sense of shock on watching the French film *Irreversible*, as being triggered not only by its graphic and sexually violent subject matter but also by disorienting camera angles and a reverse plot, while engaging larger questions about the aesthetics of shock in postmodernity. These essays were no less scrupulous or carefully argued than the ones my students had produced earlier in the semester under the sign of suspicion. The most noticeable difference, however, was a surge of élan in the classroom, a collective sigh of relief at encountering an analytical language for reflecting on, rather than repudiating, their aesthetic attachments.

The antidote to suspicion is thus not a repudiation of theory—asking why literature matters will always embroil us in sustained reflection—but an ampler and more diverse range of theoretical vocabularies. And here, the term "postcritical" acknowledges its reliance on a prior tradition of thought, while conveying that there is more to intellectual life than the endless deflationary work of "digging down" or "standing back." Rather than engaging in a critique of critique, it is more interested in testing out alternate ways of reading and thinking. What it values in works of art is not just their power to estrange and disorient but also their ability to recontextualize what we know and to reorient and refresh perception. It seeks, in short, to strengthen rather than diminish its object—less in a spirit of reverence than in one of generosity and unabashed curiosity.

. . .

In these final pages we have opted for a language of addition rather than subtraction, translation rather than separation, connection rather than isolation, composition rather than critique. Accounting for the social meanings of art becomes a matter of multiplying actors and adding mediators rather than pruning them away. Instead of typecasting the work of art as either beaten-down sycophant of power or dauntless dissident, we have sought to make room for a more diverse cast of characters. Refusing to stay cooped up in their containers, texts barge energetically across space and time, hooking up with other coactors in ways that are both predictable and puzzling. Only by making attachments and forging alliances are they able to make a difference. Rather than stressing their otherness, autonomy, nontransferability, we point out their portability, mobility, and translatability. Instead of asking "What does this text undermine?" we inquire "What does this text create, build, make possible?" Against those who declare "The text is singular! It cannot be appropriated!" we intone our own mantra: "The text is singular! Of course it will be appropriated!"

Drawing on a variety of resources—actor-network theory, posthistoricist criticism, affective hermeneutics—I have sketched out some possible paths for literary and cultural studies. Reading is now conceived as an act of composition—of creative remaking—that binds text and reader in ongoing struggles, translations, and negotiations. The literary text is not a museum piece immured behind glass but a spirited and energetic participant in an exchange—one that may know as much as, or a great deal more than, the critic. This text *impinges* and bears on the reader across time and space; as a mood changer, a reconfigurer of perception, a plenitude of stylistic possibilities, an aid to thought.

It is not—to be quite explicit on this point—that historical knowledge is to be discarded or brushed aside. Of course we need to know about the French Revolution, medieval penitents, the Boxer Rebellion, sumptuary laws, suffragettes, nineteenth-century factory conditions, the civil rights movement, changing attitudes to death, and Indian partition. Such understanding is an indispensable corrective to the bouts of amnesia that can befall us—those moments when we forget that our institutions and ways of life, passions and prejudices, are not those around which past lives were organized. We are shocked, for a while, out of the somnolence of our temporal self-centeredness. In fact, the curatorial role of the humanities—preserving and caring for the vulnerable artifacts of the past—is, I would argue, one of its most important features. And historical modes of reading can certainly be employed in ways that avoid the pitfalls of critical contextualism, as in Sharon Marcus's subtle and illuminating account of the relations between women in Victorian England.[48]

It is not a concern with the past that is the problem but the use or misuse of the "context concept": on the one hand, as a synonym for sociohistorical generalities and critical condemnations that, in seeking to explain everything, explain very little; on the other hand, as a concerted attempt to glue a text fast to the moment of its first appearance. "Texts," a recent overview of the current state of literary studies observes, "are taken to be inseparable from context rather than existing as privileged entities that transcend their circumstances of conception."[49] That such remarks have become commonplace does not render them any less puzzling. Don't texts, after all, routinely transcend their circumstances of conception—straying into new networks that have little or nothing to do with their original meaning or purpose?

Admittedly, I have taken a few liberties with actor-network theory by grafting some of its tenets onto my own agenda. ANT, after all, is committed to multiplying mediators and including a full spectrum of human and nonhuman actors. The fate of literary works, it would insist, is tied to countless agents: publishers, reviewers, agents, bookstores, technologies of consumption (e-readers, Amazon.com), institutional frames (women's and ethnic studies, for example), forms of adaptation and translation, the physical and material properties of books ranging from fonts to photographs, and so on. From such a perspective, the reader-text relationship forms only a small part of a vast and sprawling network. Keeping this in mind, teachers of literature can certainly point their students to salient connections, while reminding them that their own selves are not fountains of infallible intuition but have been worn into shape by rubbing against countless coactors. And yet, while an occasional course on actor-network theory may sneak its way onto an English syllabus, the chances of most classes on the Victorian novel or contemporary women's fiction being refurbished as classes in the sociology of mediation are close to nil. That is not, after all, what most teachers and students come to literature *for*. What remains at the heart of the discipline—for better or for worse—is a training in advanced techniques of reading, tested out in the encounter with a corpus of significant texts. A commitment to describing the hybrid networks in which literary works are embedded must be weighed against, and balanced with, the habits, preferences, and passions that define an existing field of inquiry.[50]

Thus the alliance of actor-network theory and literary studies, like all alliances, will require translation, tinkering, fudging, and compromise. It is not a question of a heavy-handed application of ANT to literary studies—calling forth protests from those who feel that crucial dimensions of literature and literary experience are in danger of being lost—but a question of trying to speak well to fellow critics about issues of common concern. And here, perhaps, some of the ideas floated in this chapter can help us to wriggle out of the straitjacket of suspicion without giving up on interpretation or lapsing back into an aseptic and sterile formalism. Critique has long lived off the reputation of being the most rigorous and radical form of reading—a reputation, I have argued, that is not entirely deserved. There are other ways of thinking about the social lives of texts, different combinations of method and mood. Forswearing suspicion, we are confronted not only with the text but with our implication and entanglement with that text. Aggressivity gives way to receptivity, detachment mingles with an acknowledged attachment, a text's pastness does not trump its evident presentness, and aesthetic pleasures and sociopolitical resonance are intertwined rather than opposed. The aim is no longer to diminish or subtract from the reality of the texts we study but to amplify their reality, as energetic coactors and vital partners in an equal encounter.

In Short

Let me now pull together the various strands of my argument in order to be as explicit as I can about what I *am* saying and what I am *not* saying. Complete transparency is, of course, impossible. Meanwhile, as we've seen, a prevailing ethos encourages scholars to impute hidden causes and unconscious motives to the arguments of others, while exempting themselves from the same charge: "I speak truth to power, while you are a pawn of neoliberal interests!" Nonetheless, I will clarify, to the best of my ability, my *conscious* premises and intentions.

My conviction—one that is shared by a growing number of scholars—is that questioning critique is not a shrug of defeat or a hapless capitulation to conservative forces. Rather, it is motivated by a desire to articulate a positive vision for humanistic thought in the face of growing skepticism about its value. Such a vision is sorely needed if we are to make a more compelling case for why the arts and humanities are needed. Reassessing critique, in this light, is not an abandonment of social or ethical commitments but a realization, as Ien Ang puts it, that these commitments require us to communicate with intellectual strangers who do not share our assumptions.[1] And here, a persuasive defense of the humanities is hindered rather than helped by an ethos of critique that encourages scholars to pride themselves on their vanguard role and to equate serious thought with a reflex negativity. Citing the waves of demystification in the history of recent thought (linguistic, historicist, etc), Yves Citton notes that they share a common conviction: the naïvety of any belief that works of art might inspire new forms of life. We are seeing, he suggests, the emergence of another regime of interpretation: one that is willing to recognize the potential of literature and art to create new imaginaries rather than just to denounce mystifying illusions. The language of attachment, passion, and inspiration is no longer taboo.[2]

This book, moreover, is not a screed against disagreement, objection, or negative judgment. (I have engaged in all these activities in the preceding pages.) "Social criticism," writes Michael Walzer, "is such a common activity—so many people, in one way or another, participate in it—that we must suspect from the beginning that it does not wait upon philosophical discovery or invention."[3] On this point, Walzer is entirely right. The act of criticizing, as I noted in chapter 4, is an everyday aspect of our being in the world. There will always be reasons to object to things that we dislike and would like to change: social arrangements, philosophical beliefs, cultural representations, political ideas or institutions, and various mundane details of our lives. There is no question of giving up disagreement—an impossible scenario in any case. The belief that disagreement must be couched in the form of "critique" to attain legitimacy, however, is a peculiarly modern and Western prejudice.

The subject of this book, then, has been a specific genre of writing: the rhetoric of suspicious reading in literary studies and in the humanities and interpretative social sciences generally. Rather than being synonymous with disagreement, it is a specific *kind* of disagreement—one that is driven by the protocols of late twentieth- and twenty-first-century academic argument. Critique, in this sense, is the hardening of disagreement into a given repertoire of argumentative moves and interpretative methods. There are, to be sure, significant differences between critical and theoretical frameworks: critique, as we have seen, is not one thing but an eclectic array of philosophical tenets, political ideologies, and modes of interpretation. Yet an exclusive focus on these differences prevents us from seeing what forms of critique have in common: shared ways of thinking about the function of the critic and the merits of art, as well as a prevailing disposition that Christopher Castiglia, in an inspired coinage, calls "critiquiness": an unmistakable blend of suspicion, self-confidence, and indignation.[4]

Castiglia urges us to rescue and revitalize critique by disengaging it from critiquiness—to shrug off the mantle of knowing skepticism by embracing a renewed sense of idealism, purpose, and utopian possibility. A hopeful critique, he suggests, offers a way of breaking the stalemate of contemporary criticism. I confess to being less sanguine than Castiglia that the difficulties of critique can be resolved in this way; they are, in my view, not only attitudinal but also methodological and theoretical. Let me now try to draw together, in schematic form, what I see as the most salient of these difficulties.

Its one-sided view of the work of art. Critique proves to be a remarkably efficient and smooth-running machine for registering the limits and insufficiencies of texts. It also offers a yardstick for assessing their value: the extent to which they exemplify its own cardinal virtues of demystifying, subverting, and putting into question. It is conspicuously silent, however, on the many other reasons why we are drawn to works of art: aesthetic pleasure, increased self-understanding, moral reflection, perceptual reinvigoration, ecstatic self-loss, emotional consolation, or heightened sensation—to name just a few. Its conception of the uses and values of literature is simply too thin.

Its affective inhibition. Critique cannot yield to a text—a process that it perceives as a form of shameful abasement or ideological surrender. As we have seen, its affective stance is far from uniformly negative; critique can inspire a fervent sense of solidarity against a common enemy, the engrossing stimulation of an interpretative game, and an admiration for the cunning maneuvers of the contradictory text. But its overriding concern with questioning motives and exposing wrongdoing (the moral-political drama of detection) results in a mind-set—vigilant, wary, mistrustful—that blocks receptivity and inhibits generosity. We are shielded from the risks, but also the rewards, of aesthetic experience. I have tried to show that a fuller engagement with such experience does not require a surrender of thoughtfulness or intellectual rigor: that, in spite of warnings to the contrary, the alternative to critique does not have to take the form of "belle-lettrism" or mindless effusion.[5]

Its picture of society. Critique's stance of againstness, whether expressed in a digging down for hidden truths or a more ironic stance of "troubling" or "problematizing," also molds its conception of the social. Power is exposed as the invariant and overriding principle of social meaning; whatever is valued by the critic must somehow resist or defy this principle. The result is a zigzagging between categories of inside and outside, center and margins, transgression and containment, as critique tries, like a frantically sprinting cartoon rabbit, to outrun the snapping jaws of its own recuperation. (Its affinity with utopian thought is entirely congruent with this logic; affirmation can only exist in a radically disjunctive relationship to a fallen present, i.e., in a far distant future.) That art works are linked to other social phenomena, however, is not a sign of their fallenness but a precondition of their existence: to reprise Latour, "emancipation does not mean 'freed from bonds,' but *well*-attached." The degree to which these attachments are enabling or limiting (or both) is not something to be known in advance; it requires empirical investigation, a willingness to be surprised, and attention to as many actors as is feasible.

Rather than invoking the familiar picture of "literature in society," then, ANT directs our attention to the many actors with which literature is entangled and the specifics of their interaction. The specific, in this sense, is not to be confused with the local. Networks, after all, can extend over very long distances, and ANT does not prevent us from engaging many of the issues that are lumped together under the label of globalization. That a plastic card issued in Des Moines can conjure money out of an ATM in Vladivostok tells us something important about the internationalization of finance. It does not, however, authorize us to draw conclusions about the late-capitalist manufacturing of global subjectivity—not, at least, without patient and empirically grounded demonstrations of how economic links are translated, revised, transformed, or ignored as they connect with other modes of existence.

Its methodological asymmetry. In diagnosing the insufficiencies of a work of art or an intellectual argument, critique explains these insufficiencies by invoking some larger frame. It looks behind the text for some final explanation or cause: social, cultural, psychoanalytical, historical, or linguistic. The text is *derived*, in a fundamental sense, from something else. Critique itself, however, remains the ultimate horizon—it is not an object to be contextualized but is itself the ultimate context. (The call to "historicize" critique or to engage in a critique of critique does not affect this logic; critique now takes itself as its own object, while reinforcing the supremacy of its own method.) It is in this sense that critique seeks to transcend the limits of other forms of thought, seeing its gambits of distancing and self-questioning as a means of forever remaining one step ahead. By treating critique as one language game among others, with its own routines, gambits, and conditions, and as one mood among others, defined by a certain ethos or disposition, I have tried to weaken the force of this presumption of epistemological or political privilege.

In summarizing these objections, it may also be helpful to underscore the criticisms I have *not* made—given a tendency to lump together the agendas of various "postcritical" thinkers. I am not, for example, persuaded that critique is a form of symbolic violence wreaked on hapless and helpless literary texts that are in need of our protection. I have no quarrel with interpretation, even though I favor description; nor am I drawn to a language of textual surfaces over depths. I have also not leveled a certain kind of political complaint: namely, that critique is a form of faux-radical posturing that has failed to achieve any substantive goals. Rather, its role in the formation of new fields of knowledge from feminism to postcolonial studies to queer theory strikes me as crucial—even though critique's distrust of co-option and institutions means it is not always well placed to assess its own impact. That critique has made certain things possible is not in doubt. What is also increasingly evident, however, is that it has sidelined other intellectual, aesthetic, and political possibilities—ones that are just as vital to the flourishing of new fields of knowledge as older ones.

These and similar concerns are now being voiced across a variety of disciplines. I have briefly alluded to the writings of sociologists and social theorists—from Michael Billig to Luc Boltanski—who are struggling against the grip of critique. In fields from political theory to art criticism, critics are experimenting with alternatives to demystification: here I have benefited especially from the writings of Jane

Bennett and James Elkins. Meanwhile, some feminist scholars are re-assessing the language game of doubt: feminist theory has more inter-esting things to do, they venture, than to question prereflective habits and demonstrate the ungrounded nature of belief. For these thinkers, ordinary language philosophy offers the most compelling alternative to an ethos of constant suspicion—one that is inspired by a very different view of the politics of language.[6]

In literary and cultural studies, these questions seem especially pressing—no doubt because engaging with a text has the potential to be an animating encounter rather than just a diagnostic exercise. Michel Chaouli puts it well: the literary work discloses itself in the reader's experience of it—such that an effacement of that experience, in the name of analytical rigor and detachment, also fails to do justice to the work. At the same time, of course, what counts as experience is neither self-evident nor infallible but is revised and remade as we encounter texts that address us in some way. Chaouli marvels at "the lengths to which we go to keep at bay the force of artworks, the same artworks whose ability to snap us out of our torpor drew us to them in the first place. How curious it is that we dig wide moats—of history, ideology, formal analysis—and erect thick conceptual walls lest we be touched by what, in truth, lures us."[7]

Talking about the force and the lure of art works need not commit us to breathless effusions or antipolitical sentiments. It can open the way to a renewed engagement with art and its entanglement with social life—in such a way that texts are no longer typecast as either heroic dissidents or slavish sycophants of power. And here literary theory would do well to reflect on—rather than condescend to—the uses of literature in everyday life: uses that we have hardly begun to understand. Such a reorientation, with any luck, might inspire more capacious, and more publicly persuasive, rationales for why literature, and the study of literature, matter.

In a previous book, I took a preliminary stab at such an exercise. There I made a case for what I called neophenomenology—a sustained attention to the sheer range and complexity of aesthetic experi-ences, including moments of recognition, enchantment, shock, and knowledge. Such experiences speak to academic as well as lay practices of reading; they connect us to our lives as social beings, while also inviting us to reflect on the distinctive qualities of works of art: what spurs us to pick up a book or to become utterly engrossed in a film. We cannot hope to do justice to these qualities, I argued, as long as we remain in the thrall of a suspicious hermeneutics. Sometimes serious thinking calls for a judicious decrease rather than an increase of distance—a willingness to acknowledge and more fully engage our attachments.

Responses to the book were not unsympathetic, but some readers expressed a certain puzzlement—as if I had somehow failed to grasp the self-evident rigor and intrinsic sophistication of critique. I had not adequately explained to myself or others, it became clear, why this deference to a particular methodology struck me as misguided. *The Limits of Critique* is my attempt to remedy this deficit and to settle some unfinished business. As the title suggests, I have tried to show why reading critically—or what I have preferred to call reading suspiciously—should not be taken as the ultimate horizon of thought. It has no a priori claims to philosophical rigor, political radicalism, or literary sophistication. It is one way of reading and thinking among others: finite, limited, and fallible.

As a critic schooled in suspicious reading, I am hardly immune to its charms, yet I have tried, as much as possible, to avoid being drawn into a "critique of critique." That is to say, I have described widespread modes of argument without making imputations about hidden motives, diagnosing symptoms and anxieties, or attributing the rise of scholarly methods to larger social pressures or institutional forces that my fellow critics have failed to understand. Meanwhile, I have tried to avoid critiquiness by opting for different shadings of style and tone. In short, I have leaned to the side of criticism rather than critique.

Such an attempt, to be sure, can have only a partial success. To object to or disagree with critique is to be caught in the jaws of a performative contradiction; in the act of disagreeing with certain ways of thinking, we cannot help being drawn into the negative or oppositional attitude we are trying to avoid. For this reason, I wish to draw a firm line under these concluding words. Having clarified, to the best of my ability, the reasons for my dissatisfaction with critique, I want to move on: to try out different vocabularies and experiment with alternative ways of writing, to think in a more sustained and concentrated fashion about what other moods and methods might look like. The point, in the end, is not to redescribe or reinterpret critique but to change it.

NOTES

Introduction

1. Helen Small, *The Value of the Humanities* (Oxford: Oxford University Press, 2013), 26.
2. Amanda Anderson, *The Way We Argue Now: A Study in the Cultures of Theory* (Princeton: Princeton University Press, 2005).
3. Kevin Lamb, "Foucault's Aestheticism," *diacritics* 35, no. 2 (2005): 43.
4. Like most scholars working in this area, I am indebted to Eve Kosofsky Sedgwick's essay "Paranoid Reading and Reparative Reading, or, You're So Paranoid, You Probably Think This Essay Is about You," in *Touching Feeling: Affect, Pedagogy, Performativity* (Durham: Duke University Press, 2003). Other works I have found especially helpful in the course of this project include Toril Moi's *"What Is a Woman?" and Other Essays* (Oxford: Oxford University Press, 2001) and her current manuscript on literary criticism and ordinary language philosophy; Linda M. G. Zerilli, *Feminism and the Abyss of Freedom* (Chicago: University of Chicago Press, 2005); the "Surface Reading" issue of *Representations*, edited by Steven Best and Sharon Marcus, as well as Marcus's *Between Women: Friendship, Marriage, and Desire in Victorian England* (Princeton,: Princeton University Press, 2007); Heather Love, "Close but Not Deep: Literary Ethics and the Descriptive Turn." *New Literary History* 41, no. 2 (2010): 371–92; Jane Bennett, *The Enchantment of Modern Life: Attachments, Crossings, and Ethics* (Princeton: Princeton University Press, 2001) and *Vibrant Matter: A Political Ecology of Things* (Durham: Duke University Press, 2010). I have

also learned much from the work of Graham Harman and of course am deeply influenced by the work of Bruno Latour.

5. Bruno Latour, "Why Has Critique Run Out of Steam? From Matters of Fact to Matters of Concern," *Critical Inquiry* 30, no. 2 (2005): 225–48.

6. Steven Marcus, "Freud and Dora: Story, History, Case History," in his *Freud and the Culture of Psychoanalysis* (New York: W. W. Norton, 1987).

7. Gilles Deleuze and Félix Guattari, *A Thousand Plateaus: Capitalism and Schizophrenia* (Minneapolis: University of Minnesota Press, 1987).

8. On this point, see also Günter Leypoldt, "Singularity and the Literary Market," *New Literary History* 45, no. 1 (2014): 71–88.

9. Nikolas Kompridis, "Recognition and Receptivity: Forms of Normative Response in the Lives of the Animals We Are," *New Literary History* 44, no. 1 (2013): 1–24. As Kompridis remarks, receptivity should not be confused with passivity—nor does it presume that readers are blank slates or "ideologically innocent." See also Nikolas Kompridis, *Critique and Disclosure: Critical Theory between Past and Future* (Cambridge: MIT Press, 2006), pt. 5, chap. 2.

Chapter 1

1. Michael Roth, "Beyond Critical Thinking," *Chronicle of Higher Education*, January 3, 2010. The argument is recapitulated in his *Beyond the University: Why Liberal Education Matters* (New Haven: Yale University Press, 2014).

2. Judith Fetterley, *The Resisting Reader: A Feminist Approach to American Fiction* (Bloomington: Indiana University Press, 1981).

3. For an expansion of this point, see Rita Felski, "After Suspicion," *Profession* (2009): 28–35.

4. Chantal Mouffe, *Agonistics: Thinking the World Politically* (London: Verso, 2013), 96–97.

5. Claudio E. Benzecry, *The Opera Fanatic: Ethnography of an Obsession* (Chicago: University of Chicago Press, 2013), 3.

6. Peter Sloterdijk, *The Art of Philosophy: Wisdom as a Practice* (New York: Columbia University Press, 2012), 12.

7. David Rodowick, *Elegy for Theory* (Cambridge: Harvard University Press, 2013).

8. Catherine Gallagher and Stephen Greenblatt, *Practicing New Historicism* (Chicago: University of Chicago Press, 2000), 9.

9. François Cusset, *French Theory: How Foucault, Derrida, Deleuze, & Co. Transformed the Intellectual Life of the United States* (Minneapolis: University of Minnesota Press, 2008), 83.

10. Some of my phrasing here is drawn from the introduction to *New Literary History* 43, no. 3 (2012), the "In the Mood" issue.

11. Jonathan Flatley, *Affective Mapping: Melancholia and the Politics of Modernism* (Cambridge: Harvard University Press, 2008), 5.

12. Quoted in Hubert Dreyfus, *Being-in-the-World: A Commentary on Heidegger's "Being and Time," Division 1* (Cambridge: MIT Press, 1990), p. 171.

13. Cusset, *French Theory*; Gerald Graff, *Professing Literature: An Institutional History* (Chicago: University of Chicago Press, 1987); John Guillory, *Cultural Capital: The Problem of Literary Canon Formation* (Chicago: University of Chicago Press, 1995); Bill Readings, *The University in Ruins* (Cambridge: Harvard University Press, 1997); Christopher Newfield, *Unmaking the Public University: The Forty-Year Assault on the Middle Class* (Cambridge: Harvard University Press, 2011); Jeffrey J. Williams, *How to be an Intellectual: Essays on Criticism, Culture, and the University* (New York: Fordham University Press, 2014); Alan Liu, *The Laws of Cool: Knowledge Work and the Culture of Information* (Chicago: University of Chicago Press, 2004). On the history of literary theory, see, for example, Chris Baldick, *Criticism and Literary Theory 1890 to the Present* (London: Longman, 1996); Nicholas Birns, *Theory after Theory: An Intellectual History of Literary Theory from 1950 to the Early 21st Century* (Boulder, CO: Broadview Press, 2010); Press, 2014); Warren Breckman, "Times of Theory: On Writing the History of French Theory," *Journal of the History of Ideas* 71, no. 3 (2010): 339–59.

14. Bruno Latour, "The Politics of Explanation: An Alternative," in *Knowledge and Reflexivity: New Frontiers in the Sociology of Knowledge*, ed. Steve Woolgar (London: Sage, 1988).

15. Amanda Anderson, *The Way We Argue Now: A Study in the Cultures of Theory* (Princeton: Princeton University Press, 2005), 1.

16. Ian Hunter, "The Time of Theory," *Postcolonial Studies* 10, no. 1 (2007): 7. See also his "Spirituality and Philosophy in Post-Structuralist Theory," *History of European Ideas* 35 (2009): 265–75, and "The History of Theory," *Critical Inquiry* 33, no. 1 (2006): 78–112.

17. Matthew Ratcliffe, *Feelings of Being: Phenomenology, Psychiatry and the Sense of Reality* (Oxford: Oxford University Press, 2008).

18. Howard Becker, *Tricks of the Trade: How to Think about Your Research While You're Doing It* (Chicago: University of Chicago Press, 1998).

19. Rita Felski, "From Literary Theory to Critical Method," *Profession* (2008): 108–116; see also David Bordwell, *Making Meaning: Inference and Rhetoric in the Interpretation of Cinema* (Cambridge: Harvard University Press, 1991).

20. Antoine Compagnon, *Literature, Theory, and Common Sense* (Princeton: Princeton University Press, 2004), 6. On literary studies as a "pluralist bazaar," see Baldick, *Criticism and Literary Theory*, 205.

21. Deidre Lynch, *Loving Literature: A Cultural History* (Chicago: University of Chicago Press, 2014), 10.

22. Sianne Ngai, *Our Aesthetic Categories: Zany, Cute, Interesting* (Cambridge: Harvard University Press, 2012).

23. Alan McKee, "The Fans of Cultural Theory," in *Fandom: Identities and Communities in a Mediated World*, ed. Jonathan Gray, Cornel Sandvoss, and C. Lee Harrington (New York: New York University Press, 2007).

24. Dorothy Hale, "Aesthetics and the New Ethics: Theorizing the Novel in the Twenty-First Century," *PMLA* 124, no. 3 (May 2009): 899.

25. For a good discussion along these lines, see Steven Goldsmith, *Blake's Agitation: Criticism and the Emotions* (Baltimore: Johns Hopkins University Press, 2013).

26. See *Poetics Today* 25, no. 2 (2004), the special issue "How Literature Enters Life," edited by Els Andringa and Margrit Schreier.

27. C. Namwali Serpell, *Seven Modes of Uncertainty* (Cambridge: Harvard University Press, 2014), 17–19.

28. Rita Felski, *Literature after Feminism* (Chicago: University of Chicago Press, 2003).

29. Robyn R. Warhol, *Having a Good Cry: Effeminate Feelings and Pop-Culture Forms* (Columbus: Ohio State University Press, 2004); Karin Littau, *Theories of Reading; Books, Bodies, and Bibliomania* (Cambridge: Polity, 2006).

30. Janice Radway, *A Feeling for Books: The Book-of-the-Month Club, Literary Taste, and Middle-Class Desire* (Chapel Hill: University of North Carolina Press, 1999), 13. See also Winfried Fluck's important essay "Aesthetics and Cultural Studies," in *Aesthetics in a Multicultural Age*, ed. Emory Elliott, Louis Freitas Caton, and Jeffrey Rhyne (Oxford University Press, 2002); and Rita Felski, "The Role of Aesthetics in Cultural Studies," in *The Aesthetics of Cultural Studies*, ed. Michael Bérubé (New York: Blackwell, 2004), and "Everyday Aesthetics," *Minnesota Review* 71–72 (2009): 171–79.

31. José Muñoz, *Cruising Utopia: The Then and There of Queer Futurity* (New York: New York University Press, 2009); Heather Love, "Close but Not

Deep: Literary Ethics and the Descriptive Turn," *New Literary History* 41, no. 2 (2010): 371–91, and "Close Reading and Thin Description," *Public Culture* 25, no. 3 (2013): 401–34; Stephen Best and Sharon Marcus, "Surface Reading: An Introduction," *Representations* 108, no. 1 (2009): 1–21.

32. Some especially helpful works include Richard Kearney, *On Paul Ricoeur: The Owl of Minerva* (London: Ashgate, 2004); Boyd Blundell, *Paul Ricoeur between Theology and Philosophy: Detour and Return* (Bloomington: Indiana University Press, 2010); Don Ihde, *Hermeneutic Phenomenology: The Philosophy of Paul Ricoeur* (Evanston: Northwestern University Press, 1971); Karl Simms, *Paul Ricoeur* (London: Routledge, 2003).

33. Alison Scott-Baumann, *Ricoeur and the Hermeneutics of Suspicion* (New York: Continuum, 2009), chap. 4. For other discussions of Ricoeur's phrase, see Ruthellen Josselson, "The Hermeneutics of Faith and the Hermeneutics of Suspicion," *Narrative Inquiry* 14, no. 1 (2004): 1–28; David Stewart, "The Hermeneutics of Suspicion," *Journal of Literature and Theology* 3, no. 3 (1989): 296–307; Erin White, "Between Suspicion and Hope: Paul Ricoeur's Vital Hermeneutic," *Journal of Literature and Theology* 5, no. 3 (1991): 311–21; Anthony C. Thiselton, *New Horizons in Hermeneutics: The Theory and Practice of Transforming Biblical Reading* (Grand Rapids, MI: Zondervan, 1992), chap. 10.

34. Paul Ricoeur, *Freud and Philosophy: An Essay on Interpretation* (New Haven: Yale University Press, 1977), 33.

35. Colin Davis, *Critical Excess: Overreading in Derrida, Deleuze, Levinas, Žižek, and Cavell* (Stanford: Stanford University Press, 2010), 173.

36. Kearney, *On Paul Ricoeur*, 14, 140.

37. Eve Kosofsky Sedgwick, "Paranoid Reading and Reparative Reading, or, You're So Paranoid, You Probably Think This Essay Is about You," in *Touching Feeling: Affect, Pedagogy, Performativity* (Durham: Duke University Press, 2003).

38. John Farrell, *Paranoia and Modernity: Cervantes to Rousseau* (Ithaca: Cornell University Press, 2006); David Trotter, *Paranoid Modernism: Literary Experiment, Psychosis, and the Professionalization of English Society* (Oxford: Oxford University Press, 2001).

39. Michael Fischer, *Stanley Cavell and Literary Skepticism* (Chicago: University of Chicago Press, 1989), 98.

40. Alexander F. Shand, "Suspicion," *British Journal of Psychology* 13 (1922–23): 214.

41. Hitchcock's film has proved highly controversial, not least because of its ending. See, for example, Richard Allen, "Hitchcock, or the Pleasures of

Metaskepticism," *October* 89 (1999): 69–86; Rick Worland, "Before and after the Fact: Writing and Reading Hitchcock's *Suspicion*," *Cinema Journal* 41, no. 4 (2003): 3–26.

42. Shand, "Suspicion," 210.

43. Tim Dean, "Art as Symptom: Žižek and the Ethics of Psychoanalytical Criticism," *diacritics* 32, no. 2 (2002): 21–41.

44. Reinhart Koselleck, *Critique and Crisis: Enlightenment and the Pathogenesis of Modern Society* (Cambridge: MIT Press, 1988).

45. Kimberly Hutchings, *Kant, Critique and Politics* (London: Routledge, 1996), 120.

46. Michael Walzer, *The Company of Critics* (New York: Basic Books, 2002), 5.

47. Robert Pippin, *Modernism as a Philosophical Problem* (Oxford: Blackwell, 1991), 6.

48. Margot Norris, *Suspicious Readings of Joyce's "Dubliners"* (Philadelphia: University of Pennsylvania Press, 2003), 7.

49. See Stephen Ross, ed., *Modernism and Theory: A Critical Debate* (New York: Routledge, 2004); David Rodowick, *The Crisis of Political Modernism: Criticism and Ideology in Contemporary Film Criticism* (Berkeley and Los Angeles: University of California Press, 1995).

50. Paul Ricoeur, *Time and Narrative*, vol. 3, trans. Kathleen Blamey and David Pellauer (Chicago: University of Chicago Press, 1988), 164 (emphasis added).

51. Michel de Certeau, *The Practice of Everyday Life* (Berkeley and Los Angeles: University of California Press, 1984).

52. James C. Scott, *Domination and the Arts of Resistance: Hidden Transcripts* (New Haven: Yale University Press, 1990).

53. Ernesto Laclau and Chantal Mouffe, *Hegemony and Socialist Strategy: Toward a Radical Democratic Politics* (London: Verso, 1985).

54. Bruno Latour, "Why Has Critique Run Out of Steam? From Matters of Fact to Matters of Concern," *Critical Inquiry* 30, no. 2 (2004): 230.

55. Peter Sloterdijk, *Critique of Cynical Reason* (Minneapolis: University of Minnesota Press, 1987). See also R. Jay Magill Jr., *Chic Ironic Bitterness* (Ann Arbor: University of Michigan Press, 2007).

56. Jeffrey C. Goldfarb, *The Cynical Society: The Culture of Politics and the Politics of Culture in American Life* (Chicago: University of Chicago Press, 1991).

57. Amanda Anderson, *The Powers of Distance: Cosmopolitanism and the Cultivation of Detachment* (Princeton: Princeton University Press, 2001).

58. Liu, *The Laws of Cool*, 33.

59. Lorraine Daston and Peter Galison, *Objectivity* (New York: Zone, 2010), 52.

60. Pierre Bourdieu, "The Historical Genesis of the Pure Aesthetic," in *The Rules of Art: Genesis and Structure of the Literary Field* (Stanford: Stanford University Press, 1996). See also Andrew Goldstone, *Fictions of Autonomy: Modernism from Wilde to de Man* (Oxford: Oxford University Press, 2013).

61. Here, however, Bourdieu conflates the historically specific notion of autonomous art with aesthetics *tout court*. People of different social backgrounds experience aesthetic pleasure from things that are not autonomous art works.

62. Anderson, *The Powers of Distance*, 152.

63. Walzer, *The Company of Critics*, chap. 11.

64. Christian Thorne, *The Dialectic of Counter-Enlightenment* (Cambridge: Harvard University Press, 2009).

65. Susie Linfield, *The Cruel Radiance: Photography and Political Violence* (Chicago: University of Chicago Press, 2010), 10.

Chapter 2

1. See Zoltán Kövecses, *Metaphor: A Practical Introduction* (Oxford: Oxford University Press, 2002); Janet Martin Soskice, *Metaphor and Religious Language* (Oxford: Clarendon, 1985); and Elena Semino, *Metaphor in Discourse* (Cambridge: Cambridge University Press, 2008).

2. Stephen Best and Sharon Marcus, "Surface Reading: An Introduction," *Representations* 108, no. 1 (2009): 9, 16.

3. Richard Shusterman, *Surface and Depth: Dialectics of Criticism and Culture* (Ithaca: Cornell University Press, 2002).

4. Fredric Jameson, *The Political Unconscious* (Ithaca: Cornell University Press, 1981), 45.

5. David Bordwell, *Making Meaning: Inference and Rhetoric in the Interpretation of Cinema* (Cambridge: Harvard University Press, 1991), 72.

6. For an illuminating discussion, see Donald Kuspit, "A Mighty Metaphor: The Analogy of Archaeology and Psychoanalysis," in *Sigmund Freud and Art*, ed. Lynn Gamwell and Richard Wells (Binghamton: SUNY Press, 1989), and also Sabine Hake, "*Saxa loquuntur*: Freud's Archaeology of the Text," *boundary 2*, 20, no. 1 (1993): 146–73.

7. Sigmund Freud, "Constructions in Analysis," in *The Standard Edition*

of the Complete Psychological Works of Sigmund Freud, vol. 23 (London: Hogarth Press, 1953–74), 260.

8. Alan Sinfield, "Art as Cultural Production," in Julian Wolfreys, *Literary Theories: A Reader and Guide* (New York: New York University Press, 1999), 640.

9. Erik D. Lindberg, "Returning the Repressed: The Unconscious in Victorian and Modernist Narrative," *Narrative* 8, no. 1 (2000): 74.

10. Peter Brooks, "The Idea of a Psychoanalytic Criticism," in *The Trial(s) of Psychoanalysis*, ed. Françoise Meltzer (Chicago: University of Chicago Press, 1987), 145.

11. E. Ann Kaplan, *Women and Film: Both Sides of the Camera* (London: Methuen, 1983), 24.

12. Marjorie Garber, *Symptoms of Culture* (New York: Routledge, 1998), 9.

13. Mary Ann Doane, Patricia Mellencamp, and Linda Williams, eds., *Re-vision: Essays in Feminist Film Criticism* (Frederick, MD: University Publications of American, 1984), 11.

14. Kimberly Devlin, "The Eye and the Gaze in *Heart of Darkness*: A Symptomological Reading," *Modern Fiction Studies* 40, no. 4 (1994): 713.

15. Ruth Robbins, "Introduction: Will the Real Feminist Theory Please Stand Up?" in *Literary Theories: A Reader and Guide*, ed. Julian Wolfreys (Edinburgh: Edinburgh University Press, 1999), 54.

16. On the idea of "saving" films by emphasizing their contradictory dimensions, see also Bordwell, *Making Meaning*, 88–89.

17. Claire Kahane, "Medusa's Voice: Male Hysteria in *The Bostonians*," in Wolfreys, *Literary Theories*, 60.

18. Terry Eagleton, *Criticism and Ideology: A Study in Marxist Literary Theory* (London: Verso, 1976), 312.

19. Bruno Latour, "An Attempt at a 'Compositionist Manifesto,'" *New Literary History* 41, no. 3 (2010): 475.

20. George Steiner, *After Babel: Aspects of Language and Translation* (Oxford: Oxford University Press, 1998), 296–301.

21. Annette Kuhn, *Women's Pictures: Feminism and Cinema* (London: Routledge, 1982), p. 84.

22. Bordwell, *Making Meaning*, chap. 2.

23. "Where are the unconscious structures of primitive myths? In Africa? In Brazil? No! They are among the filing cards of Lévi-Strauss's office. If they extend beyond the Collège de France at the rue des Ecoles, it is through his books and disciples." Bruno Latour, *The Pasteurization of France*, trans. Alan Sheridan and John Law (Cambridge: Harvard University Press, 1988), 179.

24. On this point, see also Mary Thomas Crane, "Surface, Depth, and the Spa-

tial Imaginary: A Cognitive Reading of *The Political Unconscious*," *Representations* 108, no. 1 (2009): 76–97.

25. Garber, *Symptoms of Culture*, 9.

26. Arthur Danto, "Deep Interpretation," in *The Philosophical Disenfranchisement of Art* (New York: Columbia University Press, 1986), 51.

27. Stefan Collini, "Introduction: Interpretation Terminable and Interminable," and Umberto Eco, "Overinterpreting Texts," in *Interpretation and Overinterpretation*, ed. Stefan Collini (Cambridge: Cambridge University Press, 1992).

28. Jacques Rancière, "Dissenting Words: A Conversation with Jacques Rancière," *diacritics* 30, no. 2 (2000): 114.

29. Pierre Macherey, *A Theory of Literary Production* (London: Routledge and Kegan Paul, 1978), 154.

30. Lis Moller, *The Freudian Reading: Analytical and Fictional Constructions* (Philadelphia: University of Pennsylvania Press, 1991), ix.

31. Timothy Brennan, "Running and Dodging: The Rhetoric of Doubleness in Contemporary Theory," *New Literary History* 41, no. 2 (2010): 277–99.

32. Jennifer Fleissner, "Reading for the Symptom: Beyond Historicism," unpublished paper.

33. Rosemarie Garland-Thomson, "Disability, Identity, and Representation," in *Extraordinary Bodies: Figuring Physical Disability in American Culture and Literature* (New York: Columbia University Press, 1996), 5.

34. Kobena Mercer, "Black Hair/Style Politics," in *Welcome to the Jungle: New Positions in Black Cultural Studies* (London: Routledge, 1994), 109.

35. Paul Giles, *Virtual Americas: Transnational Fictions and the Transatlantic Imaginary* (Durham: Duke University Press, 2002), 2.

36. Rey Chow, "Poststructuralism: Theory as Critical Self-Consciousness," in *The Cambridge Companion to Feminist Literary Theory* (Cambridge: Cambridge University Press, 2006), 201.

37. Charles Baudelaire, *"The Painter of Modern Life" and Other Essays* (London: Phaidon, 1995), 32.

38. Edmund Husserl, *The Crisis of European Sciences and Transcendental Phenomenology* (Evanston: Northwestern University Press, 1970), 152.

39. See Ian Hunter, "The Time of Theory," *Postcolonial Studies* 10, no. 1 (2007): 5–22.

40. Eve Kosofsky Sedgwick and Adam Frank, "Shame in the Cybernetic Fold: Reading Silvan Tomkins," in *Shame and Its Sisters: A Silvan Tomkins Reader*, ed. Sedgwick and Frank (Durham: Duke University Press, 1995), 16.

41. There is, to be sure, another side to Foucault's work that has received less

attention. In this context, see Lynne Huffer's excellent book *Mad for Foucault: Rethinking the Foundations of Queer Theory* (New York: Columbia University Press, 2009).

42. Roland Barthes, *Mythologies* (New York: Farrar, Straus & Giroux, 1972), 121, 143.

43. Ibid., 11, 9.

44. Roland Barthes, "Change the Object Itself," in *Image-Music-Text*, trans. Stephen Heath (New York: Hill & Wang, 1977), 166.

45. Roland Barthes, *The Grain of the Voice: Interviews 1962–1980* (Evanston: Northwestern University Press, 2009), 331. See also Ellis Hanson, "The Languorous Critic," *New Literary History* 43, no. 3 (2012): 547–64.

46. Richard Rorty, *Contingency, Irony, and Solidarity* (Cambridge: Cambridge University Press, 1989), 74.

47. On the tradition of theory as suspended animation, see Peter Sloterdijk, *The Art of Philosophy* (New York: Columbia University Press, 2012), chap. 3.

48. "Theorizing Queer Temporalities," *GLQ* 13, nos. 2–3 (2007): 195.

49. Bill Ashcroft, Gareth Griffiths, and Helen Tiffin, *Postcolonial Studies: The Key Concepts*, 2nd ed. (Abingdon: Routledge, 2000), 173. For a helpful overview of relevant debates, see, for example, Neil Lazarus, ed., *The Cambridge Companion to Postcolonial Studies* (Cambridge: Cambridge University Press, 2004), especially the essays by Lazarus, Benita Parry, and Simon Gikandi.

50. Bruno Latour, *Reassembling the Social: An Introduction to Actor-Network-Theory* (Oxford: Oxford University Press, 2005), 92; Ian Hacking, *The Social Construction of What?* (Cambridge: Harvard University Press, 1999).

51. Toril Moi, "Reading as a Feminist," unpublished essay.

52. Judith Butler, "Imitation and Gender Insubordination," in *Inside/Out: Lesbian Theories, Gay Theories*, ed. Diana Fuss (New York: Routledge, 1991), 2.

53. Raphael Samuel, "Reading the Signs," *History Workshop* 32 (1991): 89.

54. Judith Butler, *Gender Trouble: Feminism and the Subversion of Identity* (New York: Routledge, 1999), xx. For an alternative to the rhetoric of identity and its deconstruction, see Toril Moi's discussion of "situation" in *"What Is a Woman?" and Other Essays* (Oxford: Oxford University Press, 1999), 65–68.

55. On black boxes, see Graham Harman, *Prince of Networks: Bruno Latour and Metaphysics* (Melbourne: re.press, 2009), 36–47.

56. For a questioning of the opposition between the natural and the conventional, see Richard Shusterman, "Convention: Variations on the Nature/Culture Theme," in *Surface and Depth*.

57. David R. Hiley, "Foucault and the Analysis of Power: Political Engagement without Liberal Comfort or Hope," *Praxis International* 4, no. 2 (July 1984): 198. I take the metaphor of the spiderless web from Leslie Paul Thiele, "The Agony of Politics: The Nietzschean Roots of Foucault's Thought," *American Political Science Review* 84, no. 3 (1990): 908.

58. Hubert L. Dreyfus and Paul Rabinow, *Michel Foucault: Beyond Structuralism and Hermeneutics* (Brighton: Harvester, 1982), xix.

59. Michel Foucault, "Nietzsche, Freud, Marx," in *Transforming the Hermeneutic Context: From Nietzsche to Nancy*, ed. Gayle L. Ormiston and Alan D. Schrift (Albany: SUNY Press, 1990), 62.

60. Jim Merod, *The Political Responsibility of the Critic* (Ithaca: Cornell University Press, 1987), 160. For an argument that Foucault does not abandon hermeneutics but recasts it as a "negative hermeneutics of refusal," see John D. Caputo, *More Radical Hermeneutics: On Not Knowing Who We Are* (Bloomington: Indiana University Press, 2000).

61. Alexander Nehamas, *Only a Promise of Happiness: The Place of Beauty in a World of Art* (Princeton: Princeton University Press, 2007), 123.

Chapter 3

1. Ernst Bloch, "A Philosophical View of the Detective Novel," in *The Utopian Function of Literature and Art* (Cambridge: MIT Press, 1989), 246.

2. Marjorie Nicholson, "The Professor and the Detective," in *The Art of the Mystery Story*, ed. Howard Haycraft (New York: Simon and Schuster, 1946), 126.

3. Richard Alewyn, "The Origin of the Detective Novel," in *The Poetics of Murder: Detective Fiction and Literary Theory*, ed. Glenn W. Most and William W. Stowe (New York: Harcourt, Brace, Jovanovich, 1983).

4. Dennis Porter, *The Pursuit of Crime: Art and Ideology in Crime Fiction* (New Haven: Yale University Press, 1981), 239.

5. Stephen Kern, *A Cultural History of Causality: Science, Murder Novels, and Systems of Thought* (Princeton: Princeton University Press, 2004).

6. On the link between explanation and accusation, see Bruno Latour, "The Politics of Explanation: An Alternative," in *Knowledge and Reflexivity: New Frontiers in the Sociology of Knowledge*, ed. Steve Woolgar (London: Sage, 1988), 155–77.

7. Hayden White, *Metahistory: The Historical Imagination in Nineteenth-Century Europe* (Baltimore: Johns Hopkins University Press, 1975);

Roger C. Schank, *Tell Me a Story: Narrative and Intelligence* (Evanston: Northwestern University Press, 1990).

8. Peter Brooks, *Reading for the Plot: Design and Intention in Narrative* (New York: Vintage, 1984), 113.

9. D. A Miller, *The Novel and the Police* (Berkeley and Los Angeles: University of California Press, 1989), 30.

10. Djelal Kadir, *The Other Writing: Postcolonial Essays in Latin America's Writing Culture* (West Lafayette: Purdue University Press, 1993), 2.

11. Peter Brooks, *Troubling Confessions: Speaking Guilt in Law and Literature* (Chicago: University of Chicago Press, 2001), 41.

12. Carlo Ginzburg, "Clues: Roots of an Evidential Paradigm," in *Clues, Myths, and the Historical Method* (Baltimore: Johns Hopkins University Press, 1989).

13. Franco Moretti, *Signs Taken for Wonders: On the Sociology of Literary Forms* (London: Verso, 2005).

14. J. B. Priestley, *An Inspector Calls* (New York: Dramatists Play Service, 1972). For a discussion of the play's Broadway staging, see Wendy Lesser, *A Director Calls: Stephen Daldry and the Theater* (Berkeley and Los Angeles: University of California Press, 1997).

15. Most and Stowe, introduction to *The Poetics of Murder*, xii.

16. Tzvetan Todorov, *The Poetics of Prose*, trans. Richard Howard (Ithaca: Cornell University Press, 1977), 46.

17. Mark Seltzer, *Henry James and the Art of Power* (Ithaca: Cornell University Press, 1984), 14.

18. On this point, see James Simpson, "Faith and Hermeneutics: Pragmatism versus Pragmatism," *Journal of Medieval and Early Modern Studies* 33, no. 2 (2003): 228.

19. Catherine Belsey, *Critical Practice* (London: Methuen, 1980), 107, 111.

20. Ibid., 108, 107, 111.

21. Erik D. Lindberg, "Returning the Repressed: The Unconscious in Victorian and Modernist Narrative," *Narrative* 8, no. 1 (2000): 76.

22. Belsey, *Critical Practice*, 117.

23. Fredric Jameson, "On Raymond Chandler," in Most and Stowe, *The Poetics of Murder*, 132.

24. Roland Barthes, *Leçon* (Paris: Seuil, 1978), cited in Antoine Compagnon, *Literature, Theory, and Common Sense* (Princeton: Princeton University Press, 2004), 91.

25. Miller, *The Novel and the Police*, 2, 17.

26. Simon Stern, "Detecting Doctrines: The Case Method and the Detective Story," *Yale Journal of Law and the Humanities* 23 (2011): 363.

27. Arthur Conan Doyle, *The Sign of the Four* (Oxford: Oxford University Press, 1993), 7.

28. Franco Moretti, "The Slaughterhouse of Literature," *Modern Language Quarterly* 61, no. 1 (2000): 218.

29. Yumna Siddiqi, *Anxieties of Empire and the Fiction of Intrigue* (New York: Columbia University Press, 2008), 15–16.

30. Ibid., 16.

31. See my discussion of this question in "Modernist Studies and Cultural Studies: Reflections on Method," *Modernism/Modernity* 10, no. 3 (2003): 512, and Lawrence Grossberg's remarks in *Bringing It All Back Home: Essays on Cultural Studies* (Durham: Duke University Press 1997), 107.

32. Moretti, *Signs Taken for Wonders*, 143.

33. Seltzer, *Henry James and the Art of Power*, 34.

34. Bloch, "A Philosophical View," 246.

35. Pierre Bayard, *Sherlock Holmes Was Wrong: Reopening the Case of the Hound of the Baskervilles* (New York: Bloomsbury, 2008), 49.

36. Peter Brooks, "'Inevitable Discovery' — Law, Narrative, Retrospectivity," *Yale Journal of Law and Humanities* 15 (2003): 71–102.

37. Elisabeth Strowick, "Comparative Epistemology of Suspicion: Psychoanalysis, Literature, and the Human Sciences," *Science in Context* 18, no. 4 (2005): 652.

38. Witold Gombrowicz, "The Premeditated Crime," in *Bacacay*, trans. Bill Johnson (New York: Archipelago, 2004), 47, 52.

39. Shoshana Felman, "Turning the Screw of Interpretation," in *Literature and Psychoanalysis: The Question of Reading—Otherwise*, ed. Shoshana Felman (Baltimore: Johns Hopkins University Press, 1982), 189, 175.

40. Ibid., 193, 176.

41. Ibid., 16.

42. Heta Pyrhönen, *Mayhem and Murder: Narrative and Moral Problems in the Detective Story* (Toronto: University of Toronto Press, 1999).

43. Strowick, "Comparative Epistemology of Suspicion," 654.

44. Stefan Zweig, *"The Burning Secret" and Other Stories* (London: Pushkin Press, 2008), 52.

45. Frank Kermode, *The Sense of an Ending: Studies in the Theories of Fiction* (Oxford: Oxford University Press, 2000).

46. Arthur Frank, *Letting Stories Breathe: A Socio-narratology* (Chicago: University of Chicago Press, 2010), 48.

47. Kate McGowan, *Key Issues in Critical and Cultural Theory* (Buckingham: Open University Press, 2007), 26.

48. Elizabeth Bruss, "The Game of Literature and Some Literary Games," *New Literary History* 9, no. 1 (1977): 162.

49. Matei Calinescu, *Rereading* (New Haven: Yale University Press, 1993), 151.

50. Anna Maria Jones, *Problem Novels: Victorian Fiction Theorizes the Sensational Self* (Columbus: Ohio State University Press, 2007).

51. Robert M. Fowler, "Who Is 'the Reader' in Reader Response Criticism?" *Semeia* 31 (1985): 9.

52. Deidre Lynch, *Loving Literature: A Cultural History* (Chicago: University of Chicago Press, 2014), 77.

53. W. H. Auden, *The Dyer's Hand* (New York: Vintage, 1968), 147.

54. Louis Althusser, *Reading "Capital"* (London: Verso, 1979), 14–15.

55. T. J. Clark, *The Sight of Death: An Experiment in Art Writing* (New Haven: Yale University Press, 2006), viii.

56. Sarah Kofman, *Freud and Fiction* (Cambridge: Polity, 1991). That texts are not persons—with human qualities of vulnerability—does not mean that they are not agents or actants, as we will see in the final chapter.

57. Richard Rorty, *Consequences of Pragmatism: Essays, 1972–1980* (Minneapolis: University of Minnesota Press, 1982), 151.

Chapter 4

1. Wendy Brown and Janet Halley, introduction to *Left Legalism/Left Critique*, ed. Brown and Halley (Durham: Duke University Press, 2002), 27; Robert Con Davis and Ronald Schleifer, *Criticism and Culture: The Role of Critique in Modern Literary Theory* (London: Longman, 1991), 2.

2. David Bordwell, *Making Meaning: Inference and Rhetoric in the Interpretation of Cinema* (Cambridge: Harvard University Press, 1991), xi.

3. Gianni Vattimo, "Postmodern Criticism: Postmodern Critique," in *Writing the Future*, ed. David Wood (London: Routledge, 1990).

4. Useful resources for an intellectual history of critique include Reinhart Koselleck, *Critique and Crisis: Enlightenment and the Pathogenesis of Modern Society* (Cambridge: MIT Press, 1988); Giorgio Tonelli, "'Critique' and Related Terms Prior to Kant: A Historical Survey," *Kant-Studien* 69, no. 2 (1978): 119–48, Werner Schneider, "Vernünftiger Zweifel und wahre Eklektik: Zur Entstehung des modernen Kritikbegriffes," *Studien Leibnitiana* 17, no. 2 (1985): 143–61; and Paul Connerton, *The Tragedy of Enlightenment: An Essay on the Frankfurt School* (Cambridge: Cambridge University Press, 1980). On critique in political theory and philosophy, see, for

example, Seyla Benhabib, *Critique, Norm, and Utopia: A Study of the Foundations of Critical Theory* (New York: Columbia University Press, 1986); Raymond Geuss, *The Idea of a Critical Theory: Habermas and the Frankfurt School* (Cambridge: Cambridge University Press, 1981); Michael Kelly, ed., *Critique and Power: Recasting the Foucault/Habermas Debate* (Cambridge: MIT Press, 1994).

5. René Wellek, *Concepts of Criticism* (New Haven: Yale University Press, 1963), 35; Drew Milne, "Introduction: Criticism and/or Critique," in *Modern Critical Thought: An Anthology of Theorists Writing on Theorists*, ed. Milne (Oxford: Blackwell, 2002), 5.

6. Raymond Williams, *Keywords* (London: Flamingo, 1976), 86.

7. Robert Koch, "The Critical Gesture in Philosophy," in *Iconoclash: Beyond the Image Wars in Science, Religion, and Art*, ed. Bruno Latour and Peter Weibel (Cambridge: MIT Press, 2002), 531.

8. Tom O'Regan, *Australian National Cinema* (London: Routledge, 1996), 339.

9. Michel Serres and Bruno Latour, *Conversations on Science, Culture, and Time*, trans. Roxanne Lapidus (Ann Arbor: University of Michigan Press, 1995), 48.

10. Audrey Jaffe, "Spectacular Sympathy: Visuality and Ideology in Dickens's *A Christmas Carol*," *PMLA* 109, no. 2 (1994): 254–65; John Martin Evans, *Milton's Imperial Epic: "Paradise Lost" and the Discourse of Colonialism* (Ithaca: Cornell University Press, 1996).

11. Liam Kennedy, "American Studies without Tears," *Journal of Transnational American Studies* 1, no. 1 (2009).

12. For a questioning of this paradigm, see Joel Pfister, *Critique for What? Cultural Studies, American Studies, Left Studies* (Boulder, CO: Paradigm Press, 2006).

13. These remarks have benefited from Alex Woloch's unpublished paper "Critical Thinking."

14. Theodor Adorno, "Cultural Criticism and Society," in *Prisms*, trans. Samuel Weber and Shierry Weber (Cambridge: MIT Press, 1967), 33.

15. Keith Robinson, "An Immanent Transcendental: Foucault, Kant and Critical Philosophy," *Radical Philosophy* 141 (January–February 2007): 21.

16. Alan Liu, *Local Transcendence: Essays on Postmodern Historicism and the Database* (Chicago: University of Chicago Press, 2008).

17. I am thinking here, for example, of Rodolphe Gasché's attempt to distinguish a "bad" critique (based on separating and judging) from a more desirable, because more ambiguous, "hypercritique." This distinction

would seem to require the very act of separating and judging that is being repudiated. See his *The Honor of Thinking: Critique, Theory, Philosophy* (Stanford: Stanford University Press, 2007).

18. Theodor Adorno, *Aesthetic Theory*, trans. Robert Hullot-Kentor (Minneapolis: University of Minnesota Press, 1998), 251.

19. Raymond Geuss, "Genealogy as Critique," *European Journal of Philosophy* 10, no. 2 (2002): 209; Koch, "Critical Gesture in Philosophy," 531; Diana Coole, *Negativity and Politics: Dionysus and Dialectics from Kant to Poststructuralism* (London: Routledge, 2000), 55.

20. Cary Wolfe, *Animal Rites: American Cultures, the Discourse of Species, and Posthumanist Theory* (Chicago: University of Chicago Press, 2003), 182.

21. Giovanni Porfido, "*Queer as Folk* and the Spectacularization of Gay Identity," in *Queer Popular Culture: Literature, Media, Film, and Television*, ed. Thomas Peele (New York: Palgrave Macmillan, 2007), 63.

22. For a spirited defense of the killjoy feminist, see Sara Ahmed, *The Promise of Happiness* (Durham: Duke University Press, 2010).

23. Judith Butler, "The Sensibility of Critique: Response to Asad and Mahmood," in *Is Critique Secular? Blasphemy, Injury, and Free Speech* (Berkeley, CA: Townsend Center for the Humanities, 2009), 116.

24. Barbara Johnson, translator's introduction to Jacques Derrida, *Dissemination* (London: Continuum, 2004), xv–xvi.

25. Marcelo Dascal, for example, points out that the supposedly nonevaluative model of historical or genealogical critique retains a negative or demystifying force in tracing ideas back to causes invisible to the actors themselves. See "Critique without Critics?" *Science in Context* 10, no. 1 (1997): 39–62.

26. Coole, *Negativity and Politics*, 41. See also Sanford Budick and Wolfgang Iser, eds., *Languages of the Unsayable: The Play on Negativity in Literature and Literary Theory* (New York: Columbia University Press, 1989).

27. Susan Neiman, *Moral Clarity: A Guide for Grown-up Idealists* (Princeton: Princeton University Press, 2009), 4.

28. Coole, *Negativity and Politics*, 74. On the distinction between the stand and the stance, see John S. Nelson, "Stands in Politics," *Journal of Politics* 46 (1984): 106–30.

29. Stephen Ross, "Introduction: The Missing Link," in *Modernism and Theory: A Critical Debate*, ed. Stephen Ross (Abingdon: Routledge, 2009), 10.

30. Brown and Halley, introduction to *Left Legalism/Left Critique*, 28.

31. Coole, *Negativity and Politics*, 231.

32. Marshall Berman, *All That Is Solid Melts into Air: The Experience of Modernity* (London: Verso, 1983).

33. Pierre Schlag, *The Enchantment of Reason* (Durham: Duke University Press, 1998).

34. Ian Hunter, *Rethinking the School: Subjectivity, Bureaucracy, Criticism* (New York: St. Martin's Press, 1994), 167.

35. Hengameh Irandoust, "The Logic of Critique," *Argumentation* 20 (2006): 134. Iain McKenzie also argues that "critique is not criticism: it is precisely that which calls criticism to account as opinion," in *The Idea of Pure Critique* (London: Continuum, 2004), 89.

36. Editors' introduction to *The Routledge Companion to Critical Theory*, ed. Simon Malpas and Paul Wake (Abingdon: Routledge, 2006), x.

37. Trinh T. Minh-ha, *Woman, Native, Other* (Bloomington: Indiana University Press, 1989), 16–17.

38. Denis Dutton, "Language Crimes," *Wall Street Journal*, February 5, 1999.

39. Jonathan Culler and Kevin Lamb, introduction to *Just Being Difficult? Academic Writing in the Public Arena*, ed. Culler and Lamb (Stanford: Stanford University Press, 2003), 9.

40. Paul Bové, *Mastering Discourse: The Politics of Intellectual Culture* (Durham: Duke University Press, 1992), 167.

41. Judith Butler, "Values of Difficulty," in Culler and Lamb, *Just Being Difficult?*, 201, 203.

42. Ien Ang, "From Cultural Studies to Cultural Research: Engaged Scholarship in the Twenty-First Century," *Cultural Studies Review* 12, no. 2 (2006): 190.

43. Michael Warner, "Styles of Intellectual Publics," in Culler and Lamb, *Just Being Difficult?*, 117.

44. Bruno Latour, *Reassembling The Social: An Introduction to Actor-Network-Theory* (Oxford: Oxford University Press, 2005), 57.

45. Luc Boltanski and Laurent Thévenot, *On Justification: Economies of Worth*, trans. Catherine Porter (Princeton: Princeton University Press, 2006).

46. Luc Boltanski, *On Critique: A Sociology of Emancipation* (Cambridge: Polity, 2011), 27. For a very helpful assessment, see Robin Celikates, "From Critical Social Theory to a Social Theory of Critique: On the Critique of Ideology after the Pragmatic Turn," *Constellations* 13, no. 1 (2006): 21–40.

47. Foucault, "What Is Critique?," 194.

48. Kimberly Hutchings, *Kant, Critique and Politics* (London: Routledge, 1996), 190.

49. Francis Mulhern, *Culture/Metaculture* (London: Routledge, 2000).

50. Max Horkheimer, "Traditional and Critical Theory," in *Critical Sociology*, ed. Paul Connerton (Hardmondsworth: Penguin, 1976), 224.

51. Rita Felski, "Modernist Studies and Cultural Studies: Reflections on Method," *Modernism and Modernity* 10, no. 3 (2003): 501–18.

52. David Couzens Hoy, *Critical Resistance: From Poststructuralism to Post-Critique* (Cambridge: MIT Press, 2004), 2.

53. Brown and Halley, introduction to *Left Legalism/Left Critique*," 25.

54. Nancy Fraser, "What's Critical about Critical Theory? The Case of Habermas and Gender," *New German Critique* 35 (1985): 97.

55. Ibid., 97.

56. Ewa Plonowska Ziarek, *The Rhetoric of Failure: Deconstruction of Skepticism, Reinvention of Modernism* (Albany: SUNY Press, 1996).

57. Bruce Robbins, *Secular Vocations: Intellectuals, Professionalism, Culture* (London: Verso, 1993). See also Claudia Ruitenberg, "Don't Fence Me In: The Liberation of Undomesticated Critique," *Journal of Philosophy of Education* 38, no. 3 (2004): 341–50.

58. Robyn Wiegman, "The Ends of New Americanism," *New Literary History* 42, no. 3 (2011): 385–407.

59. Latour, *Reassembling the Social*, 218.

60. Chantal Mouffe, *Agonistics: Thinking the World Politically* (London: Verso, 2012), 104.

61. Milne, "Introduction: Criticism and/or Critique," 18.

62. Joan Scott, "Against Eclecticism," *differences* 16, no. 5 (2005): 122.

63. Bové, *Mastering Discourse*, 87.

64. Michael Billig, "Towards a Critique of the Critical," *Discourse and Society* 11, no. 3 (2000): 292.

65. Talal Asad, "Free Speech, Blasphemy, and Secular Criticism," in *Is Critique Secular? Blasphemy, Injury, and Free Speech* (Berkeley, CA: Townsend Center for the Humanities, 2009), 33. On the postcolonial challenge to the rhetoric of disenchantment, see, for example, Saurabh Dube, "Introduction: Enchantments of Modernity," special issue of *South Atlantic Quarterly* on "Enduring Enchantments," 101, no. 4 (2002): 729–55; Saba Mahmood, *Politics of Piety: The Islamic Revival and the Feminist Subject* (Princeton: Princeton University Press, 2005).

66. Asad, "Reply to Judith Butler," 140. Elsewhere, Asad discusses forms of criticism that cannot be assimilated to a Western tradition of critique. See, for example, "The Limits of Religious Criticism in the Middle East: Notes on Islamic Public Argument," in *Genealogies of Religion: Discipline and Reasons of Power in Christianity and Islam* (Baltimore: Johns Hopkins

University Press, 1993). I am grateful to Michael Allan for bringing this text to my attention.

67. Eve Kosofsky Sedgwick, "Paranoid Reading and Reparative Reading, or, You're So Paranoid, You Probably Think This Essay Is about You," in *Touching Feeling: Affect, Pedagogy, Performativity* (Durham: Duke University Press, 2003), 131.

Chapter 5

1. Michael D. Snediker, *Queer Optimism: Lyric Personhood and Other Felicitous Persuasions* (Minneapolis: University of Minnesota Press, 2009); Doris Sommer, *The Work of Art in the World: Civic Agency and Public Humanities* (Durham: Duke University Press, 2014); James O. Pawelski and D. J. Moores, eds., *The Eudaimonic Turn: Well-Being in Literary Studies* (Madison, NJ: Fairleigh Dickinson University Press, 2012).

2. Bruno Latour, *Reassembling the Social* (Oxford: Oxford University Press, 2005), 148.

3. See, for example, John J. Joughin and Simon Malpas, eds., *The New Aestheticism* (Manchester: Manchester University Press, 2004); Elaine Scarry, *On Beauty and Being Just* (Princeton: Princeton University Press, 2001); Alexander Nehamas, *Only a Promise of Happiness: The Place of Beauty in a World of Art* (Princeton: Princeton University Press, 2010).

4. See, for example, Jonathan Goldberg and Madhavi Menon, "Queering History," *PMLA* 120, no. 5 (2005): 1608–17; Carolyn Dinshaw et al., "Theorizing Queer Temporalities: A Roundtable Discussion," *GLQ* 13, nos. 2–3 (2007): 177–95; Hugh Grady and Terence Hawkes, eds., *Presentist Shakespeare*; (London: Routledge, 2006); Jeffrey J. Cohen, *Medieval Identity Machines* (Minneapolis: University of Minnesota Press, 2003); Jennifer Summit and David Wallace, "Rethinking Periodization," *Journal of Medieval and Early Modern Studies* 37, no. 3 (2007): 447–51; Jonathan Gil Harris, *Untimely Matter in the Time of Shakespeare* (Philadelphia: University of Pennsylvania Press, 2009); Carolyn Dinshaw, *How Soon Is Now? Medieval Texts, Amateur Readers, and the Queerness of Time* (Durham: Duke University Press, 2012); and *New Literary History* 42, no. 4 (2011), "Context?" special issue.

5. Wai Chee Dimock, "A Theory of Resonance," *PMLA* 112 (1997): 1061.

6. Bruno Latour, *We Have Never Been Modern* (Cambridge: Harvard University Press, 1993), 75.

7. Harris, *Untimely Matter*, 2.

8. Jennifer Fleissner, "Is Feminism a Historicism?" *Tulsa Studies in Women's Literature* 21, no. 1 (2002): 45–66.

9. Karl-Heinz Bohrer, "The Tragic: A Question of Art, Not Philosophy of History," *New Literary History* 41, no. 1 (2010): 35–51.

10. Dimock, "A Theory of Resonance," 1061.

11. Bruce Robbins, "Afterword," *PMLA* 122, no. 5 (2007): 1650. See also Eric Hayot's insightful "Against Periodization," *New Literary History* 42, no. 4 (2011): 739–56.

12. Christopher Lane, "The Poverty of Context: Historicism and Nonmimetic Fiction," *PMLA*, 118, no. 3 (2003): 450–69.

13. Compare, for example, Latour's rejection of reductionism with the theory of articulation in cultural studies as "an attempt to avoid reduction." The latter is well described in Jennifer Daryl Slack, "The Theory and Method of Articulation in Cultural Studies," in *Stuart Hall: Critical Dialogues in Cultural Studies*, ed. David Morley and Kuan-Hsing Chen (London and New York: Routledge, 1996), 112–27.

14. Lawrence Grossberg, *Bringing It All Back Home: Essays on Cultural Studies* (Durham: Duke University Press, 1997), 255.

15. Howard S. Becker, Robert R. Faulkner, and Barbara Kirshenblatt-Gimblett, eds., *Art from Start to Finish: Jazz, Painting, Writing, and Other Improvisations* (Chicago: University of Chicago Press, 2006), 3.

16. Latour, *Reassembling the Social*, 71, 72.

17. Ibid., 40.

18. James J. Gibson, "The Theory of Affordances," in *Perceiving, Acting, and Knowing: Toward an Ecological Perspective*, ed. Robert Shaw and John Bransford (Hillsdale, NJ: Lawrence Erlbaum, 1977), 68; and Gibson, *The Ecological Approach to Visual Perception* (New York: Psychology Press, 2015).

19. C. Namwali Serpell, *Seven Modes of Uncertainty* (Cambridge: Harvard University Press, 2014), 9, 22. For another valuable account of the parallels between texts and buildings as forms of induction, see Elizabeth Fowler's development of the notion of ductile space in "Art and Orientation," *New Literary History* 44, no. 4 (2013): 595–616.

20. A separate model of the agency of artworks—though with intriguing parallels—is developed by Alfred Gell in *Art and Agency: An Anthropological Theory* (Oxford: Clarendon Press, 1998). See Eduardo de la Fuente's interesting discussion, drawing on both Gell and Latour, in "The Artwork Made Me Do it: Introduction to the New Sociology of Art," *Thesis Eleven* 103, no. 1 (2010): 3–9.

21. Latour, *Reassembling the Social*, 236.

22. Tony Bennett, "Texts in History: The Determination of Readings and Their Texts," *Journal of the Midwest Modern Language Association* 18, no. 1 (1985): 7.

23. Tony Bennett and Janet Woollacott, *Bond and Beyond: The Political Career of a Popular Hero* (London: Macmillan, 1987), 64.

24. On this question, see also James Simpson, "Faith and Hermeneutics: Pragmatism versus Pragmatism", *Journal of Medieval and Early Modern Studies*, 33, 2 (2203): 233–234.

25. *Bond and Beyond*, cited in note 23 above.

26. Franco Moretti, "The Slaughterhouse of Literature," *Modern Language Quarterly* 61, no. 1 (2000): 207–27.

27. Tia DeNora, *Music in Everyday Life* (Cambridge: Cambridge University Press, 2000), 22.

28. Bernard Lahire, *The Plural Actor* (Cambridge: Polity, 2011).

29. Derek Attridge, "Context, Idioculture, Invention," *New Literary History* 42, no. 4 (2011): 682–83.

30. Timothy Bewes, "Reading with the Grain: A New World in Literary Criticism," *differences* 21, no. 3 (2010): 1–33; Sharon Marcus, *Between Women: Friendship, Desire, and Marriage in Victorian England* (Princeton: Princeton University Press, 2007).

31. Casper Bruun Jensen, "Experiments in Good Faith and Hopefulness: Toward a Postcritical Social Science," *Common Knowledge* 20, no. 2 (2014): 361. For some other pertinent discussions of the postcritical, see Janet Wolff, *The Aesthetics of Uncertainty* (New York: Columbia University Press, 2008); Antoine Hennion and Line Grenier, "Sociology of Art: New Stakes in a Post-Critical Time," in *The International Handbook of Sociology*, ed. Stella R. Quah and Arnaud Sales (London: Sage, 2000). A classic text is Michael Polanyi, *Personal Knowledge: Towards a Post-Critical Philosophy* (Chicago: University of Chicago Press, 1974).

32. Walter F. Otto, *The Homeric Gods: The Spiritual Significance of Greek Religion* (New York: Octagon, 1978), 104.

33. Richard E. Palmer, "The Liminality of Hermes and the Meaning of Hermeneutics," http://www.mac.edu/faculty/richardpalmer/liminality.html.

34. Adam S. Miller, *Speculative Grace: Bruno Latour and Object-Oriented Theology* (New York: Fordham University Press, 2013), 109.

35. Latour, *Reassembling the Social*, 245.

36. The wording in this paragraph overlaps with my essay "Latour and Literary Studies," *PMLA* 130, no. 3 (2015).

37. Marielle Macé, "Ways of Reading, Modes of Being," *New Literary History* 44, no. 2 (2103): 214. This essay contains excerpts from Macé's book

Façons de lire, manières d'être (Paris: Gallimard, 2011), translated by Marlon Jones.

38. Richard Kearney, "What Is Carnal Hermeneutics?," *New Literary History* 46, no. 1 (2015).

39. Macé, *Facons de lire*, 192, 190.

40. For other helpful discussions of this point, see Cristina Vischer Bruns, *The Value of Literary Reading and What it Means for Teaching* (New York: Continuum, 2011); and Jean-Marie Schaeffer, "Literary Studies and Literary Experience," trans. Kathleen Antonioli, *New Literary History* 44, no. 2 (2013): 267–83.

41. Yves Citton, *Lire, interpréter, actualiser: Pourquoi les études littéraires?* (Paris: Éditions Amsterdam, 2007).

42. Citton, *Lire, interpréter, actualiser*, 155–56.

43. Deidre Lynch, *Loving Literature: A Cultural History* (Chicago: University of Chicago Press, 2014), 14.

44. Latour, *Reassembling the Social*, 236.

45. On this question, see Thom Dancer, "Between Belief and Knowledge: J. M. Coetzee and the Present of Reading," *Minnesota Review* 77 (2011): 131–42.

46. As John Guillory remarks, "Scholarly reading can be said to preserve within it an encysted form of lay reading, a necessary recollection of the pleasures and rapidity of lay reading." See "How Scholars Read," *ADE Bulletin* 146 (Fall 2008): 12.

47. For a helpful discussion of this issue, see Murray Smith, *Engaging Characters: Fiction, Emotion, and the Cinema* (Oxford: Oxford University Press, 1995).

48. Marcus, *Between Women*.

49. Daniel Carey, "The State of Play: English Literary Scholarship and Criticism in a New Century, "*Cadernos de Letras* 27 (December 2010): 19.

50. Felski, "Latour and Literary Studies."

In Short

1. Ien Ang, "From Cultural Studies to Cultural Research: Engaged Scholarship in the Twenty-First Century," *Cultural Studies Review* 12, no. 2 (2006): 190.

2. Yves Citton, *L'avenir des humanités: Économie de la connaissance ou cultures de l'interprétation* (Paris: La Découverte, 2010), 133.

3. Michael Walzer, *Interpretation and Social Criticism* (Cambridge: Harvard University Press, 1987), 35.

4. Christopher Castiglia, "Critiquiness," *English Language Notes* 51, no. 2 (2013): 79–85. See also Steven Maras, "Communicating Criticality," *International Journal of Communication* 1 (2007): 167–86.

5. The aesthetic, moreover, also has an ethical dimension. As Jane Bennett points out, experiences of enchantment are not reducible to critical accusations of mindlessness or naïve optimism: rather, they are a means by which we come to experience wonder and pleasure in the world and to care deeply about its condition. Jane Bennett, *The Enchantment of Modern Life* (Princeton: Princeton University Press, 2001), 10.

6. *New Literary History* 46, no. 2 (2015), special issue, "Feminist Interventions."

7. Michel Chaouli, "Criticism and Style," *New Literary History* 44, no. 3 (2013): 328.

INDEX

CPSIA information can be obtained
at www.ICGtesting.com
Printed in the USA
LVHW02s1042150118
562888LV00001B/2/P